CW01625419

An Introduction to
COMPARATIVE POLITICS

An Introduction to

COMPARATIVE POLITICS

Peter Calvert

Professor of Comparative and International Politics,
University of Southampton

HARVESTER WHEATSHEAF

New York London Toronto Sydney Tokyo Singapore

First published 1993 by
Harvester Wheatsheaf
Campus 400, Maylands Avenue
Hemel Hempstead
Hertfordshire, HP2 7EZ
A division of
Simon & Schuster International Group

Typeset in 10½/12½pt Meridien
by The Midlands Book Typesetting Company, Loughborough

Printed and bound in Great Britain by
T J Press Ltd, Padstow

British Library Cataloguing in Publication Data

A catalogue record for this book is available from the British Library

ISBN 0-7450-1075-X

1 2 3 4 5 97 96 95 94 93

Contents

Acknowledgements

The author would like to thank the following for permission to reproduce copyright material:

Table 2.1 reprinted with kind permission of Oxford University Press, Inc., New York; Table 7.2 reprinted with the permission of the American Enterprise Institute for Public Policy Research, Washington, DC; Material in Table 7.1 reproduced from *The Times Guide to the House of Commons 1945–70* by kind permission of Times Newspapers Limited; Table 7.4 reproduced from *The Sunday Tribune*, Dublin; Figure 1.1 reprinted with the permission of University of Chicago Press; Figure 3.1 reproduced from Jean Blondel, *An Introduction to Comparative Government* (1969) with permission of Weidenfield & Nicolson, publishers; Figure 11.2 reproduced by permission of The American Sociological Association.

Glossary

politics: the art of getting others to do the things you want them to do

government: an organisation composed of individuals who collectively, though in different degrees, participate in the making of decisions, and have a successful claim to have the legitimate monopoly of the use of force

state: the organised community within which a government claims obedience as of right of all citizens

nation: group of people having a sense of identity through the possession of a common language, religion and/or culture

international relations: the study of the relations between states

political science: the study of politics

political scientists: those who study politics professionally

politicians: those who take an active part in politics

political system: that common whole of related parts and functions that is concerned with the making of decisions within a society

function: a task performed by a system that contributes in some way to its survival

structure: any recurrent pattern of behaviour in a political system that persists over time

PART ONE
Introduction

1 The comparative study of politics

INTRODUCTION

Politics, which Aristotle described as the 'master science' (Aristotle, *Ethics*, I, 1, 1094a, cited in Barker, 1968: 354), is the key to everything else that human beings do. It is so central and so complex that its importance can hardly be overstated. Politics is concerned with the *making of decisions* in society. But politics is not action, but interaction; it is both what decision-makers do to people, and what people do to try to influence the decision-makers. Hence it is to be found everywhere in society where decisions have to be made, and nowhere more so than where the most fundamental and crucial questions have to be resolved.

The principal institution of any society dealing with political matters, and the key to understanding its politics as a whole, is its *government*. By a government is meant an organisation which has established a *successful claim to have the legitimate monopoly of the use of force* (Weber, 1965: 154). Once secured, this monopoly is the ultimate sanction that the decisions of government can be made effective; in other words, that it has *power*.

By *force* is meant any use of physical coercion, whether by government, other groups or private citizens. The emotive term 'violence' is quite often used, but since this has a definite implication that it is not controlled and channelled, it is better avoided.

By *power* is meant *the ability to get others to do what you want*. In practice, though this rests on the sanction of force, the sanction is never completely, and often very incompletely, secured. Though most writers have assumed that some form of organised government is essential to the maintenance of society, this is not an assumption which it is necessary, nor even helpful, to make. In addition, there are always a number of (subordinate) levels of government in any society; there is not, indeed, any such thing as an absolute dictatorship, and politics exists at all levels.

The organised community, within which a government claims obedience as of right of all citizens, has traditionally been known as a *state*. Present-day states, covering a relatively wide area, are commonly termed *nation states*. Originally, this was to distinguish them from earlier forms of political organisation covering relatively small areas, such as tribes or city states. It is true that in modern states the majority of inhabitants generally identify themselves with one another, by the possession of a common language, religion and/or culture. A people with this sense of identity is a *nation*. However, the term *nation state* is a misleading one, for there is no exact correspondence between state and nation; there are states with more than one nation (Britain), nations with more than one state (ethnic Albanians, Hungarians, Serbs etc.), states with no definite national identity (Chad) and nations with no definite state (the Palestinian Arabs) (Seton-Watson, 1977). The reason why it is so popular is that in nineteenth-century Europe there emerged the concept of *nationalism*, the belief that the only appropriate basis for a state was the nation. To this day, therefore, states which lack a sense of national identity try very hard to inculcate it, as for example did the United States (Lipset, 1979).

The study of the relations between states is commonly known as *international relations*, and forms an academic discipline so closely allied to politics that the two are normally taught together. Indeed, the fact that the disciplines have become separated is largely fortuitous, and there is everything to be gained by bringing the study of comparative politics and international relations as close together as possible. The fact is that the practice of international relations was established in a political climate which held that states were in every sense quite distinct and separate from one another, treating with one another as equals, and owing no duty to any outside earthly authority. This notion, which is termed *sovereignty*, has been regarded as one of the attributes of a state since the time of Jean Bodin (Frankel, 1964: 13).

All central governments are, in theory, still sovereign. Taken literally, for the people whose destinies they control, this would mean that there was no appeal to any higher level. However, the concept of sovereignty is not 'real', simply a convenient, and indeed very important, legal fiction. In practice, ever since the concept of the state emerged, in or around the sixteenth century, states have interacted with one another and so – at least to some minor extent – have been dependent on others. In the twentieth century, and especially since 1945, states have given up substantial proportions of their former freedom of action to transnational and supranational organisations and, indeed, to one another. These states are therefore bound by international obligations to respect certain minimum standards of behaviour and to avoid certain types of action.

Yet this should not lead to the belief that there is a general decline of the state. On the contrary, there are more states now than ever before, and in almost all of them the spirit of nationalism seems as strong as ever. Since the whole inhabitable world is now parcelled out between them, it is quite impossible for anyone to ignore their existence, or escape from the influence of one or another of them (Frankel, 1964: 28, 126, 156). Furthermore, with modern communications the actions of different states are now so intertwined that international relations, in the old sense, has had to expand its boundaries to include all sorts of relations with and between *non-governmental organisations (NGOs)*. This term is a wide one, ranging from technical bodies such as the Universal Postal Union (UPU) to pressure groups such as Greenpeace and the World Wide Fund for Nature (WWF).

Hence sovereignty, for obvious physical reasons, is not a fact but a fiction, which is retained because it is convenient from the point of view of governments and lawyers. It is, however, intimately bound up with two other ideas: those of legitimacy and authority, with which it is often confused (Friedrich, 1972: 14–15, 47–8).

Legitimacy means that a government is generally recognised to have the right to do what it does. It depends, therefore, not on what the government claims, but on whether or not that claim is recognised. The fact that a government is recognised as legitimate, whether by its own citizens or by its peer states, gives it authority, which is the assurance that its commands will be obeyed.

Authority itself, however, is not absolute or unlimited. To have authority to do something is the right to do that thing, and be obeyed; it is not a general grant of power to do anything you want. Authority, therefore, can be delegated, divided or shared. In fact, all operation of complex governments depends on this fact, since the delegation, division or sharing of the tasks of government depend on it.

Authority and power

The question of authority was treated by Max Weber as being central to the evolution of the modern state (Weber, 1965: 132, 324ff.). Originally, Weber believed, the authority of government stemmed from what he termed *charisma*; that is to say, the outstanding personality or personal qualities of an individual. In more developed societies, charisma was 'routinised', or subjected to legal forms and controls. It could be either *traditional* – accepted because it had always been accepted – or *legal-rational*, which is to say, accepted as being conferred by formal rituals involving some kind of choice or recognition by or on behalf of the society as a whole. Weber therefore distinguished these three types of authority – charismatic, traditional and legal-rational – from one another, while treating them as 'ideal types' which were not necessarily found in pure form. Thus a person of outstanding personal qualities may come from an old family, which lends traditional authority, and legally be elected president, a position which confers legal-rational authority. An interesting example of this duplication was Prince Norodom Sihanouk, who in the 1950s gave up his throne to become Prime Minister of Cambodia and since 1991 has again emerged as the one figure in that unhappy country who can command a measure of general support.

The fact is that, in all but a few modern states there was a specific moment in time when a government seized power, and all other governments after that time claim part or whole of their authority by virtue of being successors to that government. Even in states such as Australia and New Zealand, which achieved independence peacefully, conquest formed the basis of the colonial state. In Canada and Malaysia self-government was conceded because of the threat that they might otherwise succumb to force, and additionally in Nigeria and Ghana force has been used since independence to instal a series of military governments. All Weber's forms of authority, therefore, amount to the same thing: the habit of obedience. The collective habit of obedience gives a tendency to inertia in social systems. Social systems, once established, will tend to continue unaltered either until society decides to change them, or until it discovers that it has forgotten any need for them. By extension, the longer a social institution continues in existence, the longer it is likely to continue.

So it is with the key social institution, that of government itself. The habit of obedience is perpetuated the more easily since very few people, if any, see or are in the habit of seeing the government as a whole, and thus may be, and frequently are, protected by encapsulation from the attentions of the government. All that is not central to them is regarded as being peripheral. So the bulk of governmental operations survive war, invasion, revolution, civil war, earthquake, flood or pestilence, joining together after the event to repair the damage as well as possible in the accustomed mould. Changes of major importance in government only take place either incrementally, by slow changes over a long period of time, or, as in the case of Japan or Eastern Europe after 1945, by imposition from without.

It is important to stress that the initial seizure of power does not confer either authority or legitimacy. Nor are the motives relevant. Governments which seize power always claim to be acting under the authority of some superior law – be it divine right, the will of the people, or the mission of the armed forces to protect the state. But such arguments have to be recognised as fallacious. A man who steals a loaf has still committed theft whether he eats it himself or gives it to his aged mother. In this sense, then, no modern government has legitimacy by virtue of its past history, and all governments depend on the active or passive consent of their subjects to their actions, which gives them a lot of scope to coerce their subjects into accepting those actions.

POLITICS AS A SOCIAL SCIENCE

Politics can be defined first as an art, because for those who practise it (*politicians*) that is what it is, a skill which they generally learn by trial and error, and not by study. But the study of politics is termed *political science*, and those who study it professionally are known, correctly, not as politicians but, in a rather cumbersome phrase, as *political scientists* – terms that in each case go back to the earliest years of the American Republic.

At that time the term 'science' covered all forms of systematic knowledge. More recently the term has come to be associated particularly with the so-called 'exact' sciences: e.g. physics, chemistry, biology, which are based on *experimental evidence* from which they derive regular *laws* giving them the ability to *predict* future events.

Clearly the study of human political behaviour cannot be reduced to propositions with the inflexible regularity of the so-called laws of Nature. There is scarcely a rule of politics that is not broken successfully at one time or another, and there is no reason to suppose that there are in fact any that cannot be broken. Statements about social phenomena cannot be predictive in the 'If A then B' sense (Runciman, 1963: 2–3). All statements in the social sciences are statements of probability. Consequently, any statement about human behaviour can be true only for individuals in groups at the most, and can say nothing about the certainty of action by a single individual. Additionally, in dealing with human beings as opposed to natural phenomena, knowledge of the results of an investigation into a pattern of behaviour will lead to changes in that behaviour pattern in the future – assuming a pattern to be discernible in the first place.

Hence philosophers such as Winch (1958) have asserted that there is no possibility whatsoever of developing a predictive science in the social sciences. Is it true that political science cannot be scientific? No, for two reasons.

1. Not all sciences can make such predictive statements and, in fact, the belief that they can stems from a common failure to understand the nature of the so-called exact sciences. Medicine, for example, is undeniably a science, yet many statements in medicine about the effect of one or another treatment can only be couched in terms of *probabilities* (Lessnoff, 1974). It can be said that a treatment usually helps patients with a certain condition to a complete recovery, but it cannot be certain that it will help any *one* patient to whom the treatment is administered.
2. As in medicine, the weighing of probabilities in politics is seldom a simple matter; the more serious any problem, the less likely

> it is that it will occur on its own, and the more likely it is that it will occur in conjunction with other problems to which it is closely related (Brodbeck, 1968; Przeworski and Teune, 1970). In such circumstances, a decision on one problem will necessarily have consequences for the others which may well make their solution much more difficult, and in extreme cases it may seem very difficult to make any useful decision at all. Just as the exact sciences (including medicine) have had to build up their basic store of information over many generations, and often by trial and error, so too political scientists are doing the same. The fact that the road may be a long one is no excuse for not setting out on it boldly. As the Chinese proverb has it: 'The journey of a thousand *li* begins with a single step.'

In what respects, if any, then, should political science be regarded as a science?

First, it has a defined and unique field of study. It is not, for example, history, sociology or philosophy, though it has both borrowed from and contributed to each of these disciplines in what has been a fruitful interchange for all.

Second, it does seek to build up a body of knowledge which is as *comprehensive* and *exact* as techniques permit (Easton, 1965b; Mayer, 1989; Parsons and Shils, 1962; Stanyer, 1976).

Comprehensiveness is limited by two problems. Political phenomena are very short-lived, and it requires intensive study to keep up with a developing political situation. As with the politicians themselves who are actively involved, it may occupy all a working day for days on end. In addition, information is constantly becoming outdated. Hence books on politics cease to fulfil their original purpose and soon become history books.

Exactness is limited by the very nature of the art of politics. In so far as political activity is to be realised in the form of decisions, it involves the amassing of a given amount of *support*. There are no dictators so powerful that their decisions do not have to be carried out by others. In an assembly, a committee, a meeting, or an election support may take the very specific form of committed votes. The stock-in-trade of the successful politician, therefore, is the recollection from moment to moment of the balance of advantage or disadvantage to his or her own side, together with the tally of obligations amassed in the course of bargaining for support. However, this knowledge is in itself a valuable part of the ability to bargain, and so is jealously guarded. Hence the political scientist in this respect too is aware of a barrier protecting information. Other difficulties exist. As a result of the large number of individuals involved, there are problems of collecting, maintaining and above all recalling large amounts of information culled from many different sources. This information has to be reduced to a standard form. In addition, much of it is not numerical, but in nominal form, that is to say, certain information is either present in a given category or it is not. This problem restricts the range of possibilities for analysing it. Nevertheless, in itself, none of these problems is strange to the exact sciences.

Third, it makes use of the *hypothetico-deductive method* to derive regular principles from observing the behaviour of both individuals and groups. It is possible to understand enough about the motivation of politicians to be able to make reasonably reliable predictions concerning their most likely courses of action, together with the probable consequences of alternative courses of action or inaction. Even if it is true that a politician may break all the rules of politics and get away with it, nevertheless, to say this is to say that there are rules that do apply to the majority of cases. In the long run, it may even be possible to discern regular laws.

THE COMPARATIVE METHOD

Politics has to be studied comparatively because there is no other way in which to obtain the raw data on which to base informed judgements. It is certainly possible and, indeed, most desirable for political philosophers within particular societies or political systems to think constructively about how people ought to act in ideal situations. Indeed, the only way to explore the full range of possibilities implicit in any given situation is to think about it as an abstract problem. But this can be done only in the light of general principles about human behaviour which are derived from experience, as in the problem itself. At best, that necessary experience will be broad, but the more systematic it is the broader it is also likely to be.

In one sense, then, there is no study of politics that is not comparative (Dogan and Pelassy, 1984). All political science, as all other sciences, involves learning by measuring and examining events which are comparable, so that first impressions of how the results might vary from one case to another (hypotheses) may be tested, and, if supported, may then gain acceptance as regular statements of future probability (theories). Only the comparative method, moreover, shows up regular patterns in the behaviour of both individuals and groups.

The difficulties outlined above dictate the choice of method. The comparative method is the clinical one: to examine cases of the phenomenon which is to be investigated, cases which will be complicated by irrelevant information and misleading statements by the various participants, and by a wide range of other differing factors which just have to be tolerated. Where one begins is largely a matter of individual choice. After all, the subject matter is the same however it is approached. Nevertheless, to be fully effective any study must be undertaken in an informed knowledge of the range of possible variation that can take place. It must also embody a sufficient depth of historical knowledge to show how the society and its political system have evolved and are evolving, and this demands awareness not only of the techniques of the political scientists but also those of the historian. This done, the student then orders the resulting set of findings by the use of shorthand expressions for general concepts such as are implied by the use of technical terms and systems of classification.

Hence what value any research may have depends entirely on the adoption of a satisfactory *research design* (Allan and Skinner, 1991). This has a number of stages.

First, clearly formulate the problem to be investigated.

Next, establish the hypotheses to be tested. These hypotheses, however, must be capable of being analysed in terms of the data that have been obtained and will be sought in the future. These hypotheses will have to be formulated in such a way that a precise relationship can be identified between the *dependent* variable, the change to be explained, and the *independent* variables which are believed to affect it.

Next, the validity of hypotheses must be tested against the data. In political science, as in sociology or weather forecasting, it is very seldom possible to use either of the two methods by which scientific research can be validated. Experiments are rarely possible, both for reasons of time and for ethical reasons, and for the same reasons the researcher cannot arrange for observations, other than in surveys of individuals, to be randomised. So the choice of analytical techniques must reflect the limitations of the material, though this does not mean that political scientists should not at all times strive for greater accuracy.

In the end, the results of the work must be set out clearly and made available to other researchers, showing how and why those conclusions have been obtained.

SCHOOLS OF INTERPRETATION

The study of comparative politics rests on a fundamental assumption: that human behaviour is, broadly speaking, constant, that it will be the same in the same circumstances. Without this assumption the philosophical problems of studying politics in a comparative context would be immensely complicated, if not insoluble. However, this is not in itself sufficient reason for making that assumption. The overwhelming weight of evidence is that *homo sapiens* is an extremely consistent species (Howells, 1971; Dobzhansky, 1971). Such differences as exist between the populations of different parts of the world are trivial, and such as exist are in any case easily accounted for by accidental factors, such as the relatively temporary isolation of small units of population on remote islands. And between the sexes such differences as exist appear minor compared with those obtaining in many animal species. Hence variations in fundamental behaviour patterns between different communities in different parts of the world are likely to be so slight that they may be safely ignored in planning comparisons even between widely separated communities.

Such similarities of behaviour, however, are often concealed by the fact that they are described in very different ways in different languages. This is the first and most important reason why political science needs to develop a standard vocabulary in which to talk about politics in a comparative context (Almond, in Almond and Coleman, 1960; Almond, 1968; Sartori, 1970). The act of comparison, too, will help researchers in turn to escape from the assumptions of their own times and their own society (Dogan and Pelassy, 1984: 5).

Political scientists have prejudices like other people, and the most persistent of these are their own political views. It comes as no surprise to find, therefore, that their writings on politics can be grouped in the main in one or another of three competing schools of interpretation.

(i) Historical/descriptive

Despite criticisms that have been levelled at the historical/descriptive method by the supporters of other schools, it still lies at the basis of all work in political science and, it may be said with confidence, provides 90 per cent of the information on which all the more ambitious approaches in each of the schools depend. Work that neglects the basic principles of historical research produces valueless data, so political scientists, if their work is not to be over-dependent on others, must understand the value and significant features of different historical sources. They will learn three things from the best historians: to take account of all the information available to them, even if they do not agree with it; to give due weight to the factor of time in the development of events; and to show clearly to the reader the source of their ideas. Certainly the weakness of many historical studies is the tendency to historicism, the explanation of events in terms only of themselves. Political scientists must do more than the historians. They must translate their works into a set of common concepts before they can hope to make meaningful comparisons. Interestingly enough, in the historical/descriptive tradition, such common concepts have most often been supplied by lawyers, though legal terminology was in the first instance developed for very different purposes.

(ii) Marxist

Marxism contributes to modern interpretation the powerful and seductive idea of a common path of development for all societies. This is not an original idea, but it was one which gained considerable impetus from the onset of the Industrial Revolution, since Marx himself, who asserted the primacy of economic causes in determining human behaviour, was the first to seek to explore these in relation to an overall philosophy of history, which he hoped – and repeatedly asserted – had in itself a predictive value. Although – where they were not so vague as to be meaningless – Marx's own predictions have consistently been proved wrong, his own emphasis on two points is of the greatest value to the study of comparative politics: the fact that the political cannot be detached from the economic and social aspects of a community, and the need for hard data as the essential foundation for any serious future research.

The weaknesses of the Marxist approach are traceable to the undue respect his disciples continue to attribute to the diverse writings of a mid-nineteenth-century writer, and the trivialisation of his most interesting propositions by unthinking repetition. Marxism is most fruitful where it has been incorporated into the general body of human knowledge, of which no one school of thought has a monopoly.

(iii) Functionalist

The adherents of this school derive from the natural sciences an emphasis on clinical study of behaviour in very small groups and in the individual. This fills an essential void in Marxist theory, which is concerned above all with very large groups and movements. As has been demonstrated by biologists, propositions derived from the behaviour of one size of group are simply not valid for other sizes of groups (the so-called ecological fallacy). As much of politics involves small-group behaviour, the political scientists' use of the work done in this area, which has been slow to be accepted other than at the most superficial level, is hardly excessive, though it is also true to say that obsessions with methodological purity have had a stultifying effect on actual research.

Biology has specifically contributed to political science the concept of social entities as *systems* performing specified functions. Again, this is not a new idea, for the notion of the 'body politic', familiar in medieval times, is but an earlier version of the same idea. The expansion of the concept of system in political science has, however, been much aided by the cybernetic revolution and by the success of engineers in developing artificially intelligent machines. Though it may not look like it at first sight, 'cybernetics' comes from the same Greek root as 'government' and means 'the science of steering' (Weiner, 1967: 11). A *political system* is simply that common whole of related parts and functions concerned with the making of decisions within a society.

System concepts have considerable advantages over traditional terms derived from legal terminology. They can be applied on any scale, to a local community or to a whole modern state, utilising the concepts of regionally or functionally distinct subsystems within one common whole of interrelated parts (Dahl, 1964a: 9). Increasingly, therefore, political scientists have come to talk of *political systems* rather than of states.

In addition, systems analysis has contributed two essential ideas to political science. First is the notion of *function*. A function is simply a task performed by a system that contributes in some way to its survival. The same functions may be performed in different systems by different structures – a worm, for example, 'sees' with its skin (Almond, in Almond and Coleman, 1960: 13). Second is the idea of *structure*. A structure is any recurrent pattern of behaviour in a political system that persists over time. It is function that determines structure, though it has too readily been assumed from this that all structures will have useful functions. In fact, they do not necessarily do so, since they may merely represent the residual traces of a function that is no longer performed, as in the case of the appendix in human physiology, or the American Electoral College in politics.

THE POLITICAL SYSTEM

Modern states are so large and complex that at any one time only a few comparisons can be selected for study, either because of their *importance* (general value to society) or their *salience* (urgency to find a solution to a problem). The first task is to specify the boundaries of the *political system*. The political system might be regarded, following Talcott Parsons, as one of a number of subsystems of the overall social system; or, following Easton, it can be distinguished as an entity for study on its own, engaged in transactions with the social system which constitutes the nearer part of its environment (Davies and Lewis, 1971: 22–3). The choice is an open one. Whichever is selected, it must be remembered at all times that the political system is not a real entity, but a conceptual one. The political system is not a group of people, a huddle of buildings, or even a carefully constructed machine. It is a set of social relationships, and its boundary is set by the limit of those relationships, wherever that happens to fall.

It is partly for this reason that the broader concept of political system is attractive, since that way its boundary appears to coincide with that of the state, and from the point of view of a student of international relations this would seem to be convenient. But unfortunately it is misleading for the student of comparative politics, in two ways. On the one hand, the political system of many states – Brazil, for example – does not impinge directly on the lives of a significant fraction of its inhabitants. They live their lives in what the anthropologists call an encapsulated society: one which exists within the territory of the state without forming part of it (Vogt, 1969: 582; cf. Rose, 1971: 27, 31). On the other hand, the boundary of the nation state of today, as already noted, is penetrated from outside by many different influences (Herz, 1959: 64). Indeed, over the past two decades it has been increasingly common to regard domestic and international politics as only aspects of one interrelated whole.

The term *political system* here, therefore, will be used as a synonym for *government* – that is to say, that system of interaction which forms the fundamental control mechanism within a society. The boundary between it and the rest of society is not a clear-cut one. It runs not between individuals, but between the different roles they play. Most people, most of the time, do not participate in making demands in politics. But they cannot opt out of it when it makes demands upon them, at least when they are called upon to pay their taxes. Politics is an essential part of modern societies; it is certainly never absent.

The political system is political because it is concerned with the making of decisions about the allocation of *power resources*. This allocation is disputable because power resources are limited. By power resources is meant those things which people want, which if controlled by governments enable them to maintain their power over those they rule. In material terms this means food, clothing, housing and energy, or the equivalent cost of those items, the supply of which is, at any given point in time, itself limited. Control of such resources gives political power, which in turn means the ability to use force to control them, the habit of exercising authority which is referred to as *status*, and the limitations on access to authority which are often loosely and inaccurately termed *class*.

The political system is that part of the social order in which the ultimate decisions of society are made. Approaching the problem of steering mechanisms from the viewpoint of cybernetics, Deutsch identified important properties of any political system. A cybernetic system is a self-steering mechanism guided by analysis of consequences of its own decisions. Knowledge of these consequences, which is termed *feedback*, is literally 'fed back' from the output to the input side of the process. Hence, just as inputs are converted into outputs, in turn the outputs are monitored for specific inputs. Deutsch points out that a mechanism such as a gunsight will have to have the capacity to anticipate what the future course of events may be, and to modify the information received by the input side accordingly. The gun must fire, not at the aircraft, but in front of it, so that by the time the shell arrives the aircraft will be at the correct position in space to be hit by it. In this instance this correction is known as *gain*, an allowance for the delay in response to a decision which is known as *lag* (Deutsch, 1966: 90, 106)

To be able to 'steer', there must be two categories of *inputs* to the system. On the one hand there will be *demands* on which the decision-makers are asked to act, and information to enable them to decide. On the other, they must also receive *support* of various kinds for their decisions. This consists both of personnel to make the decisions, and a great deal of resources, both material and moral, with which to make them effective.

The decisions themselves, the rules by which they are enforced and the way in which they are interpreted, form the *outputs* of the system.

Similar reasoning lies behind Easton's (1965b) model of the political system (see Figure 1.1), which forms the basis for many later variants.

The first attempt to adapt the systems approach for the purposes of *comparative politics* was made in 1960 by Almond and Coleman (1960: 17). As they pointed out, the outputs of government were already familiar as the 'powers' set out by the makers of the American Constitution, and since followed by most other constitutional lawyers. However, to distinguish the functions from the bodies set up to embody them, Almond and Coleman labelled them, rather than the legislative, executive and judicial powers, the functions of rule-making, rule-application and rule-adjudication. By doing so they made it easier to discern that, for example, when Congress, which is formally a legislature, impeaches the president of the United States, it is actually exercising the function of rule-adjudication. There are many other such examples of overlapping functions in all constitutions, some deliberate ('checks and balances') and some accidental.

Almond and Coleman broke new ground when they turned to the

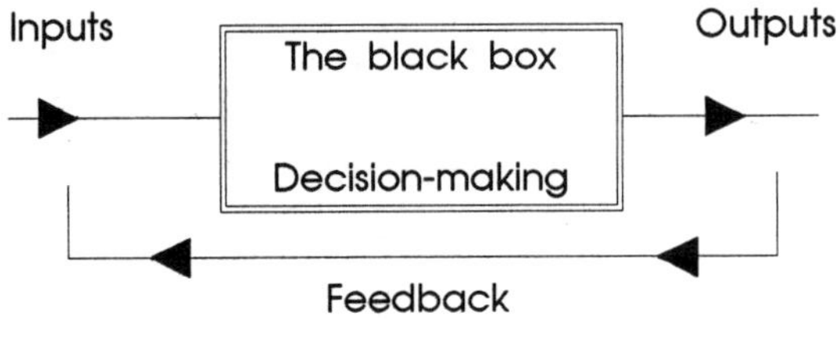

Figure 1.1 *The political system (after Easton)*

inputs, as these had been largely ignored by earlier writers. One of them they termed political communication (cf. Deutsch, 1966). However, strictly speaking, this is neither an input nor an output, but a method by which inputs and outputs are conveyed. It will be dealt with separately in Chapter 4.

Almond and Coleman's other three categories are: (i) political socialisation and recruitment; (ii) interest articulation; and (iii) interest aggregation.

Political socialisation and recruitment, which are rather odd but not incompatible bedfellows, consist of the process of formal and informal shaping of citizens' attitudes to politics, and those structures that exist for the recruitment of people into political or administrative office.

Interest articulation refers to the process by which people express their needs and wishes. They can be divided into demands upon the system and expressions of support for it.

Interest aggregation means the process of linking together various interests into a more or less coherent programme of action on which a decision can be taken.

In a later adaptation of this classification, Almond and Powell (1966) distinguished interest articulation and interest aggregation, together with political communication, and the three output functions of rule-making, rule-application and rule-adjudication, as *conversion functions*, that is, those processes which enable the political system to convert demands and supports into political decisions. Among these decisions are some, undoubtedly, affecting political socialisation and recruitment, which are seen by Almond and Powell as *pattern maintenance functions*

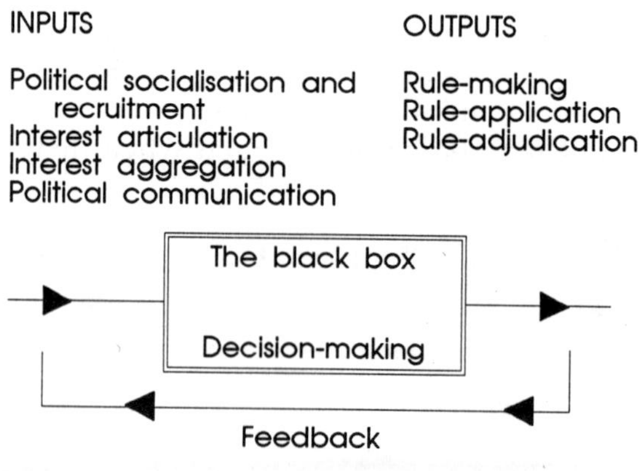

Figure 1.2 *The political system (after Almond and Coleman)*

(see Figure 1.2). The efficiency of the system in doing each of these things they describe as its *capabilities*.

What is not at all clear, however, even in the revised model, is just why these, *and not any other categories*, should have been chosen. This often leads Almond and Coleman, in their earlier work, to equate greater efficiency with greater technical complexity, and at the same time to obliterate what seems to be an essential distinction between demands and supports, for it is impossible to imagine a control system that does not convert one, demands, into the other, supports. Certainly they do recognise that inputs may arise within the ranks of the decision-makers themselves. These they term variously 'withinputs' and 'intraputs'. But there remains an impression that the initiative for political action comes in the main from outside, and that is something which this categorisation renders difficult to avoid.

A simpler and more effective way of looking at inputs to the political system is simply to regard them as *positive* and *negative*. Positive inputs, which enable the government to perform its functions at all, include support in the widest sense, but more particularly the resources to make decisions. Negative inputs are demands on government for action or payment.

There are also only two main types of outputs. Political decisions as such are not outputs, any more than a tap is water, or a switch electricity. Positive outputs are rewards; negative outputs are sanctions or punishments. The prime purpose of the political system is to survive. Like any other system, it can either adapt to changes in its environment, it can change its environment to suit it, or it can, and usually does, do both. It utilises its outputs to maximise support for it, and to minimise the demands made upon it, within the parameters of the society in which it operates, and under the general constraint of the principle of economy of effort. Given unlimited resources, there would be no problem in maintaining support indefinitely. Scarcity, population growth, natural disasters and international influences, however, limit resources in almost all modern political systems, so that the allocation of resources is the fundamental task they face. It is the curious characteristic of politics that a very small amount of power, correctly used, can be sufficient to gain control over a very large quantity of resources, both physical and human. To understand fully how any individual government is actually operating, therefore, it is necessary to trace the direction and intensity of all the possible functional flows, and of their interactions – a simple equation of power between government and society would not only be misleading, but meaningless. To trace them, they must first be identified and labelled.

The government puts *out* resources to perform the function of *power resource extraction* by which, in turn, it takes in necessary *support*.

Being challenged continuously concerning its right to do this, it puts *out* more resources in *input control* in order to regulate and, where necessary, screen out *demands* coming *in*.

It will, further, regulate society in its own interests, through the general function of interest arbitration which can be either positive or negative. By *positive interest arbitration* it strengthens interests and thus attaches them to itself, at the same time depriving the society at large of the resources implied; by *negative interest arbitration* it does the reverse. However, the strengthening of interests soon implies a challenge to the authority of the government itself and will lead to corrective action being applied, so that the two processes are in fact continuous. The principal means employed can be simplified into taxes on the strong and subsidies for the weak, but since the resources for the maintenance of the system in each case are drawn from the social system and the political system of itself produces nothing, the maintenance of the political system in its existing form is possible only for as long as sufficient groups within the society have an expectation of getting something out of it.

In Table 1.1 the symbols P and F refer to inputs to and outputs from the political system respectively; Q and E to inputs to and outputs from the social system with which it is conterminous. The symbols + and – (read 'positive' and 'negative') identify the direction of flow.

The principle of economy of effort goes right to the heart of the system, however. Thus, though all governments owe their origins at some time, and their continued maintenance ultimately, to their faculty of coercion, they do not choose to operate in the coercive mode for most purposes because it involves a disproportionate drain on their resources and weakens them for their ultimate task: their own defence against an external attack or natural disaster. What happens when they do operate in coercive mode will be the subject of a later chapter. Basically, however, a government depends on force in the way that banks depend

Table 1.1 *The political and social systems*

	Input	*Output*
Political	P+ support	F– power resource extraction
	P– demands	F+ input control
Social	Q– taxes	E– negative interest arbitration
	Q+ subsidies	E+ positive interest arbitration

Source: Calvert (1969b)

on their reserves. No government has anything like enough force at its disposal to subdue all its citizens if they all rise in revolt simultaneously. But since they rarely, if ever, do so, governments can continue to operate for very long periods of time with very small reserves of support, and the longer they have operated, the greater the confidence that they will continue to do so, and the greater the degree of actual positive popular support on which they can count.

Popular support will be maximised if, in addition, the government can be seen to be doing visibly useful things for its citizens. However, to do this requires a great deal of money, and in consequence the first task of government is to extract from the society it governs the resources it requires not only for its own maintenance but for its chosen programme. The principal way in which this is done is by taxation, which in the modern state has almost completely superseded the system of individual fees and charges for specific services which earlier governments used. Taxes are not paid voluntarily; they are extracted from citizens more or less painlessly with the aid of a series of bargains to supply remedies for specific demands which the citizens or their representatives present, but they are extracted nevertheless, and the first task of a successful government is to maintain the function of power resource extraction.

Given adequate resources, the government can then embark on a strategy of maximising supports and minimising demands in which its use of positive and negative outputs is very keenly attuned to the needs of the situation. A government which in this way is keenly aware of the desires of its citizens is commonly called a *democracy*; one that does not is loosely termed a *dictatorship*, particularly if coercion is used to limit demands upon the system. The problems of classifying systems, however, will be dealt with further in Chapter 3.

COMPARISON

The basic unit of study in comparative politics, then, is the state or political system. There are quite a number of them – 179 are currently members of the United Nations (1992), but some long-established states (Monaco, Andorra) are not and some newer states (Palestine, Taiwan) have been unable to gain recognition. More than 200 entities are expected to be represented at the 1996 Olympic Games in Atlanta, Georgia. This number is in theory quite large enough for meaningful analysis in statistical terms. However, the universe of states is not a random sample, and its members differ drastically in all kinds of obvious ways.

At one end of the scale there is the gigantic Russian Federation. It stretches across eleven time zones, and covers 17,075,000 square kilometres, or one-eighth of the world's land surface. At the 1989 Soviet census, it had a population of 147,021,869. At the other end of the scale is the Pacific island of Nauru, with a population of 8,100 (1983 census) on an area of 21.3 square kilometres (2,130 hectares), most of it bare jagged coral (*Statesman's Year Book, 1992–3*). Clearly any comparison between Russia, on the one hand, and Nauru on the other must be almost meaningless, even if the formal legal status of each is the same. The disparities are so great that a small handful of cases – the United States, Russia, Japan, for example – invalidate the generalisations about the rest.

Hence, having first defined the unit for study, the second general principle of comparison is to ensure that as many variables as possible are held in common. One could compare, for example, the United States and the former Soviet Union, and it soon becomes clear why the former has survived and the latter has not. Britain (area 241,705 square kilometres, population 57.41 million (1990 estimate)) is comparable with France (area 543,965 square kilometres, population 56.61 million (1990 census, provisional)) because they are, by world standards, very similar in population and basic levels of development, located in the same temperate region of the world, have many similar geographical features, share a common historical tradition, exhibit rather similar economic and social structures and have banded themselves together in an association called the European Community. There are many interesting generalisations that can be made about all Western European states, both big and small (Gallagher, Laver and Mair, 1992). But there can be considerable problems in trying to make comparisons between widely separated states even where they have some obvious similarities: between, say, France and Thailand (area 513,115 square kilometres, population 55.89 million (1989 estimate)), or Ireland (area 68,895 square kilometres, population 3.52 million (1991 census, preliminary)) and Sri Lanka (area 65,610 square kilometres, population 14.84 million) (*Statesman's Year Book, 1992–3*).

Political scientists, therefore, have suggested a number of possible strategies or approaches to the general problems of comparison, and one of these may well have advantages over all the others in considering any given problem.

1. *Whole-unit approach*. The examples given so far are of a whole-unit approach. Their authors try, more or less successfully depending on the space available, to compare all relevant structures in two modern states that have important aspects in common. However, when comparing more than two countries at a time (pair-wise comparison), the whole-unit approach generates so much information that handling it can be very troublesome.

2. *Competing-power-centres approach*. Other writers have borrowed from anthropologists the technique of comparing different societies known as the competing-power-centres approach. This involves, for politics, identifying centres of political power in given societies, and finding out with whom they compete and for what. Certain patterns recur again and again, the best known of which is generally known as the conflict between the *centre* and the *periphery* (Galtung, 1971; see also Clapham, 1985; Migdal, 1988). Conflict between centre and periphery is a basic pattern operating both between states and within states.

   In the latter case it commences whenever political unification takes place, whether this is by the voluntary linking of states in alliance or confederation, the federation of states of common heritage, or the conquest of imperial possessions by a colonising power. Generally speaking, the stronger the resistance put up by the periphery to the pretensions of the central authority, the weaker the structure of the whole. Hence, by examining more closely the nature of the competing centres, greater insight can be gained into the special conditions that gave rise to federalism in the United States or Germany, as opposed to its abandonment in Colombia or Venezuela; federalism being, in fact, a very special case of a stalemate in the conflict between centre and periphery. In Switzerland the balance between centre and periphery is weighted much more decisively in favour of the periphery, while in the European Community the bulk of the strength of the institution continues to reside with the periphery and the centre has only very limited powers for specific purposes. There is, for example, no *general* power of the Community to intervene in individual planning disputes, for example, and provided that the state concerned has conformed to the specific requirements of the treaty, it can otherwise do what it likes. Consequently the Community cannot as yet be regarded as a state in its own right.
3. *Local-community approach*. Another level again is the local-community approach. In this, reasonably sized areas defined as forming communities with some sort of individual coherence are compared across national boundaries. Rokkan and Valen used this technique to identify differences in size, scale, potential for political organisation, specialisation etc. which have obvious implications for the comparison of the countries concerned (Rokkan and Valen, in Rose, 1974: 315). Studies of towns in different countries have been made for various purposes, usually by geographers or town-planners, and these too have obvious value for the understanding of comparative politics (Whiteford, 1964). An obvious weakness, however, springs from the very

different organisation, powers and capabilities of units in different countries.

CONCLUSION

Finally, it is, of course, quite legitimate to study any one country or any one aspect of politics on its own, in the hope that one's findings may be interesting in themselves, and it is a sobering fact that at least a third, and probably over half, of all published work in 'comparative' politics is still of this kind (Mayer, 1989). But such studies will be much more valuable if they are done in the awareness that there is value to others in recording results in a form that will make later comparison easier, while there is also an advantage to oneself in using knowledge of other countries to formulate a wider range of questions to ask of the data. There is no advantage to anyone, either, in piling up so much material that no one handling it can do anything useful with it, or, on the other hand, spending so much time deciding on an approach that the journey never begins.

KEY CONCEPTS

authority: to have the right to do something or to instruct others to do something.

government: an organisation which has established a successful claim to have the legitimate monopoly of the use of force.

international relations: the study of relations between states.

legitimacy: the fact that a government is generally recognised to have the right to do what it does.

nation: people identified by the sense of possession of a common language, religion, culture or ethnic origin.

non-governmental organisations (NGOs): organisations having an existence independent of government.

politics: the making of decisions in society.

power: the ability to get others to do what you want.

sovereignty: the belief that states are in every sense quite distinct and separate from one another, treating with one another as equals, and owing no duty to any outside earthly authority.

state: the organised community within which a government claims obedience as of right of all citizens.

SAMPLE QUESTIONS

Candidates should expect questions on a comparative politics paper to be explicitly comparative. If a question names a specific country, they can expect the question to be designed to test their knowledge of a specific problem area. In all cases, however, they should expect to *compare* and *contrast* two or more political systems (or types of political systems) in such a way that they demonstrate awareness of the wider issues involved. They will also get credit for showing an understanding of current events relevant to the question.

Candidates should be careful to note whether the syllabus allows them to draw upon examples from countries outside the list of those specified for more detailed study. The University of London GCE syllabus for Paper 6, for example, allows them to do so in Part B, but not in Part A, though as ever the examples would have to be relevant to the topic under discussion.

Some possible topics for examination questions on this chapter would be:

What is the comparative method, and how can we apply it to the study of politics?
Can the study of comparative politics be 'scientific'?
What are the differences between government, state and nation?

FURTHER READING

On the definition and scope of politics see Crick (1964) and Runciman (1963). Dogan and Pelassy (1984) give a crisp and interesting overview of the comparative method at work.

The functionalist approach is dealt with by Almond in his introduction to Almond and Coleman (1960). Sartori (1970) deals with the necessity for accurate identification of concepts. On the differences between state and nation see Seton-Watson (1977).

Methodology and research design in the social sciences generally are dealt with in Allan and Skinner (1991).

The student should be encouraged from the beginning to seek and find the most up-to-date data available. The most comprehensive ready reference, published annually, is the *Statesman's Year Book*, used above. Both the United Nations and UN organisations such as UNESCO publish regular year books or similar compilations of statistics on a comparative basis. Unfortunately, however, not all countries publish their own statistical year books, such as the *Annual Abstract of Statistics* in the United Kingdom, and many countries fail to report important data, for example, unemployment figures or the national rate of homicide, even to the UN.

PART TWO
Environment and Development

2 Environment and development

INTRODUCTION

The context of politics is to be found in the environment. As this chapter shows, the environment today is the product of human economic development. Politics, however, has not necessarily developed in the same sense. What then is meant by the notion of political development?

ENVIRONMENT

The history of human political organisation has been shaped by the *environment.* By environment is meant two things: generally, the world and all that is in it and, specifically, that part of it in which a specific political system is located. It can be divided into the natural environment, the built environment and the social environment.

1. The *natural environment* consists of the physical topography of a country, its climate, its soils, its water resources and its vegetation. However, much of what people today regard as the 'natural' environment has in fact been determined by human activity. The deserts of Iraq and the Sahel, the great American dust-bowl and the Dorset heathlands are all the end-product of imperfect farming techniques. The bare hills of Croatia and the Philippines were once covered with forest. They are quite as artificial as cities such as Rijeka or Manila.
2. The *built environment* of cities and towns is designed for human comfort and convenience, though with ever-increasing size it frequently falls short on both counts. The one thing it lacks, however, is the ability to produce the food on which its residents depend. To control supplies of food it must control the countryside.
3. The *social environment* both determines and is determined by the physical environment, whether natural or artificial. With the

development of human societies the social environment for all has changed accordingly.

Early societies

The environment of early human beings was certainly very unlike that of modern times. Fortunately, populations were small and, since humans are omnivores, they were able to adapt to a wide range of climates and conditions. The unromantic characteristic of human beings that has ensured their survival has been an unspecialised digestive system, capable of tackling most foods that come to hand.

Early human beings lived in very small communities. The exact size of these communities is unknown; they were probably bands, that is to say groups not as small as the nuclear family units of gorillas, nor as big as the tribes of baboons. The government of the band, therefore, was not a specialised function, and there really was no clear distinction between the family and the community. Recently, DNA analysis has indicated that all living human beings may be descended from a single female who lived in Africa some 200,000 years ago, which is the very recent past in terms of evolution.

Moreover, it appears that different bands must have interacted with one another, and that mating between individuals of different bands was normal. The complex rules needed to secure this in primitive communities survive in a number of forms, and they constitute the basis for the incorporation of new members of the band and hence its possibilities for growth into a tribe.

Significantly, this process coincided with the emergence of larger permanent settlements, termed towns or cities, based on a regular food supply. At or soon after the end of the last Ice Age (c. 10,000 B.C.) an accidental mutation between two wild grasses in Anatolia gave rise to emmer, the primitive form of modern cultivated wheat, the basis of the civilisation of the Mediterranean basin. Somewhat later, a similar mutation and crossing of strains in what is now Guatemala gave rise to maize, the foundation of the civilisation of the New World (Farb, 1968: 257–9). Together with the development of the wet cultivation of rice in Asia, these developments, quite independently, made it possible for large human communities to emerge and to remain in one place, engaged in common tasks over a considerable period, by generating a considerable surplus of food which could be stored (and indeed had to be stored during the winter). These large-scale communities became the basis of one of the most important social and political inventions: the town or city (Bury, 1956: 74–5). Indeed the word city – *polis* in Greek – gave its name to politics.

At the same time, this social reorganisation necessitated large-scale storage and the defence of the supplies thus won. For ever since cities came into existence, they have had to live in conflict with their envious neighbours, who have always tried to subject them to their political control so that they too could draw on the resources they generated. However, war seems to have been a characteristic feature of human organisation from the earliest times, and a great deal of human social and all human political organisation is strongly conditioned by it. It is possible that, at least at first, it had a eugenic effect in that the accidents of evolution had eliminated many of the creatures who might have become human beings' most persistent natural enemies, and the few such animals which were left were just dangerous enough to require co-operation to tackle them, but not dangerous enough to eliminate the human race entirely. This had a very important consequence for politics: political leadership tended to be derived from military leadership.

The development of larger-scale forms of social organisation derived from a number of sources. Conquest was one, but it was not the whole story. The attraction of greater food resources, the fame of a successful leader, and the endless growth of towns, all played a part.

Of course, in the absence of written records or inscriptions there is no direct first-hand evidence, even in the most advanced cultures, for the existence of politics. Scholars *infer* the political development of modern societies from what limited material remains survive, and such inferences depend – too heavily for comfort – both on the prejudices of the investigator and on his or her own knowledge of primitive cultures. This knowledge can be obtained only from present-day societies.

Politics in early societies

What, then, do present-day anthropologists actually say about the origins of modern society? To begin with, they confirm that no society, however primitive, lacks politics. There may be, as the Nuer of the Sudan illustrate, no actual discernible government; no one gives instructions to the rest of the tribe and all disputes are resolved by *arbitration* (Evans-Pritchard, 1940: 4–5). Yet decisions are made. They may not be made through the setting up of a distinct separate organ of decision-making, but they are made nevertheless. And it is significant, perhaps, that they are almost invariably ascribed to the male members of society. This is not to say that there are not decisions of political importance made among the female section of such communities, it may mean only that they are not noticed by anthropologists, who are mostly male.

Second, they suggest that there is no one form of development followed by all primitive societies. The emergence of the state, as anthropologists tend to call it, or government, as it will be termed here, does not follow an unchanging pattern. As a matter of fact, the very idea of a state is historically peculiar to Europe; there is no exact parallel to it in Islamic thought, where the identity of state and belief was originally seen as axiomatic (Rosenthal, 1962: 3–4). And there is no exact correspondence with it in China either, for Chinese thought allowed for only one universal society, focused on the emperor (Bloodworth, 1969: 325–7).

The most general form of government adopted, however, is that of the tribal chiefdom. Modern tribal societies purport to be based on kin groups. It is not known whether or not these correspond to real relationships. It is probable that they do not, on the grounds, as already stated, that intermarriage is one of the fundamental characteristics of human societies. What complicates the question is that, certainly in many historical cases, the concept of kinship was a retroactive fiction. As Henige convincingly shows in *The Chronology of Oral Tradition*, kinship is primarily a ceremonial relationship, and is normally adjusted to allow for political changes (Henige, 1974: 4). Most important is the fictitious incorporation into the kin structure not just of individuals but of groups. When the tribe goes to war and fights another tribe and the other tribe is beaten then the lesser, defeated tribe tends to be incorporated over a period of time into the structure of the state. It can be found not only among primitive communities in the sense in which anthropologists study them, but also historically, for example in the *Anglo-Saxon Chronicle*, where the West Saxons incorporated the followers of Withgar in the Isle of Wight and of Port, the eponymous founder of Portsmouth.

If human beings, as some now argue, have always been hierarchical animals, then they can be expected to replicate in their tribal social structure the basic structure of the extended family. Hence there probably has been, since pre-human times, some kind of surrogate 'head of the family' in most tribes, and this post was almost certainly hereditary in one family.

In some surviving states membership of a specific family is still a requisite for access to real political power: in Kuwait, the al-Sabah family, in Qatar the al-Thani family, and in Bahrein the al-Khalifa family. In Saudi Arabia the state actually takes its name from the ruling family.

Rules of succession

These states vary, however, in the extent to which the *rules of succession* are predetermined; in Saudi Arabia, for example, a family deliberation can alter the order of succession. In all states in which the order is not defined by general agreement – in republics as much as, if not more so than, in monarchies – the rules still have to be settled afresh at each transition of power. The way in which this is usually done is by armed conflict.

Similar conflicts lie at the heart of the constitutional order in all countries. In the United Kingdom, for example, where collective force has not been used to alter the disposition of political power since 1688–91, the fact that Queen Elizabeth II is directly descended from King Alfred can easily be misunderstood as confirming the hereditary basis of the monarchy. She is also descended from Charlemagne, Louis IX and Rodrigo the Cid, but she is not Queen of Germany, France or Spain, and in constitutional theory her position in England (though not Scotland) depends ultimately on an act of conquest.

Today, of course, though the majority of these families survive, they have almost invariably lost their powers. In Western Europe and Japan their survival has depended on the willingness of their incumbents to play a constitutional role as heads of state. Where they have recently disappeared, in Iran, Greece, Afghanistan and Ethiopia, they still had, or claimed to have, power. As Aristotle put it, 'the less the area of the prerogative, the longer will the authority of a king last unimpaired' (Aristotle V, ii, 1312, in Barker, 1968: 243). Today, as in his day, monarchy is not fashionable. Nevertheless, the fact that almost all modern states have passed through a period of monarchical rule, and that this has been very much longer in sum than any period of republican rule, is bound to be significant. It is from this age that modern heads of state, now generally called *presidents*, inherit the reserve powers of their office.

Nor are presidents of most modern states presidents in the sense of the chief officer of a golf club, or a debating society. They are often – very often – people like the Sforza, the Visconti or the Medici of the time of Machiavelli, who owe their control of state power to the direct or indirect use of force – people like Jerry Rawlings of Ghana, Ibrahim Babangida of Nigeria, Fidel Castro of Cuba.

Yet the states which they control have inherited the notion of *law* which was established in a monarchical framework. Arbitrators approach each problem separately, guided at most by basic principles of fairness which they determine in a given situation. Law, on the other hand, means a continuity through time over a much longer period and, more importantly, it is necessary for the extension of the tribe beyond a certain point. However, until comparatively modern times the law was regarded as being a fixed, indivisible entity; something given, the product of divine order and backed by divine sanction. The lawgivers, the men who codified law, the Solons of this world, did not, on this view, *invent* laws. They were simply the individuals who recognised the existence of the law and made it available to all. The law itself already existed and had always existed and would always exist. The idea that law could actually be created was a recent invention, apparently of the medieval thinker Marsiglio of Padua (Ullmann, 1965: 67).

The prime function of law is to regulate disputes. Inside the tribe, war is regulated by law of some kind. Outside the tribe there are, in primitive circumstances, no laws of war as such. There may be customs which hold good at certain times and certain places. But between tribes war has always been a bloodthirsty affair. Only inside the tribe does it appear that fighting was inhibited, and necessarily so; in other words, the structure of a community cannot long survive if people spend all their time fighting each other. The war of all against all is in fact completely contrary to the maintenance in practical terms of all orderly society, and the only result of it is that the tribes split up.

Of what, then, does the law consist? First, it must contain rules by which disputes can be regulated. These rules concern the three properties of the tribe: people, pigs and gardens, to borrow a striking phrase from the anthropologist Roy Rappaport (1968: 3). (By pigs can be understood herd animals of all kinds, such as goats and cows.) Second, it must contain established *rules* for the maintenance of the system as a whole.

The game of politics

These rules are the rules of a game, the game of politics. The game is a complex one, for it consists of competition within the tribal boundaries for access to each of the principal resources. Part of the complexity stems from the nature of the resources themselves, for it is necessary to point out straight away that the first has a unique property – that people are divided into two groups, each in competition for the other. From a male point of view, women are resources, but they are also players; and to women, men are not only players, they are also resources, though men may find it beneath their dignity to think so.

A second complication arises from the fact that the various resources may be traded off between players, not according to their 'intrinsic' value, but according to the saliency of the need for each felt by the players in question, in each of the series of transactions of which the game of politics consists. Since the game of politics lasts a very long time – much longer than any human lifetime – there develops a very complex awareness of the network of bargains and consequent relationships involved which acts as the fundamental underpinning of all other human relationships within society.

Why does the game take so long? It is tempting to answer: because without it life cannot go on, or the species be reproduced – but that seems too great an oversimplication. In pre-modern times there seems little evidence that people had to participate in politics simply in order to live. This is not to say that politics did not intrude itself upon them, and more frequently as time went on, but simply that unless one lived in a city there seems to be have been little need, simply to earn one's livelihood, to take part in politics at all. Nor, for the reproduction of the species to have been quite effective over a space of more than two million years, was it apparently necessary for mankind to develop settled communities. One is forced back to the explanation that people take part in politics not because it is essential to them, but because they like it; that, in short, it enables them to *structure* time. Human beings are a long-lived species (among animals only the blue whale lives longer), and many of them are already forgetting how hard they had to work to structure time before television was invented.

For politics is not just a game, it is the ultimate game, a game played with real people and real things. Consequently, as Bailey points out, its rules are different in nature from other games in that you as a player have three options about how to treat them. You may play according to the rules and seek to win that way. You may seek to bend the rules in your favour, or even to break them when others are not looking, for there is no umpire to tell you that you cannot. Or, you can work to change the rules, so that you can make the game more congenial (Bailey, 1969: 32–3).

GOVERNMENT AND TERRITORY

Government begins by some individuals establishing a claim to the monopoly of the use of force over others. It seems only prudent, therefore, to ask whether or not there is any natural predisposition in human beings towards the use of force. Among philosophers, Thomas Hobbes in particular believed that there was. Without strong government, therefore, human beings would soon relapse into savagery – 'the war of all against all'. Some modern ethologists agree that human beings, in common with other animal species, have an innate instinct of aggression. Lorenz (1966) remains a well-known exponent of this view.

Aggression is, he suggests, an essential drive which defines the community and protects it against outside attack. In other words, if the community has a boundary (and it may be a highly mobile boundary), that boundary is defined as the line at which the aggressive response is triggered off by an intruder. It is a fail-safe mechanism in that it is safer to respond aggressively to someone who turns out to be a friend than it is to accept as a friend someone who turns out to be an enemy.

This seems a highly plausible argument, and a simple mechanism of this kind could be a reasonable explanation of the aggressive actions of animals. But there are weaknesses in it. First of all, for animals aggression does not mean actual fighting. Baboons, for example, get up every morning to go down to the edge of their territory and jump up and down and howl at their neighbours for half an hour, but they rarely come to blows with them. This aggression, therefore, is ritual aggression, and a similar ritual element can be observed in human societies. Significantly, these rituals are not innate, they are *learned,* for there is abundant evidence that one of the great characteristics of primate species is their social organisation. Social behaviour, which requires *co-operation,* not only enhances the chances of survival for the group as a whole but also for every member of it. What applies to other primates is even more true of humans, for the long period it takes for a human baby to become an adult gives even more opportunity for behaviour to be learned.

Hence, few modern psychologists would agree that there is an innate instinct or *drive* of aggression. The opponents of the idea of the aggressive drive argue that human beings are *instinctively underdetermined* – that is to say, there are very few things they *must* do. They go on to argue that there is really no evidence that human aggression is instinctive. The evidence is entirely consistent with aggression being *socially conditioned.* It derives from an unfavourable environment, and in particular from overcrowding.

Many of those who reject the idea of an aggressive drive follow the view of John Dollard and his colleagues, who asserted that 'aggression is always a consequence of frustration' (Dollard *et al.,* 1939). The *frustration–aggression thesis* is still widely popular, despite more than a decade of derision from the New Right. Among political scientists, Ted Gurr has made use of it to develop a theory of how internal conflict arises in a political system (Gurr, 1970: 24). Though such lines of research still look promising, they present considerable difficulties, since the concept of frustration is a very subjective one. Overcrowding and bad social conditions can undoubtedly be trying, but circumstances which one person finds frustrating may strike another as perfectly reasonable.

In any case, why should overcrowding and bad social conditions necessarily lead to an aggressive response? Alternative possibilities exist: withdrawal, accommodation or, in extreme cases, mental breakdown. The point is, surely, that people do behave aggressively in certain social conditions, and the relevance today is that these are the conditions in which modern societies have to function. Aggression begins with their personal relations with one another, so the ways in which those relations may be modified are of fundamental importance to their political development. If 'an Englishman's home is his castle', does the separation from his neighbours which this brings help him to develop a society in which his level of aggression is relatively low? Or can he shrink his horizons to the walls of a French, American or Russian apartment and still get on well with the people next door, and vote accordingly? Certainly there is some evidence that alteration of the physical environment in which people live can bring about a marked decline in violence.

The modern phenomenon of competition for the control and use of territory is to a great extent the artificial product of human social conditions and can be explained under the frustration–aggression thesis by competition for food in conditions of growing scarcity and serious overcrowding (Crook, in Montagu, 1973: 183ff.).

Overcrowding in giant cities has been the most striking social development of the twentieth century, as the continuing growth of Tokyo, Shanghai and Mexico City demonstrates. Overcrowding may indeed lead to sudden complete biological collapse in some species – rabbits, for example. The correction of such problems is a vast political problem, with implications for government control and use of land throughout the community. Most developed countries in Europe and North America have in the past fifty years come to acknowledge some of the problems involved, and have adopted elaborate systems of planning and control of development, or zoning as it is known in the United States. However, during the 1980s many of these controls were again abandoned, in the belief that all such matters can safely be left to the free market. The major disturbances in Los Angeles in 1992 suggest that they cannot. RUBBISH

Land ownership and reform

The expansion of towns is only a special case of the control of land and its capacity to generate wealth. The Industrial Revolution was preceded, and made possible by, an agricultural revolution which dramatically increased the productivity of a given amount of land. Control of political power was used to take productive land away from country-dwellers and to create large estates. In turn, the Industrial Revolution gave rise to transport systems which made possible the conquest of the countryside by town-dwellers. As this control has been extended in the present century, it has resulted in the industrialisation of agriculture (agribusiness). The impact on the environment of the 'internal colonisation' of the countryside can be plainly seen in the replacement of traditional subsistence agriculture by large farms or plantations managed for export and/or commercial sale of a single product or limited range of products.

There is no *direct* relationship between unequal land ownership and dictatorial government. Australia, a democratic country, has one of the most unequal land-distribution patterns in the world. However, land ownership had historically given rise to a degree of political control over others which they could not effectively be challenged. Hence the redistribution or reorganisation of land has been a major factor in breeding resentment against incumbent governments over the last two hundred years, and all reforming programmes have had to take account of it.

The Marxist model called for the common ownership of land, as with other forms of property. However, things did not go in practice as Marx had forecast. In the Soviet Union under Stalin (1924–53), agricultural land was reorganised into collective farms under state ownership. Great suffering was occasioned to millions of peasants, and a catastrophic drop in production followed, bringing hardship and even starvation to many parts of the country. Peasants living on collective farms were, however, permitted to retain a small plot for their own use, and during the 1980s these private plots contributed a disproportionate amount to the overall level and variety of production. In China, however, during the Great Leap Forward (1958–61) private property in agriculture was wholly abolished by the formation of communes, only to be restored by allowing private plots openly from 1961 to 1966. During the Great Proletarian Cultural Revolution 'rectification campaigns' were used to induce the peasants once more to surrender their plots, with some success, but evidently not without cost in terms of economic disruption. More recently, under the 'open-door' policy of economic liberalisation promoted by Deng Xiaoping, peasants have again been allowed to sell produce from private plots, with a significant increase in their standard of living as a result. In Cuba no allowance was made for private plots, and the country has conspicuously suffered from a serious decline from levels of pre-revolutionary production which, even during the 1960s, forced it to import black beans, a staple food in the Caribbean area (Goldenberg, 1965: 227).

A common charge against land reform schemes is that they lead to inefficient production. It is true that (in theory) this problem can be solved and more food produced from existing land for a considerable time into the future. However, this is not a solution, for three reasons. First, it requires high inputs of energy which the world ecosystem is just not capable of absorbing. Second, it will exhaust the soil, and once that happens the situation will get steadily and irremediably worse. Last, in the meanwhile the existing levels of inequality will have to be maintained. Conflict, therefore, can arise from the fact that advanced industrial development is at least in part a *positional good* (Hirsch, 1977); that is to say, something whose desirability to others stems from the fact that only a few people at a time can have it.

This global conflict arises, in part, from the external colonisation of the rest of the world by the European powers, between the fifteenth and twentieth centuries. It is natural to blame colonisation, despite the subsequent collapse of these empires, for the very unequal pattern of economic development among today's independent states. Under this assumption, it was common in the 1970s to group states in one of three 'worlds', according to their level of economic development.

The advanced industrial nations of Western Europe, the United States and Canada, Japan and Australia formed what was termed the 'First World'. These states continued to dominate the world economy and, if anything, to become richer in relation to the others. The 'Second World', consisting of the Soviet Union, its allies in Eastern Europe and elsewhere, and China, had effectively isolated themselves from the world economy. They claimed to have an effective alternative model of development which other states could follow. All other states formed the 'Third World'. Most, but not all, were former colonies. What they tended to have in common was that they were relatively poor and dependent on the production of primary products for the world market for what income they did have. Once independent, their prime aim was to follow the path of economic development already trodden by the advanced industrialised nations.

ECONOMIC DEVELOPMENT

Economic development refers to a process by which societies increase their capacity to produce. In practice, economists tend not to draw distinctions between what they produce, so that the standard measure of economic development is the *gross national product (GNP)*, the sum total of all that is produced by economic activity in a single year. Since states vary so much in size and productive resources, it is often best to distinguish between more or less 'wealthy' states in terms of their GNP *per capita*.

This immediately shows that the world is a much more complicated place than the 'Three World' model would suggest. First of all, it makes clear that the majority of states are indeed very poor and that there are relatively few rich ones. However, in income terms they form a continuum, not a set of separate categories, though the World Bank has found it useful to divide them into four groups: low-income countries (including China), lower-middle-income countries, higher-middle-income countries and high-income countries. Data on GNP for the 'Second World' has not so far been generally available. However, where it is, the figures suggest that the 'Second World' is a political, not an economic concept, a view supported by the collapse of the Soviet Union and with it the notion of a distinctive path to economic development. Today, therefore, for a variety of reasons, it is more usual to speak of two main categories according to their rough positions on the globe: the 'North', the advanced industrialised countries, and the 'South', the rest.

There is no doubt that the Industrial Revolution, which began first in Britain, then spread to other parts of Europe and later to the rest of the world, marks a radical transformation in economic processes and as such a major step in economic development. For us, states that have achieved this level of economic development are 'modern'; the others are not.

Older theories of national differences in terms of economic development were based on the concept of *modernisation*. This was a *unilinear* model which envisaged development as a single continuum, along which societies moved slowly from traditional to modern. As modernity, mainly in the form of technology, industry and capital investment, was diffused to the less developed countries (LDCs), it was once generally believed that they would achieve similar levels of development.

In the model advanced by the economic historian W.W. Rostow (1960, 1971), the process of economic modernisation takes a considerable, though diminishing time to get under way, but accelerates into self-sustaining growth after a certain stage of development (the *take-off* point) has been reached. However, not all countries do achieve sustainable growth, and the classic example is Argentina. It reached what Rostow believed was its take-off point in the 1920s and was at that stage among the half-dozen richest nations in the world. Today it ranks eightieth (*Buenos Aires Herald*, 15 July 1990).

It is no coincidence that it was in Argentina and Brazil, where economic development was expected but failed to take place either in the way or to the extent expected, that writers proposed an alternative model of development generally known as *dependency theory* (Cardoso and Faletto, 1979). Drawing some of its inspiration from the Marxist critic Paul Baran (1957), it was soon widely adopted in Europe, Asia and Africa. One of the best known of the European dependency theorists, André Gunder Frank (1978), drew an important distinction between *undeveloped* and *underdeveloped* countries. Arguing that the rich Western nations were now the global 'bourgeoisie' exploiting the Third World 'proletariat', he claimed that capitalism was actually *causing* underdevelopment. Underdeveloped countries had economies that had actually been *distorted* by capitalism. Capitalism, for Frank, promotes uneven growth in the form of both national and regional polarisation. Funds flow, not from the rich nations to the poor as aid agencies would like, but rather from the poor nations to the rich, as they pay for expensive imported manufactured goods, and the multinational corporations (MNCs) operating on their territory repatriate their profits. Far from being destined to follow the same pattern of development as the industrialised countries, the LDCs are the victims of the world economic system. Their lack of development is not something natural; it is actually caused by the existence of the developed economies, which has ensured that they remain suppliers of the primary raw materials the developed economies need. Only through a major change in the balance of power in the world system and a radical shift in the terms of trade in their favour can they be enabled to break out of this condition of dependency.

However, in 1973 the Organisation of Petroleum Exporting Countries (OPEC) tried to engineer just such a change by restricting production and forcing up the price of crude on the world market. Though this brought about a brief recession in Western Europe and the United States, both this first 'oil shock' and the second that followed in 1979 had a much more serious effect on the majority of Third World economies that did not have petroleum. By 1990, despite a failure to implement effective conservation measures, the advanced industrial countries had become much less dependent on imported petroleum, and the collapse of the world coffee and sugar agreements, which had existed since the 1930s, demonstrated that similar attempts to maintain prices in other commodities were even less likely to be successful. On the other hand, the so-called 'tiger' economies of Singapore, Thailand, Taiwan and South Korea, developed in co-operation with the advanced industrialised countries on the basis of low-cost production, had brought about very rapid rates of economic growth and a substantial degree of prosperity for the peoples of those countries.

Certainly, economic development depends on a number of preconditions, and the variety of the world's states means that no one pattern is likely to be applicable to all. On the other hand, the pessimism of the dependency theorists appears to be misplaced. It is possible for states in the Third World to develop. However, in the meanwhile for most of their inhabitants the gap between their living conditions and those of the inhabitants of the advanced industrialised countries is continuing to widen – but not for all. The figures in Table 2.1 make clear just how much variety there is between the experiences of different states, despite very similar levels of economic development.

POLITICAL DEVELOPMENT

It was, inevitably, tempting to try to analyse the development of political systems in terms of modernisation. The theme espoused by

Table 2.1 *GNP per capita of selected states in US dollars, 1988*

Range	*Population 1988*	*GNP per capita 1988 $*	*Growth 1965–88*	*Life expectancy*	*Adult illiteracy*
Low income	2,884.0	320	3.1	60	44
1 Mozambique	14.9	100	—	48	62
17 Nigeria	110.1	290	0.9	51	58
21 China	1,088.4	330	5.4	70	31
22 India	815.6	340	1.8	58	57
29 Ghana	14.0	400	–1.6	54	47
31 Sri Lanka	16.6	420	3.0	71	13
Lower-middle income	741.7	1,380	2.6	65	27
43 Bolivia	6.9	570	–0.6	53	26
57 Thailand	54.5	1,000	4.0	65	9
60 Jamaica	2.4	1,070	–1.5	73	—
65 Turkey	53.8	1,280	2.6	64	26
71 Mexico	83.7	1,760	2.3	69	6
76 Brazil	144.4	2,160	3.6	65	22
Upper-middle income	326.3	3,240	2.3	68	24
80 S. Africa	34.0	2,290	0.8	61	—
84 Argentina	31.5	2,520	0.0	71	5
88 Trinidad	1.2	3,350	0.9	71	4
90 Portugal	10.3	3,650	3.1	74	16
91 Greece	10.0	4,800	2.9	77	8
93 Libya	4.2	5,420	–2.7	61	33
High income	784.2	17,080	2.3	76	—
97 S. Arabia	14.0	6,200	3.8	64	—
100 Israel	4.4	8,650	2.7	76	5
104 Australia	16.5	12,340	1.8	76	a
105 UK	57.1	12,810	1.8	75	a
112 France	55.9	16,090	2.5	76	a
118 USA	246.3	19,840	1.6	76	a
120 Japan	122.6	21,020	4.3	78	a
121 Switzerland	6.6	27,500	1.5	77	a

a = UNESCO data, illiteracy less than 5 per cent
Source: World Bank (1990)

modernisation theorists, that all societies tend to move from more traditional forms of organisation towards a single, more modern form, is to be found in the work of Marx, Weber and Durkheim, among others.

Building on the work of the eighteenth-century economists, Marx and Engels (1848) argued that the political order derived directly from the prevailing *mode of production*. Hence there would be an appropriate political order for each stage of economic development, in a linear progress towards modernity, though one cut across with specific moments of transition. For them, societies were scattered at various stages along the road leading to socialism, but all were moving at greater or lesser speed towards the same place, a place where satisfaction of material needs would rest on the large-scale production associated with industrialisation. Thus the economic stage of *primitive accumulation* characterised by nomadic society was, they argued, displaced when slave labour became generally available by *feudal* society. This in turn gave way to *capitalist* society, in which, by a revolutionary seizure of power, rule passed from the aristocracy to the new *bourgeoisie*. Capitalist society, however, would in turn bring its own nemesis. By calling into existence an industrial working class, the *proletariat*, it created the class which would ultimately supplant it, and build on its ruins a *socialist* society in which 'the exploitation of man by man' would come to an end.

For Weber (1965, written *c.* 1919), the tendency towards the complexity of mass industrial society increasingly required societies to move from traditional and charismatic forms of authority towards legal-rational authority and bureaucratic organisation. Durkheim (1964, first published 1893) saw modern society as increasingly characterised by a division of labour and interdependence. These themes come together in the work of the post-Second World War structural functionalists, working under the influence of the American sociologist Talcott Parsons. For Apter (1965) *political modernisation* was a process of adaptation to the changing needs of economic development. The starting point was traditional society, which proved strongly resistant even to the impact of Western colonisation. 'Secular-libertarian' societies tended to emerge because of the particular needs and requirements of industrial society.

But political modernisation proved a very troublesome concept to define, let alone to apply systematically. Perhaps as you read this you are looking out on the glass, steel and concrete of a college, factory or block of flats which represent, in visual terms, a stage of the development of building techniques. As you look, you are aware that in turn this depends on a process of economic development, involving such trends as the growth of corporations, economies of scale, mass production, greater use of machinery, and substitution of natural products by synthetic ones. But it is not clear that the government of the town in which that building stands, or indeed the political system of any country in the world, has changed in the sense that builders have changed from the use of stone and wood to the use of concrete and glass, and the growth in size of political units is not in itself a guarantee of greater political effectiveness, and may well be the reverse. The term 'modernisation' was increasingly seen in the late 1960s as ethnocentric and misleading, even by those who continued to use it (Kautsky, 1972). The emergence of authoritarian regimes in post-independence Africa and in Latin America was seen as an alternative route to modernisation, and the notion of the universality of liberal democracy as a model seemed to be discredited (Huntington, 1968; see also Apter, 1987; Lenz and Shell, 1986).

Political development, the term that took its place, was from the outset a controversial term, with many definitions (Huntington, 1965). There was, and is, moreover, a tendency to assume that political development must in some way be related to if not actually *caused* by economic development. The theme that rational economic production required a well-educated and democratically controlled workforce was strongly in evidence in *convergence theory*, which argued (against very strong opposition on both sides) that the political systems of the USA and USSR were bound in time to get more like one another (Brzezinski and Huntington, 1964). After a long eclipse, a somewhat similar view has been enjoying a new vogue in the aftermath of the changes in Eastern Europe and the collapse of the former Soviet Union.

Convergence suggests that all societies are en route to industrialisation and hence that similar Western-style democratic political systems will displace authoritarian and state-socialist arrangements. The emerging societies will reflect the 'logic' (or needs) of industrialism, including urbanisation, advanced technology, well-developed communications, enhanced educational opportunities and high social mobility. Increased economic interdependence and increasing cultural similarity will reduce conflict between states and make the world a more stable and peaceful place.

Of course there are arguments that can be raised against the convergence model. There are many societies in the world that it would be difficult to see as moving towards industrialisation. Many parts of the world – Africa south of the Sahara, for example – have so little infrastructure (good roads, railways, adequate power supplies etc.) and so many social problems (not least, feeding their populations) that industrial development must be very limited for the foreseeable future. Industrial development itself, in any case, takes many forms, and the oil-producing states of the Middle East vary markedly in social structure from the 'high-tech', manufacturing states of the Far East, such as Taiwan and South Korea. Both are different, again, from older industrialised nations. The professional and technical expertise accorded most respect in any hierarchy of occupations varies a good deal too, as does the degree of status attached to education. Education is often least valued in the most industrialised nations, and the convergence model does not explain this. Authoritarian and personalist rulers remain, and only when they openly and flagrantly violate international law, as in the case of the 1990 Iraqi invasion of Kuwait, do they attract much attention from the world community. The emergence of fundamentalist Islamic regimes in countries such as Iran and the Sudan has also provided evidence against the convergence hypothesis.

Nevertheless, the convergence argument, in a rather specialised form, is still being used by the proponents of the so-called *free market* in both Western and Eastern Europe. Not only do they believe that the free market is a prerequisite for democracy, but they argue that the existence of the market in itself renders democracy inevitable. Better knowledge of a century and a half of Latin American political history suggests that this idea should be treated with the greatest possible caution.

However, there are two senses in which it is still not only possible but necessary to talk of political development, as a common theme which links together the political systems of the modern world within an historical framework.

1. With time there has been a tendency for political systems to become more *complex*.
2. Over the past two hundred years most, if not all, systems have been modified to allow for greater *participation* by the general mass of the people.

The concept of sovereignty in the modern sense is inseparable from the idea of the representation of the people, in an *assembly* which has successfully asserted its right to take part in the making of new laws.

> By 'assembly' is meant here a grouping together of people representing the society as a whole. They do not have to be elected by any specific system of election. There only has to be general acceptance that the assembly as constituted represents the people as a whole. It stands for all classes and all interests and acts on their behalf – and, they must obey it. (Verney, 1961: 3)

CONCLUSION

Political development, therefore, is a term which should be used very carefully. However, present-day politics can be understood only in a developmental context. Modern complex societies are built up out of relatively simple elements. The relationships within modern complex societies obviously reflect the nature of economic production, and the overarching framework of the global system determines the economic relationships not only between but within modern states. However, there is still substantial room for variation in the political arrangements within any given society, and the influence of political ideas such as freedom and participation has been so great as at times to override considerations of economic productivity.

KEY CONCEPTS

aggression: propensity to use force.

arbitration: listening to the views of two contending parties and proposing a solution which they have previously agreed to accept.

assembly: a group of people representing society as a whole.

convergence: the view that the logic of industrialisation is that all societies will become more alike.

development: in economics, the increase in a society's capacity to produce; in politics, the tendency of political systems to become more complex.

environment: generally, the world and all that is in it, and, specifically, that part of it in which a specific political system is located.

law: an authoritative code of rules for a society expressed in written form.

rules: principles which determine action, e.g. in a game.

Third World: those countries that are neither advanced industrial countries nor part of the former Eastern bloc.

SAMPLE QUESTIONS

Examination syllabuses require candidates not only to show that they know how systems work now, but to explain why, in terms of the historical, social and economic development of those systems. Candidates are unlikely, however, to be required to answer questions on political anthropology or primitive government, unless the syllabus specifically indicates that this is likely.

Where examination questions concern an aspect of the politics of only one country, it is still generally true that the categories used will have a wider comparative context, and awareness of the relevant debates would be an advantage.

How far can a developmental perspective enhance the understanding of politics?
What factors favour the unification of states into larger groupings?
'Communism is essentially a programme for the economic and social development of backward countries.' Discuss.
Is the nation state in Western Europe an historical anachronism?

FURTHER READING

On the global environment and its crisis see C. Thomas (1992). The concept of the environment in political analysis is discussed by Deutsch (1966) and Easton (1965b), as well as by other writers. Early warnings of today's environmental crisis came from Falk (1970) and Meadows *et al.* (1974).

Political anthropology is a specialist field not easily accessible, but Bailey (1969) uses an anthropological approach and introduces the concepts of rules and of the 'game' of politics. A clear and well-organised introduction to 'Third World' politics is given by Randall and Theobald (1985). On economic development Gauhar (1983) forms a useful introduction, while Rostow (1960) and Myrdal (1972) are classic statements of developmentalist theory. On the notion of political development see Huntington (1968) and Lenz and Shell (1986). Cardoso and Faletto (1979) was one of the first statements of dependency theory, and retains its interest well despite many later critics, while C. Thomas (1987) discusses the nature of present-day economic constraints on Third World states in the international arena.

3 Classification

INTRODUCTION

From the beginning of the study of politics, observers have tried to order their ideas by the use of various systems of classification. Modern systems utilise the basic concept of participation, in conjunction with other criteria. However, political systems are in constant evolution. Static typologies are therefore of little use compared with developmental models.

WHY CLASSIFY?

Classification as a means of organising information is essential, and the first system of classification propounded for states was that used by Aristotle himself, who divided them between those ruled by the One, by the Few, and by the Many (Aristotle, ed. Barker: 113). This distinction, even though it was not developed for use on modern complex states at all, is still useful, but only in a limited sense. It appeals to the most important of popular feelings about politics, the sense of how far – if at all – the system appears to respond to one's own individual wishes, and in an age when democracy is almost universally espoused as the ambition of each and every political system, it still operates as the chief criterion for determining just how far any given state or political system can be truly regarded as democratic.

But the mere number of the rulers (read decision-makers) in a modern system is not an adequate guide to the way in which the system as a whole actually operates, even assuming that the exact number could be determined. Concepts such as the Few and the Many are irritatingly imprecise. One of the few definite things that can be said, for example, about the 'Fourteen Families' traditionally said to control El Salvador is that intermarriage and breeding combine to make the actual number quite meaningless. For another thing, the capacity of the ultimate decision-makers is determined by their effectiveness. This depends both on the amount and accuracy of the information that reaches them, and on their capacity to implement their decisions once taken. Even 'Ramfis'

Trujillo of the Dominican Republic, who in 1962 personally shot his political prisoners with a machine-gun, had in other, more complex respects, to depend on others to act on his orders and so found himself forced to flee the country regardless (Diedrich, 1978: 248).

Once a ruler depends on others, autocracy is qualified, and so, in practice, the rule of the One becomes the rule of the Few. Not only must the others continue to render their services, but they may and do act in the name of the one person who bears the responsibility for all decisions of government. Under the Reagan administration in the United States (1981–9) this led to the doctrine of 'plausible deniability', by which subordinate officers acted in the name of the President in the belief (but without the formal assurance) that they had his authority. To understand other countries, therefore, one has to identify a set of criteria by which they can be sorted into recognisable categories.

Participation

The key concept for this purpose is the concept of *participation*. Almost all states nowadays consider that they are either democratic or aspiring to democracy. That is to say, their rulers believe that under their form of government, as far as human fallibility allows, the ultimate decisions are either taken by the people at large, or will be, as soon as they can be taught how to do it. Unhappily, there are two basic strands of thought concerning what is meant by democracy. The fact that these differences involve differences of technique rather than belief makes them of as much interest to the student of comparative politics as to political philosophers, and indeed they reflect the observations by those who first formulated them of the political systems of their own day.

Both views are concerned with the process of choice by which the people select their representatives and that by which people or representatives reach decisions on specific issues. The older view, represented in ancient times by Roman practice, and in modern theory by the writings of Rousseau, see both as aspects of what Rousseau termed 'the general will' (*volonté générale* – Rousseau, 1958: 20, 22–30). The general will of the people is not just the will of the majority, nor even of all individual people, it is a coherent expression of the feeling of the society as a whole. It is therefore possible to say that the general will cannot be understood and interpreted by a series of individual choices, but that anyone who can perceive what the general will is can point it out and advocate its support to his fellows. This was the view of Robespierre and the Jacobins, and it is one congenial to individuals or groups under the 'mixed' constitutions of most modern societies.

The more modern view, represented by Locke and Mill among theorists, is that all government is a process of compromise, and that the general will – if it exists – cannot be arrived at except by approximation. This approximation can be arrived at by accepting the decision of the majority in all processes of choice involving large numbers, but in the self-restraint also of that majority in tolerating the views of the minority (Locke, 1956: 49–50, 95–8; Mill, 1958: 102–3). Thus a series of shifting coalitions becomes possible on individual issues. Recent American writers, beginning with Dahl (1964a, b) and Kornhauser (1959), have increasingly emphasised the importance of keeping the process of choice essentially one of bargaining in a 'free market' of ideas.

Competitive vs. non-competitive systems

As already pointed out, the belief of the Communists in the absence of antagonistic conflict within their states and the role of the party as vanguard of the proletariat necessarily implied their adherence to the concept of the general will. A similar argument has been used by various self-appointed rulers to justify their actions as being guided by a superior form of legitimacy. Writers on these aspects of government have therefore propounded a number of schemes of ideological classification which takes these facts into account. Some have chosen to focus on the location of power in the system, others on the degree to which theory is reflected in a valid attempt to replace counting heads by a system for reaching a consensus of views. Thus Talmon distinguishes between 'representative' and 'totalitarian' democracy in his study of the conflict of the emergent ideas in the French revolutionary period (Talmon, 1961), while Almond and Coleman distinguish in Asia and Africa between 'Western' systems based on the acceptance of majority decision, and 'non-Western' systems in which attempts are made to include criteria of value on the process of decision, and to promote the solidarity of turbulent states by making decisions only when they command universal assent (Almond and Coleman, 1960: 17). Both terminologies, however, are highly unsatisfactory, and '*competitive*' and '*non-competitive*' are better.

Whatever the terminology employed, the fact is that structures of similar names perform different functions in each type of system. Thus political parties, which for some 'competitive' systems are largely concerned with articulating and aggregating interests, are for the 'non-competitive' systems primarily a means of mobilising support. 'Non-competitive' systems, abhorring overt conflict, do not allow for *interest groups* openly to operate as *pressure groups*, abolish or co-opt competing parties and predetermine the result of elections by various devices designed to monopolise political power for those favoured by the regime, often with the ideological justification that, because of their special knowledge, such matters should be the preserve of a small group or *elite*.

But these facts are not the product of the differences in terminology; the terminology has been selected to reflect just those differences.

Participation may be either *qualitative* or *quantitative.* A football match involves twenty-two players, a polo match eight. That is a quantitative difference. A football match may also involve the participation of a handful of spectators, if amateur, or of thousands, if professional, but the differences may have little impact on the performance of the players compared with the quantitative difference in the teams themselves if a member of one is sent off the field. Participation can also be further restricted or enhanced, other than by simple, clean-cut numerical criteria. Thus the fact that a goalkeeper's function is to remain within a defined area of the field is counter-balanced by allowing him increased freedom to handle the ball, while the fact that other players have greater freedom on the field is limited by the fact that the goal is only of a certain size, and so on.

In politics the most important differences between modern states are the number of *levels* on which, and *channels* through which, participation can take place.

There are many possibilities of participation in European states short of taking part in government itself, the actual decision-making process. There are the possibilities of, first of all, interest in politics; second, voting; third, political organisation – taking part in some kind of mechanism designed to influence the political process, party membership, possible candidature for the assembly, and actual choice to be a member of the government itself. These are all *levels* of participation involving greater involvement in the system and a greater say in what goes on.

But at each level, except at the top, there are a number of alternative *channels* through which participation can be effective; these include elections or referenda, interest groups, political parties and local-government organs. The same is true even in such apparently unpromising instances as, for example, China under the Cultural Revolution, but there the channels included such unfamiliar devices as the wall poster, the Red Guards, and the revolutionary committees (Robinson, 1969). In addition, when one system is compared with another, what varies is not simply participation, but what is considered to be political. In other words, political participation varies with the definition of what is properly the concern of politics and what the proper way of being political is.

It is for this reason that one has to make a functional separation between one aspect of government and another, rather than a purely institutional one, because what is defined as being one thing in one country may be defined as being something quite different in another. To take the obvious case, in almost all modern countries people 'participate' in elections. But what this *means* in terms of the individual varies from country to country, depending on what the actual likely outcome of the vote is – that is, the degree to which it is connected to the rest of the political process.

Liberal democracy

The overwhelming majority of modern states have what Aristotle would have called 'mixed' constitutions; that is to say, they combine elements of monarchy, oligarchy and democracy in differing proportions. Rule-application is vested primarily in the hands of one person (a president) or a few (a cabinet, a praesidium or a junta); the need to sanction rule-making in many (a popularly elected legislature, be it a parliament, a congress or a supreme soviet). Most of them claim to be what are usually termed *liberal democracies. Liberal democracies* are states in which government is limited in its powers by a written constitution, a system of law and/or an independent judiciary, and in which it is responsive to the popular will as expressed through elections. Under such a government certain basic freedoms (often termed *human rights*) will be guaranteed to the individual (Holden, 1988).

Liberal democracy is well established in Western Europe, North America, Japan and other leading countries. However, economic development is not a prerequisite, as is demonstrated by the persistent reappearance of the liberal tradition in Latin America over the past century and a half, and some striking examples from South Asia, the Middle East and the Caribbean. Liberal democracy has proved adaptable and responsive to the pressures of survival in a competitive world, and with the collapse of the rival Soviet model, it currently has no effective competitor. However, this does not mean that all liberal democracies are the same.

Since the nineteenth century, it has been a widespread assumption, particularly in English-speaking countries, that stable democratic systems required a high level of social consensus. Where this was achieved, political stability was enhanced and society unified. Where it was not, there was a tendency for political order to break down and democracy to collapse. More recently it has been suggested that the key determinant of political stability is the number and nature of *social cleavages* in society (Lane and Ersson, 1991; Rae and Taylor, 1970). There are many factors dividing groups in all societies. However, it was argued, if the dividing lines between these groups do *not* coincide with each other, competitive democratic politics can and does take place without endangering the whole structure.

Nevertheless, there are several states which are among the most democratic in Europe in which, on the contrary, a high level of agreement is obtained in divided societies. Hence special interest attaches to what is now termed *consociational democracy*, a term originally formulated by a Dutch political scientist, Arend Lijphart, as a result of comparative studies by other political scientists of Austria, Belgium, the Netherlands and Switzerland (Lembruch, 1967; Lijphart, 1969, 1974, 1977; Steiner, 1972, 1974).

This system has two characteristics:

1. Consociational democracy exists in societies which are clearly and apparently permanently divided vertically into a number of communities, whether ethnic, religious or linguistic. These communities, after Dutch practice, are often referred to as 'pillars' and their division as 'pillarisation' (*verzuiling*).
2. It is characterised by an elaborate process of *negotiation* between the elites of the different 'pillars' leading to *accommodation* and *compromise*. In fact, as Table 3.1 shows, Lijphart's argument is that it is the behaviour of the elite that makes this system possible. What is of particular interest is that the strategy of seeking agreement should apparently be so successful. Not only has it served to maintain unity in the highly unpromising circumstances of Belgium, where ethnic, linguistic and religious cleavages between Flemings and Walloons coincide with a clear-cut geographical split, but there is evidence that where the same strategy has been adopted in other states – Germany in Europe, Canada in the Americas, Malaysia in South East Asia – it has achieved a much higher degree of political stability than might otherwise have been expected. Conversely, its abandonment in Colombia, Cyprus, Lebanon and Nigeria has led to political instability, unrest and even civil war.

This reminds us that all states, even liberal democracies, exist in an evolutionary context and may well have diverged considerably from the ideal types they profess to represent (see Macpherson, 1977). Moreover,

Table 3.1 *Lijphart's typology of democratic systems*

	Political culture – homogeneous	*Political culture – fragmented*
Elite behaviour – coalescent	Depoliticised democracy	Consociational democracy
Elite behaviour – competitive	Centripetal democracy	Centrifugal democracy

on many occasions in the present century rulers have argued that for reasons of national security, or otherwise, they have found it 'necessary' to suspend or dispense with any or all of the notions of individual rights, limitation of government power or the right to a fair trial.

Authoritarianism

It was in the age of the Cold War (1946–90) that a new term, *totalitarianism,* came into use in the West to describe a syndrome of features believed to be characteristic of both *fascism* in Hitler's Germany and *Communism* in the Soviet Union, China and Eastern Europe. These states, it was thought, differed from all previous states as having both the will and the ability to exercise unlimited control over their populations (Friedrich and Brzezinski, 1975). By contrast an older word, *authoritarian* gained a new popularity as a convenient term to designate more traditional dictatorships. The beliefs which underpinned such systems included: belief in the transcendental importance of the principle of authority; an emphasis on the exclusive use of political power, unfettered by juridical restraint or civil liberties; and a tendency to excuse the excesses either of arbitrary decision-making or of despotic methods of political and social control.

Consequently, various writers have since 1960 sought to identify a number of criteria by which to distinguish between the two broad types of political system, democratic and authoritarian, which they see as opposites.

Thus Dahl, who in his *Modern Political Analysis* began with the Aristotelian criterion as his point of departure (Dahl, 1964a, 26), distinguishes between two broad types of political systems which he has termed *polyarchies* and *hierarchies,* according to such criteria as the existence of a separation of powers, the independence or otherwise of the judiciary and civil service, the existence or otherwise of competitive parties, and formally organised pressure groups with open access to the decision-makers (Dahl, 1964b: 84–7).

In a key study Linz defines the new authoritarian states as

> political systems with limited, not responsible, political pluralism; without elaborate and guiding ideology (but with distinctive mentalities); without intensive nor extensive political mobilization (except at some point in their development); and in which a leader (or occasionally a small group) exercises power within formally ill-defined limits but actually quite predictable ones. (Linz, in Allardt and Rokkan, 1970: 255).

On the basis of Linz's definition it is possible to distinguish as he does between new and old authoritarian regimes. The longer established an authoritarian regime is, the less it needs to rely on the overt use of force and the more it tends to develop new forms of legitimacy. However, for Linz authoritarian government is always a transitional state, either towards democracy or towards totalitarianism.

In addition, Sahlin (1977) suggests that it is useful to distinguish between protective authoritarianism and promotional authoritarianism. Protective authoritarianism is the argument of those who intervene by force simply to protect the status quo and the position of those who benefit from it. Following a traditional military coup, which has the limited aim of displacing the existing government, a period of emergency rule normally follows in which the armed forces emphasise the power available to them, their limited ambitions in making use of it, and their intention to return the country to civilian rule as soon as possible. Some regimes of this type, for example that of Franco's Spain, do survive for a long period and, Sahlin notes, become 'old' authoritarian regimes in Linz's terms, gaining a degree of legitimacy through force of habit and, generally, needing to depend less on the overt use of force. However, their principal aims remain the same: the depoliticisation of issues and the demobilisation of the masses.

Promotional authoritarianism, by contrast, is characterised by a desire to promote change, by supplanting the existing government and establishing one which will stay in power for a period of years to pursue certain stated aims. Chief among these aims is economic development, the desire for which is in itself rooted in a nationalistic belief in the value of a strong state. But this requires a certain degree of mobilisation of the masses in the interests of productivity. For such neo-authoritarian regimes this can most safely be achieved by appealing to nationalism. However, even this does not resolve, but only postpones, a fundamental conflict between the desire for economic mobilisation and the fear of political mobilisation. There are two possible ways in which this can be done; each, significantly, involves maintaining and not jettisoning the forms of democracy.

Some authoritarian regimes are prepared to mobilise the popular sector for both political and economic purposes, and to live with the consequences. Regimes of this rare type can be classed as authoritarian populist regimes. The classic case of such a regime is to be found in Argentina under General Juan Domingo Perón (President 1946–55, 1973–4). Its success can be gauged by the fact that ever since the coup that displaced the regime in 1955, no government survived long that did not come to terms with the Peronists. Despite his authoritarian ideology and emphasis on the role of the leader (known as 'verticalism'), Perón was constitutionally elected and re-elected, and it took several attempts for the armed forces to overthrow him.

Other regimes have been able to achieve such a degree of economic success that their citizens are prepared to wait for democracy. It is probably not just coincidence that the so-called 'tiger' economies of East and South East Asia – Singapore, Taiwan, South Korea, Malaysia and Thailand – are in states where, for a variety of reasons and in varying degrees, the governing style, and often the substance, is authoritarian.

Oligarchy or totalitarianism?

Other writers have sought to utilise the concept of *totalitarianism*. The word 'totalitarian' was originally coined by Mussolini to designate a state in which the power of the state worked without hindrance and the individual citizen had no rights at all. Friedrich distinguishes *totalitarian* states from others by six criteria:

(i) an *official ideology*, to which everyone is supposed to adhere;
(ii) a *single mass party*, usually led by one man, organised hierarchically;
(iii) monopoly of the effective use of all *weapons* by party and bureaucracy;
(iv) monopoly of the means of effective *mass communication*;
(v) a system of terroristic *police control*; and
(vi) central control and *direction of the economy* (Schapiro, 1972: 18).

In the late 1960s the concept of totalitarianism came under strong attack, both from writers in Eastern Europe and from specialists on Eastern Europe. The former pointed out that the six criteria were chosen to link together three principal historical instances: Mussolini's Italy (1922–44), Hitler's Germany (1933–45) and the Soviet Union under Stalin (1928–53). They rejected this linking as propagandist, principally (though not entirely) because they saw the purpose of the Soviet Union as being entirely opposed to that of the other two instances. The 'leadership principle' was not, they argued, a basic principle of Communism, but an aberration. The latter, on the other hand, had failed to find evidence that the overwhelming control claimed for the state by the proponents of the model did in fact exist in the Soviet Union at that time. They were able to identify a limited number of competing power centres and interest groups within Soviet society (Skilling and Griffiths, 1971; Hough, 1974; Kelley, 1976) and even argued that a degree of *pluralism* existed (the view that the will of the individual is best served by the multiplication of competing groups – Solomon, 1983). Hence they could dismiss the totalitarian 'rational actor' model of Soviet decision-making in favour of a 'bureaucratic politics' interpretation (Allison, 1971: 5 – see also Gustafson, 1980 and Chapter 8, this volume). Other Eastern European states, notably

Poland and Hungary, had diverged from the model substantially on the criteria of centralised control of the economy, and acceptance of the ruling ideology (Ball and Millard, 1986).

A more serious problem is presented by the difficulty of distinguishing between 'true' democracy and what S.E. Finer (1970) has helpfully called 'façade democracy'; that is to say, a system that is nominally democratic, but in fact oligarchical. Where does the dominance of an elite end and oligarchy begin?

This problem is well illustrated by Shils' well-known model which formalises concepts widely used in speech and in the press (Parsons and Shils, 1962). He distinguishes, on the one hand, the rule of the Few, which he calls oligarchy, from the rule of the Many, democracy. He then proceeds to subdivide these types by two different criteria: what he takes to be the actual effective degree to which the concept is applied, and for what purpose the government concerned advocates it.

He thus arrives at two types of democracy: *political democracy*, that is to say liberal democracy, such as exists in Western Europe and the United States, characterised by free elections, competitive parties, pressure groups, and so on; and *tutelary democracy*, such as was characteristic of Pakistan under Ayub Khan (1958–68), where the government holds many rights in abeyance on the pretext that the people need to be educated before being ready for political democracy. This category might include many military governments which, as in Bolivia, Ecuador, Peru and Brazil in the 1970s, promise free elections once they have ended illiteracy, taught everyone who to vote for, and given them an official party to support – but there must surely be serious doubts whether democracy is the right word for it.

It is, indeed, very difficult to distinguish tutelary democracy from the first of Shils' three categories of oligarchy, which he calls *modernising oligarchy*. This is where the rulers justify their restraint on public self-assertion on the grounds that to do so will promote economic development.

Naturally, modernising oligarchy can be made to look attractive, particularly if judiciously contrasted with its old-fashioned counterpart, *traditional oligarchy*, where nothing is ever done because the rulers like things the way they are.

Last, however, Shils offers a third category, that of *totalitarian oligarchy*. This is rule from the centre directed by an ideology which justifies it on the grounds that it is in the true interests of the masses and backed by a coercive apparatus which demands positive and not merely negative acceptance.

Although these three types correspond to popular ideas of differences between states – and especially to types which were fashionable in the

1950s when the scheme was outlined – the way in which the differences are drawn is not really up to the strain of actual classification. Was Brazil under General Medici (1969–74) a modernising oligarchy, as it professed to be, or a totalitarian oligarchy as Amnesty International tended to regard it? Not only is there, it seems, no very hard and fast line to be drawn between democracy and oligarchy, but the divisions between the subtypes are just as uncertain. And the scheme makes no mention of perhaps the most fruitful subtype possible, that of totalitarian democracy, which in the hands of J.L. Talmon (1961) did so much to illuminate the way in which earlier ideals found a logical development in the so-called people's democracies of Eastern Europe after the Second World War.

For unfortunately in the meantime the word 'totalitarian' continued to be widely used. By loosening the definition somewhat, Crick extends to eleven the number of criteria by which he distinguishes between *autocratic, totalitarian* and *republican* regimes (Crick, 1973: 44–81). In theoretical terms this seems a retrograde step. Understanding of the underlying processes can be reached only by establishing a framework within which the underlying relationships between the criteria can be understood. Extending the number of criteria may in itself, therefore, not be particularly informative, and in any case even those who have adhered to the totalitarian model have never been able to argue that there were very many examples in the world at large.

Despite these arguments, the notion of totalitarianism enjoyed a renaissance in the 1980s, when it was incorporated in the notorious distinction of Jeane Kirkpatrick between 'totalitarian' governments and 'moderately repressive authoritarian' governments (MRAGs). She argued that their control mechanisms were such that 'totalitarian' states could not evolve into liberal democratic states. The United States should therefore, she argued, be prepared if necessary to support 'moderately repressive authoritarian' states, such as Pinochet's Chile, rather than run the risk of allowing a state to succumb to totalitarianism (Kirkpatrick, 1982). The collapse of Soviet power in Eastern Europe in 1989 and the disintegration of the Soviet Union two years later has exposed the specious nature of this argument. The problem is, however, one common to all *static typologies* of political systems (see Table 3.2).

CRITERIA FOR CLASSIFICATION

The best approach would be to return to first principles and determine a number of *clearly defined criteria* by which states can be categorised and the different labels employed by politicians and others related to one

Table 3.2 *Static typologies of political systems*

Aristotle	Monarchy Tyranny	Aristocracy Oligarchy	Polity Democracy
Shils (Parsons and Shils, 1962)		Modernising oligarchy Traditional oligarchy Totalitarian oligarchy	Political democracy Tutelary democracy
Dahl (1964a)		Hierarchy	Polyarchy
Finer (1970)	Dynastic state	Military regime Façade Democracy Quasi democracy Totalitarian regime	Liberal democracy
Crick (1973)	Totalitarian	Autocratic	Republican

another. Blondel has proposed three axes of classification (see Figure 3.1) which he believes could enable us to link all such criteria (Blondel, 1973: 40). He identifies:

a radical-conservative dimension
a democratic-monarchical dimension, and
a liberal-authoritarian dimension.

The importance of this approach is that it makes us think clearly, not just why some 'cells' of a given typology are full, but why others are empty, and it will be helpful to bear this in mind in what follows. For this book is based on an approach which is rather different, but is, nevertheless, based on the same imperative: to relate the universe of states to underlying processes. The problem is twofold. On the one hand, the number of possible axes of classification is potentially infinite. On the other, all classifications, however detailed, will be actively misleading in so far as they distinguish categories only at one moment of historical time. For within the universe of states order can be found only if it is understood that all static typologies are only 'snapshots' of an

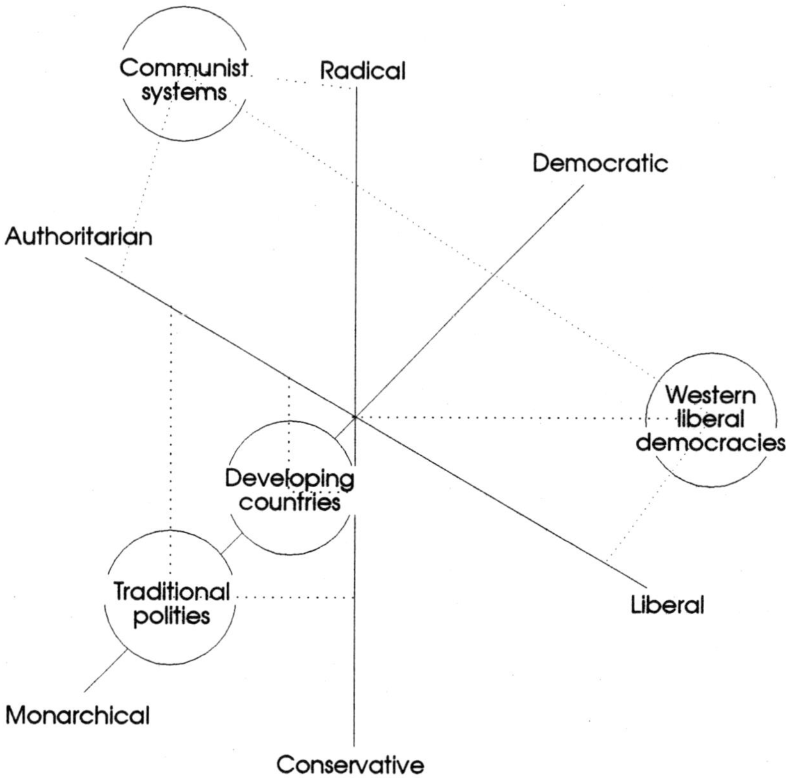

Source: Blondel (1973)

Figure 3.1 *Blondel's three dimensions of classification*

evolving pattern, and that the confusion stems from the conflict of two principles:

1. Each political system has some freedom to evolve according to its own internal political dynamics.
2. All political systems have been shaped by the influence of two successive periods of political evolution which have occurred in the last 200 years, each of which has altered (in ways that are not wholly compatible) prevailing ideas about the relationship of the individual to the state.

Thus most states today wear a formal aspect of government which is of one of two types: the parliamentary or the presidential state. Both are historical variants of what Verney has called the 'convention theory' state

(Verney, 1961: 3, 57). By 'convention theory' Verney refers to a rather rare but historically very significant form of government in which all conversion functions are exercised by a representative assembly (a 'convention', after the French Revolutionary Convention), and since in any one state this form of government either never has existed at the national level, or existed for a very brief period, it is more a theoretical model ('theory') of what government ought to be like rather than the real thing.

The relationship here between Verney's view and Aristotle's on the one hand, or Almond and Coleman's on the other, is through this differentiation between the executive and the legislative 'powers', which was first formulated by Locke, and its more sophisticated transplantation into the notions of rule-application and rule-making. Locke, however, also spoke of a third 'power', but this one has scarcely ever been specifically incorporated into the constitution of any modern state, though it is implicit in the structure of all states. This was the *federative power* – the power to conduct relations with other states (Locke, 1964: 383).

An exception was the former Soviet Union, where the 1936 constitution was amended, after the United Nations was created, to give individual union republics the right to conduct direct relations with other states. This enabled Moscow, through branch 'foreign offices' in Bielorussia (now Belarus) and the Ukraine, to have three votes in the UN instead of one, for there is no recorded instance of either state voting independently of the Soviet Union as a whole. The federative power was never found very attractive by other theorists, who were very reluctant in applying it to the actual study of states. It appeared that the federative power, such as it was, was exercised either by the executive, or, worse, by the army. Worst of all, the term 'federal' now has a meaning exactly the opposite in Britain and the US from its meaning in continental Europe. In France 'federation' means *decentralised* government; in the 'Anglo-Saxon' terminology, *centralised*.

Perhaps fortunately, the American solution to the problem was to reject the notion of a federative power altogether and instead to adopt the concept of a discrete judicial power originally identified by Montesquieu as characteristic of Britain during his visit to that country in 1739. The 1787 constitution of the United States, therefore, speaks of *three* powers: the legislative, executive and judicial. The judicial power, under the functional name of rule-adjudication, has been transplanted into modern terminology without necessarily getting away from the fact that, by and large, with the possible exception of the United States, the judiciary is usually in effect part of the executive branch of government, even where the belief exists that there is an abstract entity called law existing independently of the power of government.

However, this does not dispose of the problem of the federative power, and in fact the history of independent states in the nineteenth century was one of constant struggles to define their identity. In these struggles the major factor was the struggle between the centre and the periphery of the newly emergent states, as the centre sought to extend its control over the periphery and the peripheral provinces sought autonomy or even independence. This struggle continues today.

DEVELOPMENTAL TYPOLOGIES

Once the bases of classification are clarified in this way it should be easier to see how political systems change over time. *Developmental typologies* are those that take the time dimension into consideration.

The oldest of these typologies was that of Aristotle, as modified by the historian Polybius, who saw governments as following an endless chain of evolution: from monarchy, to aristocracy, to democracy, and then by way of tyranny, back to monarchy.

Marx's typology of economic systems, each with its appropriate form of political order, recognises the long-term effects of the contest for political power, but derives it in turn from the underlying economic order.

A recent attempt at a new classification is that of Almond and Powell (1966). Their developmental model rests in the first instance not on power, but on the concept of authority, following the distinction made by Weber between patriarchal, patrimonial and feudal authority (Weber, 1965: 346).

Patriarchal authority is authority vested solely in the representative of the lineage; patrimonial authority depends on the possession of goods, or lands having value; feudal authority involves a bargain between the holders of each of these concepts for a series of reciprocal obligations of service and protection. The most decentralised of the lot is the *feudal* system of authority, where there are two types of patrimonial authority in conflict. In other words the representatives of the lineage in the first instance hold centralised authority which is, however, counterposed by other people who have a right to authority within their own areas and over whose traditional rights they have no authority at all; the differentiation of subsystems, to use more modern terminology.

Out of the patrimonial states there has been developed, in turn, what has been called the *historical bureaucratic state*. This is the kind of state described in Eisenstadt (1963: 4), the state in which the system of government itself becomes so formalised that it operates whether or not there is a competent representative of the lineage actually in charge. In other words, every so often, human inheritance being what it is, either the inheritance fails or there is a 'time of troubles' when there are many contenders for the throne. But the bureaucratic structure by that time is such that decisions continue to be made, that the system continues to work; the field boundaries are still delimited; the harvest is still gathered, a tenth is dished out to the priests, and a pittance is dished out to the poor, if they are lucky. The whole system continues to work on the basis that it always has worked, just because the degree of sophistication of the system has become sufficiently elaborate for the system itself to continue in a state of equilibrium, regardless of dynastic considerations. And it is out of this historical bureaucratic system that modern states have evolved.

It will be noticed that Almond and Powell do not, as is done here, stress the duality of the origins of government. They accept the fact of government, and with it, implicitly, the assumption that it is beneficial to society. But there are always two elements in conflict in government: government and the people, the claim to power and its acceptance, or reward and punishment. Government is interaction, not action.

Almond and Powell provide a special category for the *secularised city states*. These are very small states such as Liechtenstein, San Marino or Monaco, but probably not Andorra or Luxembourg, because they are too large, or the more recently independent island states such as St Vincent or St Kitts in the Caribbean or Kiribati, Nauru or Tuvalu in the Pacific. Secularisation refers simply to the fact that the religious element has, in modern times, been taken out of their government, which presumably excludes the Vatican City State, but it is very hard to see why.

From this point onwards Almond and Powell view development as a process of *political mobilisation*; that is, the bringing of more and more people into the political life of the community. Certainly the mobilisation of individuals does mean at the same time taking account of their interests. To bring them into the political system, they have to be getting something out of it if they are going to be required to continue to put something in to it. It is, of course, possible to find, even today, systems in which large sectors of the population are not incorporated in the structure, and so a category is provided for *pre-mobilised modern* systems.

Finally, they conclude with two categories of *mobilised* systems, in which mass participation is both required and encouraged, and so is qualitatively different. One is the democratic state, in which the desire of the people to produce inputs is fully accepted and channelled, even when it is a question of demands rather than supports. The other is the *authoritarian* system, where the support is wanted but demands are not.

To summarise, therefore, Almond and Powell see the evolution of modern states as following an historical path from the patriarchal/

patrimonial level, through the feudal states and the historical bureaucratic states, to the pre-mobilised modern states; modern, that is, in that they still exist in today's world, but are not mobilised in the sense that the mobilised modern state requires or permits. And in these mobilised modern states, the common factor is that people participate widely in politics, some because they want to do so, some because they are made to do so, and some for both reasons (see Table 3.3).

CONCLUSION

For the present writer the possibilities are somewhat more complex (see Table 3.4). The categorisation has two distinctive features.

First of all, the dualism which Almond and Powell discern as coming into evolution of states at the division between the authoritarian and democratic states of today is here seen as running throughout the whole course of human history. Indeed, this conflict, natural because politics is institutionalised conflict, provides the basic dynamic for all experimentation with political forms. People in Western Europe or the United States may have forgotten, or become habituated to the essentially violent and self-imposed way in which their governments first emerged. But the facts are still fundamental to their understanding

Table 3.3 *Developmental typologies of political systems*

Aristotle/ Polybius (c. 146 B.C.)	Monarchy Aristocracy Democracy Tryranny Monarchy etc.	
Marx (1846)	Primitive accumulation Feudal Bourgeois Socialist	Primitive accumulation Oriental mode of production ???
Almond and Powell (1966)	Patriarchal/ patrimonial Feudal Pre-mobilised modern Mobilised modern Democratic	Patriarchal/patrimonial Historical bureaucratic Pre-mobilised modern Mobilised modern Authoritarian

of how they work today. All governments exercise just as much power as they believe they can get away with. It is in the extension or, conversely, in the limitation of these powers that all modern governments have been shaped.

Second, precisely because this dynamic is continuous and fundamental, it is consistent with the observation that the process of political change ebbs and flows. It does not follow a cycle of change from one form of government to another, returning to the beginning, as Plato and later Polybius suggested (Calvert, 1970a: 40, 43–4). Nor, as the Victorians (including Marx) would have it, is there an irresistible progress in the sense that political systems evolve along a single line towards a predictable future state. Of course, human beings learn by experience, but even with books to aid them, memories grow cold and old men die. Hence the revolutions in Eastern Europe in 1989 should have come as a surprise to no one, least of all to those who were most surprised by them.

What, above all, makes it difficult to identify discernible categories of states is the fact that, however complex they are, they are made up of very simple assemblages of horizontal and vertical links, replicating the tribe and band of primitive times. It is easy to make fun of this idea, for the notion of modern man as an ape in spaceman's clothing is richly comic. But it is, none the less, uncomfortably true.

It follows that a crisis which leads to the replacement or mutation of a relatively small number of links in the system by which interests are balanced, amounts to a fundamental change in the system as a whole. In this respect at least, the industrious constitution-makers of the nineteenth century, with their obsession with detailed legal checks and balances, were not misguided, though they failed to allow for the realities behind the systems they sought to construct. Such crises are, naturally, likely to arise in certain well-defined circumstances. Five such possibilities were identified by Binder *et al.* (1971): identification, legitimation, penetration, distribution and participation. A later section will explore in what circumstances such moments of crisis and change are likely to arise.

Table 3.4 *Varieties of government*

Primitive	*Agrarian*	*Imperial*	*Assembly*	*Apparat*
Tribe	Kingdom	Empire	Presidential	Party
	Theocracy	Tyranny	Caesarism	Praetorian
Band	Horde	Feudal	Federal	
	City	Anarchy	Parliament	

Source: Calvert (1983)

KEY CONCEPTS

authoritarian: government or state characterised by very limited participation and strong emphasis on the right of the rulers to give orders.

competitive systems: political systems in which a degree of free competition of ideas is permitted, e.g. by competitive elections.

consociational democracy: for Lijphart a political system characterised by strong and long-lasting political cleavages and an elaborate process of negotiation between the elites of the different 'pillars' leading to accommodation and compromise.

federative power: the power to conduct relations with other states.

liberal democracy: states in which government is limited in its powers by a written constitution, a system of law and/or an independent judiciary and is responsive to the popular will as expressed through elections.

mixed constitution: for Aristotle a political system that combines elements of monarchy, oligarchy and democracy.

participation: the extent to which citizens take part in politics.

'totalitarian': term coined by Mussolini to designate a state in which the power of the state worked without hindrance and the individual citizen had no rights at all (see *authoritarian*).

SAMPLE QUESTIONS

Candidates should be familiar with a representative selection of typologies of states which have been proposed since the major expansion of comparative politics got under way in the 1960s, and be prepared *critically to analyse* the strengths and weaknesses of each. Given their special relevance to liberal democratic systems, typologies of political parties are common in the literature and a favourite subject for examination questions – see Chapter 5.

How useful is a typology of states to our understanding of comparative politics?

What do we mean by the term 'liberal democracy'? Is Britain still a democratic country?

Could Marxist–Leninist regimes in the Brezhnev era accurately be described as 'totalitarian'?

How useful is the concept of 'totalitarianism' in understanding the nature of traditional Communist political systems in the 1970s and 1980s?

'The essence of Marxist–Leninist political systems is mass participation combined with the "leading role" of the Communist elite.' Discuss.

FURTHER READING

On the principles of liberal democracy see Holden (1988, second edition 1993) and for its philosophical basis Plant (1991a). Lijphart (1969) is the classic formulation of the notion of 'consociational' democracy. Rae and Taylor (1970) and Lane and Ersson (1991) discuss social cleavages in the Western European context. Dahl (1964a) is a useful starting point for the pluralist model. An excellent recent overview of competing theories is Dunleavy and O'Leary (1987).

For 'totalitarianism' see Schapiro (1972), and for a critique of its application to Eastern Europe before 1989 Ball and Millard (1986). For 'authoritarianism' and other important political concepts see Foley (1993).

The various typologies of states discussed are presented in detail in *inter alia* Almond and Powell (1966), Blondel (1973), Finer (1970) and Shils (Parsons and Shils, 1962).

4 The social environment

INTRODUCTION

The social environment of politics can be analysed in terms of communication, political culture and ideology. *Communication* is the vehicle by which politics is carried on. The range of systems of communication available and the way in which they are used help determine the nature of politics. *Political culture* describes the way in which politics is carried on. It forms part of the collective memory of a society, and is largely determined by the dominant *ideology*, the system of ideas which is taught consciously or unconsciously as part of the socialisation of new members of the society.

COMMUNICATION

Communication is *the transmission of a signal through a channel from a transmitter to a receiver* (Miller, 1963: 6). The signal, which is generally in the form of an economical statement known as a *code*, does not arise accidentally, and it must be recognised and interpreted by the receiver into a pattern of actions or statements. Communication therefore normally includes a process of coding and a process of decoding, as well as the act of transmission, which may be either direct or through third parties. An essential prerequisite, therefore, is that the code should be known to the parties at both the sending and receiving ends. Last, a communication may result either in action directly by the receiver, or in action by a relay or servomechanism communicating or creating the conditions for communication to one or more indirect recipients. However, it does not follow that all communications can be easily understood or accurately interpreted, since the codes in which they are transmitted may be complex, obscure or deliberately restricted to a select few.

Communication is the foundation of society. It begins with *language* itself. Sophisticated languages distinguish human society from that of the rest of the animal world, with the exception of the cetacea (e.g. whales and dolphins). No other land-based animal appears to have a 'vocabulary' of more than some twenty 'words'. Nevertheless, the existence of simple communication systems among animals shows that they fulfil the needs of the animals using them. Much the same kind of lesson can be drawn from human society. For each type of society, good communications are appropriate communications. A small rural community can be well integrated and interact fully by direct speech; a city such as New York or Tokyo would disintegrate under the same conditions. But conversely, the same number of farmers deprived of direct speech and dependent for integration on television and radio would not be a community at all. In fact it is just this reliance in modern states on the mass media which leads to that decentralised and demoralised condition which has been termed 'mass society'.

Types of communication

1 phatic communion
2 prevention of communication
3 recording-transmitting
4 instrumental
5 affective
6 catharsis
7 magic
8 ritual

Types of communication

Communication serves a wide range of different purposes. It is possible, however, to distinguish between eight different categories into which individual sentences can be classified: phatic communion, prevention of communication, recording-transmitting, instrumental, affective, catharsis, magic and ritual.

1. *Phatic communion.* This is the technical term applied to formal exchanges which open up the possibility of communication between two people who have just met, e.g. 'Hello. How are you?' 'Fine. How are you?'
2. *Prevention of communication.* The converse of phatic communion is a statement indicating unwillingness to communicate, usually coupled for reasons of politeness with an expression of willingness to communicate later, as e.g.: 'Hi there.' 'Hi. Sorry, can't stop now. See you later.'
3. *Recording-transmitting.* The simplest example of a communication that is concerned only with the recording-transmitting of

information is dictation, as in e.g. 'Take a letter, Ms Jones. Dear Sir or Madam, in reply to your letter of . . .' Substantial wodges of such material are to be found in formal statements to parliaments and congresses and form the staple filler of many political speeches, which otherwise would be unbearably short.

4. *Instrumental*. Instrumental statements are statements which result in physical movement or action on the part of the person addressed, as when a patient entering the consulting room is greeted by the doctor with: 'Come in. Sit down. Now what seems to be the trouble?'

   Quite a number of political communications are of this kind. However, in political speeches, particularly (but not exclusively) at election time, politicians angle their statements in order to generate emotion rather than action. In addition, many political messages are sent for the purpose of deliberately confusing or misleading the receiver, or, in other words, from preventing him or her from drawing the correct conclusions from a pattern of actions or statements.

5. *Affective*. At times of national stress or emergency the use of emotive language is particularly valuable, since it distracts attention from inconvenient facts. When on 20 December 1990 President Bush told the American people he had given orders to invade Panama, he used strongly emotive imagery to justify his action:

> Last Friday, Noriega declared his *military dictatorship* to be *in a state of war with the United States* and *publicly threatened the lives of Americans* in Panama. The *very next day*, forces *under his command* shot and *killed an unarmed American* serviceman, wounded another, arrested and *brutally beat* a third American serviceman, and then *brutally interrogated* his wife, *threatening her with sexual abuse*. That was enough. (*Congressional Quarterly Weekly Report*, 47, No. 51: 3534 – italics added).

In fact it was not Noriega, but the Panamanian Congress who had said they regarded themselves as being in a state of war with the United States, owing to a substantial previous build-up of American troops there. The American serviceman shot, who was in civilian clothes, had driven through an official checkpoint without stopping. There was no evidence that specific orders had been given to Panamanian troops to harass Americans. And what Bush did not say was no less important; that Noriega's regime, despite its corruption, was considerably less brutal than previous Panamanian regimes, and that he himself had not only been an informant for the US Central Intelligence Agency (CIA) for many years but had actually been commended for his work for the US Government, and that had his regime survived for just ten more days it would have had the right to appoint under the treaties of 1977 the first Panamanian administrator of the Panama Canal. Instead, in the war that followed, twenty-six US soldiers were killed and 323 wounded; the Panamanians lost 314 soldiers and more than a hundred wounded, and there were literally thousands of civilian casualties (Calvert, 1990c).

6. *Catharsis*. Powerful emotions, once aroused, can be hard to handle, and the experienced politician will know when and how to discharge powerful emotions, such as pain and grief, in a way that consolidates their own position. When at the time of the Falklands War Mrs Thatcher said: 'They risked their lives to defend British sovereign territory, the British way of life, and the right of British people to decide their own future,' she simultaneously recognised the magnitude of the sacrifice involved and asserted its significance in the wider context of British history.
7. *Magic*. A rain-maker who repeats often enough that it is going to rain is quite likely to be right some of the time; if so (such is the waywardness of human nature) those are the times that are remembered. Similarly, politicians who have little or no ability to influence events positively often resort to the incantation of formulae which are indistinguishable from the magic of the rain-maker. An example was when Sir Geoffrey Howe, the British Chancellor of the Exchequer (Finance Minister), 1979–85, repeatedly promised: 'Inflation will be down to 5 per cent by the year's end.'
8. *Ritual*. Ritual, both physical and verbal, serves a number of useful purposes in politics. The complicated circumlocutions obligatory in the House of Commons serve to slow and so cool the process of debate. 'Madam Speaker, the Hon. Member for Stoke Newington South has undoubtedly been guilty of a terminological inexactitude' means exactly the same as 'You are a liar', but with reasonable luck will not lead to bloodshed. It is, after all, not so many years since two Uruguayan politicians fought a duel, or a Mexican deputy opened fire with a pistol on an opponent on the floor of Congress.

Metacommunication

In interpreting all verbal communication account must also be taken, consciously or unconsciously, of *metacommunication* – information gained from *signs* (Condon, 1966: 9). Signs differ from symbols in that they are not consciously created. However, though the interpretation of signs is easy in theory, it can be quite difficult in practice. The idea that one can walk down a street in a strange town and look at it for the evidence it gives on the lives of those who live there is not a remarkable one. Whether the street is swept, what sort and size of houses it contains, whether they have gardens and what sort of plants they have in them, whether the houses are well painted, what sort of curtains show at the windows, the presence of garages, lawnmowers, scooters, bicycles, cars and children's toys – all these, given experience of that society, inform the passer-by of the social standing, income, occupation, taste and even the political sympathies of the residents. But only up to a point.

In a society in which governments are on the alert for manifestations of discontent, of course, people may take great care to assume a uniform outward appearance. Besides, they may, and frequently do, live in flats or apartment blocks; the presence of a concierge, security guard or electrically-operated door here can be a sign of the degree to which those within feel it necessary to defend their position against the outside world or, as with the Russian *dezhurnaya*, a sign of the degree to which the state may wish to keep an eye on the residents.

Distortion of communication

Otherwise all communication is subject to *distortion*, specifically of three types (Condon, 1966: 51; Miller, 1963: 257; Pierce, 1962: 25, 29). It may be subject to *bias*, *interference* or *overload*.

1. *Bias* is selectivity to certain signals rather than to others. It may occur because no one within the system recognises the significance of certain signals. Or it may result within the system from the choice of information to be passed on to the decision-makers by the selectors who first receive the communication.
2. *Interference* is the obscuring effect of the general mush of background noise, coming in the case of politics from the wider social environment: information on subjects such as the weather, sporting events or cultural activities which engage the attention irrelevantly from their very volume and persistence.
3. *Overload* selectively limits the capacity of the network to handle information flows. The problem of it is its random effect on individual communications within the total volume of messages being passed.

The German critical theorist Jürgen Habermas argues that systematic distortion of communication is in itself a way in which control can be maintained over a society, and that this distortion is the product of the dominant ideology of that society.

Levels of communication

The extent and effectiveness of each and all of these types of communication depends on the *level* at which it takes place.

At the simplest level of understanding there is *face-to-face* communication, that is to say, direct speech between two human beings. It is at this level that government alone becomes truly real to the individual person. Therefore it is not surprising to find that the essence of government to most people is not the orderly but impersonal operation of the postal service or traffic lights, but the occasional but often potentially conflict-laden encounters with policemen, local government officers or civil servants, such as welfare officers or social security clerks. These are the people with whom citizens deal directly, and it is on them that their resentments tend to get discharged.

Face-to-face communications are direct, real, present. They are the necessary foundation of systems in which interaction, characteristic of them, is replaced by action. The only other means of communication with the characteristic of interaction is the telephone, which transmits speech directly, and which like direct speech leaves no written record. It is difficult to say what the political consequences of widespread distribution of telephones may be – the leading telephone nations, New Zealand, the United States and Germany, have little enough in common, except prosperity. But two characteristics have become very clear. On the one hand, it is difficult for a society to be a completely closed one if its citizens have telephones. In the former Soviet Union this feature of the telephone was minimised as far as possible by the absence of a satisfactory telephone directory. Yet even with this limitation, Andrei Sakharov could, through the use of the telephone, retain access to the outside world and to world public opinion as long as he was not actually in prison. On the other hand, in open societies, telephones have a great advantage for the citizen over physical presence: properly used, they enable him or her to penetrate to a much higher level of decision-making than would otherwise be possible. As in face-to-face discussion, too, refutation can be advanced directly, specific points confronted, and statements demanded which cannot easily be evaded.

However, there are limitations of scale: interaction is not a feature of a mass meeting, even though communication is by voice and face-to-face. Questions may be offered, but even when answered immediately need not be revealing: the continental practice of gathering questions together and answering them in a supplementary oration gives all the advantage to the speaker. 'Heckling', as it is known in England, is forbidden in many countries; in others, such as South Africa and Australia, it is much more vigorous and inclined to cause physical harm to the speaker (Butler, 1959: 261).

Mass communication is the distinctive characteristic of modern societies. Mass communication by voice, the radio broadcast, is now proportionately very cheap and has extensive uses in spreading government propaganda both at home and abroad. The role of Radio Cairo in inflaming opinion in Algeria in 1954–6 is considered to have been a major factor in the response of the Mollet Government at the time of Suez, but it was undoubtedly just as important in integrating post-revolutionary Egypt itself (Nutting, 1967: 21; H. Thomas, 1966: 22). Mass communication by television was extensively used by Castro in Cuba to communicate the views of his regime, but not the reverse (Huberman and Sweezy, 1968: 152). On the other hand, people in the former German Democratic Republic could receive not only radio but also television broadcasts from West Germany, thus informing them about life in the West and building up popular pressure for eventual reunification.

Visual communications apart from television depend, except in rare instances, for most of their effect on the use of writing. Writing is a code for expressing on paper or other material the sounds of the code that is language. Knowledge of this code is, however, not a normal part of each individual's basic home instruction, and is imparted by specialists as the first part of a process of formal education. Literacy is therefore not a political attribute as such, but arises only as part of formal inculcation of the values of society. This point is important, since the existence of such values determines the interpretation of written material as certainly as it does the interpretation of photographic or pictorial material.

Individual visual communications are primarily letters and similar messages; mass communications include, apart from posters and handbills, newspapers and even books, all forms where the same text is multiplied by printing press or photographic means.

Such communications by their nature can be controlled and even monopolised almost completely by governments. Even clandestine printing presses are of little avail if the supply of newsprint or ink is a state monopoly, as in the former socialist countries including Cuba (Goldenberg, 1965: 202–4). Moves to create similar state monopolies in Chile under Salvador Allende (1970–3) (*The Economist*, 20 November 1971) and Peru under Velasco Alvarado (1968–75) (*The Times*, 20 January, 10 February 1970) were regarded with great suspicion by journalists and helped generate opposition abroad in each case. In Albania and Romania every typewriter had to be registered lest it be used for the dissemination of propaganda against the regime.

Television has a particular appeal to members of governments attempting to put over their point of view to the largest possible number of people. The immediacy of television has given it a special place in the folklore of politics, perhaps not entirely justified by the facts, since it has important social consequences which may not be so easy to control. Direct personal conversation may increasingly be invaded by shared television experiences, but equally the same experiences facilitate the education of young children and provide topics of conversation for people of all ages who hitherto had nothing in common (McQuail, 1969: 71ff.).

Communications and decision-making

The way in which communications are used in the process of *decision-making* can be dealt with under three headings: inputs, communications between decision-makers, and outputs.

Inputs in turn can be divided into two categories: input communication in general – that is, all influences from the environment; and *feedback*, the response monitored to actions by the decision-makers themselves.

The first step is regulation of the input, both to reduce the pressure to manageable proportions, and to distinguish the first from the second. The effect upon decision-makers of wholly unregulated input communication can hardly be imagined. It has occurred, however, for only brief periods, as in the case of the revolutionary government of students in Cuba under President Ramón Grau San Martín in 1933 (Goldenberg, 1965: 107). Sufficient to say that no one – whether individual or group – could possibly exercise any functions of decision-making if exposed to a continuous unregulated flood of inputs. It is all one whether they are pestered by people with demands, or by people with offers of support, since the one generally turns out to be conditional on the other.

Equally, it would be fatal for governments to be too effectively screened. In particular, a government must have information on the effects of its own actions on the environment. Unlike an organic body, it has no other compulsion than conscious choice to do so but, equally, its actions could be taking place in a void. For this purpose, therefore, governments find it necessary to devise systems by which they can admit the inputs they wish to admit, while continuing to exclude unregulated calls upon their time. Such role-bearers have been termed by David Easton the 'gatekeepers' (Easton, 1957).

In a democratic society, the decision-makers themselves will be expected to be seen going among the people; in President Lyndon B. Johnson's words, 'pressing the flesh' (White, 1965: 366), and obtaining apparently spontaneous responses of joy to the presence of someone associated with government policy as a whole, or a crucial sector of it. This is certainly useful as far as it goes, but as an output of government facilitating a higher level of extraction of effort rather than a genuine input mechanism.

Internal communications. Assuming that the process of regulation of inputs has been assessed, the next task is to look at the means by which the decision-makers handle communication among themselves. Decision-makers are people. Decisions are made by people, even if they are made by omission more often than by commission. And these people may, and often do, form a particularly close group; that is to say, they form an *elite* which can be identified either subjectively or objectively or both. The strength of an elite lies in its ability to communicate. They compensate for the greater mass of information they have to handle by taking advantage of their ability to communicate directly, face-to-face. This gives them not only an advantage against the mass of society, but also against the bureaucracy which may otherwise all too easily overwhelm them with its rigidity and resistance to change.

The decision-makers do not have it all their own way, however, in dealing with the general public. Members of the public only need the opportunity to communicate, to be able to put their case. The decision-maker has to reply on the assumption that his/her brief comments will go on record and may cause trouble in the future.

Outputs. Much of the process of internal communication is concealed by governments until no longer of great current interest to scholars. The importance of output communication is thus disproportionate to us, as the sector of the communications net most easily accessible to the investigator as political scientist.

Given enough records, the investigator can analyse its characteristic pattern. This varies according to the direction, the volume and the content of the communication flow, and specifically in the ways set out here.

Outputs may have two different effects. They may act directly, by delivery to a desired individual or group with a calculated emphasis and association of political pressures. Or they may act indirectly, through the instrumental effect that they cause others to act in state or local government. Local government structures are often formally independent, but respond to central instruction. This type of action is most important because without it the operation by decision-makers of a modern administrative machine would be quite impossible. Its own articulation, its internal routing of messages is therefore of fundamental importance in assessing its effects, for the way in which it affects the outside world is more often indirect than direct.

Restricted codes

The crunch comes at the most important part, discovering what (if anything) the messages are actually about. This involves understanding the code in which they are written.

As already indicated, it is in the nature of communication that messages are transmitted in code; it is not just an accident of time or place. Codes are not cyphers, that is to say, they are not meant to be secret, so there is no fundamental reason why a trained observer cannot learn them.

The first step, obviously, is to learn the language. For a student of comparative politics learning languages can become a major task in itself, for the language reflects the society which uses it; indeed it shapes society, a flexible language such as English taking on new concepts to the point of meaninglessness, while an exact language such as French implies a closer correspondence of ideas in the mind of speaker and hearer. The shaping effect of language is felt at those points at which ideas are taken for granted. Students of politics have long been locked into an earnest debate as to whether Marx expected the state to be 'transcended' or 'abolished'; the German word which he used (*aufheben*) inconveniently means both. Indeed, it also means lifted, picked up, arrested, kept or preserved (see also Merritt, 1970: 152–3).

Then, beyond the dictionary definition of words, societies employ general codes of social communication, in which words such as 'crown' or 'flag' carry wide-ranging overtones of political responsibility, and phrases such as 'the common law' in England, or 'the Fourth of July' in the United States, are heavy with meaning which the individual words of which they are composed totally lack (cf. Eysenck, 1963). Understanding of the general code of each society is, therefore, the understanding of the nature of political education.

Beyond these in each society lie *restricted codes*, applicable only within certain sectors of that society (Bernstein, 1973–6). Communication within these sectors is conducted for most purposes in terms of the restricted code. Bernstein himself is interested in the way in which working-class children are both identified and restricted in their possibilities of expression by their restricted code. Full access to power, he suggests, is possible only through learning the general code of society as a whole.

However, there are even more limited examples of restricted codes. The classic instance is the code employed by the armed forces, characterised by a small vocabulary in which each word has a very precise meaning, and hence, by two advantages, that ensure the general use of such a code by the soldiers of any country. One is that each order given to a soldier means one thing and nothing else. Under conditions of severe stress – under fire or danger from mines or aerial attack – the soldier given a command will respond instinctively without having to make a conscious and potentially fatal choice. The other advantage is that the limitations of the code deliberately leave him no room for concepts not covered by it, such as fear of flight (the latter being termed a tactical retreat). Indeed the deficiencies of the code are such that the soldier tends to supply his own two or three all-purpose words to fill gaps.

Restricted codes are most important for this quality of exclusion, which is characteristic of all forms of professionalism, nowhere more so than in government. That can indeed be implanted generally by education in political matters, so that the subject is bound to an official ideology, and is less receptive to destabilising stimuli. This can in turn be used to strengthen distinctions of status, or to impart values suggesting certain types of social patterning rather than others.

This was strikingly important in communications within and between Communist systems. For the former USSR a phrase such as 'proletarian internationalism' meant 'limited sovereignty for other Communist states', while for the Chinese 'Hold High the Banner of Marxism–Leninism' meant 'oppose Maoism' (Hong, 1978). But it is also found in liberal democratic political systems. Under Harold Wilson, for example, the phrase 'social contract' was used in the UK to refer to the control of wages by government without the formal passage of legislation, but had the additional political benefits (other than deliberate vagueness) of suggesting agreement and social value (Bosanquet and Townsend, 1979: 7–8). In the United States the phrase 'pro-life' means forcing unmarried mothers to have babies, by denying them the right to undergo an abortion. At worst, political debate may come to be filled with a series of nearly meaningless catchphrases, as in Sukarno's Indonesia, where many of the slogans chanted by the crowds included English words, such as 'ritulin' (retooling), known to Sukarno as an engineer, but not familiar to his audience.

The use of a special restricted code *within* the administrative system combines all these qualities. It depends on its capacity and precision to carry large volumes of meaning in a short space, and ensure accurate response on the part of its servomechanisms. A circular on building standards will be complied with by local authorities in a similar fashion, but with the necessary adjustments for regional variations of soil, climate, and so on. But when the same communication falls into the hands of a person who does not know the restricted code, a misinterpretation of it may lead to confusion.

By extension, tortuous and jargon-filled codes may be employed deliberately to restrict the circulation of information to administrative circles, while continuing to permit the public, in theory if not in practice, full participation in the processes of government. They form, therefore, one of the many means by which participation is actively restricted. The use of simple language, coupled with the availability of good civics classes in school or adult education, has just the reverse effect. Beyond this, though not intentionally, the use of restrictive codes can handicap feedback processes. Here the problem is that the code used within the system is not able to carry the range of meanings used by the plain language of those outside it whose opinions are being canvassed. Often this can occur because a wide range of views are reduced to a single formula. Since a great deal of uninformed hostility to government arises from just this feeling of not being understood, it is not surprising that codes play a major role at particularly crucial moments such as the consolidation period of revolutions (see Chapter 11).

Semantics and politics

Sadly, insufficient attention has been given in the past to semantic analysis in political discourse and, rather disappointingly, little progress seems to have been made as a result. The science of semantics, it is not too much to say, is in its infancy as far as the understanding of political concepts is concerned, but without its aid cross-national comparisons involving socialisation or ideology are unlikely to be valid. Even as between Great Britain and the United States – 'two nations divided by a common language' – the structure and implications of the English language vary greatly. So much we know. But how it varies, and where it varies, and what implications the variations have for political communication, are problems for semantics.

In the late 1950s psychologists interested in semantics devoted much effort to the precise location of concepts in what, with Osgood, Suci and Tannenbaum (1957: 25), can be termed 'semantic space'. Questionnaires submitted to volunteer subjects called upon them to assess the position of words and phrases in terms of pairs of opposed qualities. Some extremely interesting results emerged. It even became possible, using related techniques, to build on identifications of concepts in two or more areas or regions – as in one study between the United States and Mexico – and compare their values in terms of a single attribute such as 'respect', maintaining semantic correspondence between the concepts used to assess variations resulting from purely societal differences (Díaz Guerrero, 1975: 89ff.). However, there is a long way to go before this laborious technique can be applied to politics in general.

Nevertheless, it has been possible to make content analyses of speeches or statements by leading politicians, and to assess from elimination of ancillary matter and purely functional expressions the presence or absence of qualities such as 'hostility' or 'aggressiveness' (North *et al.*, 1963; Pool, 1957). So far these techniques have mainly focused on ascertaining what politicians are actually saying – no small task in itself – though some writers claim to be able to construct a 'cognitive map' of the decision-makers' perceptions and values. Given a sound semantic foundation, however, great expansion could be foreseen in the use of all these techniques in the next few years. The result for the study of comparative politics, and for political science in general, would be wholly beneficial.

POLITICAL CULTURE

The term 'political culture' is a controversial one. However, in making comparisons between different societies, it is hard to avoid coming back to the concept of 'culture'.

First of all, it must be clear what the term means. To a political scientist, as to an anthropologist or a sociologist, a 'culture' is *the entire pattern of behaviour of a given society*. In this sense, therefore, individual behaviour within that society will in some sense be determined by that culture, and that of politics is no exception.

In everyday use, the term 'culture' often has a much more restricted meaning. Culture in this sense, sometimes termed 'high culture', refers to specialised forms of self-expression in art, literature, music etc., produced by an educated stratum of *intellectuals*, knowledge of which acts as a strategy of 'social closure' to define this group. Despite their relatively small numbers and isolation from the rest of society, in all ages intellectuals have tended to believe that intelligence entitles them to hold and control political power. Since writers on politics are themselves intellectuals they tend to share and propagate this belief. However, education does play a key role in most societies in regulating access to the 'leading strata' (Aron, 1967), from which the political elite in due course will be drawn.

The inclusive definition of 'culture', however, has its own difficulties. The problem arises with Marx's insistence on the primacy of the *mode of production* as determining the nature of society. Even non-Marxists have long accepted that economic processes, and the consequences of economic growth, urbanisation and industrialisation, play some role in determining the nature of society. But the dominant tendency in Marxism has long been to insist on a rather deterministic view, in which culture forms only part of the 'superstructure' of society resting on an economic 'base', and this view was part of the official ideology of the Soviet Union down to its collapse in 1991. Despite this, for some years previously in other parts of Eastern Europe, Marxist thinkers had increasingly come to accept, as Marx had probably originally intended, that the culture of a society also affects and shapes its capacity for economic production. Hence the terms 'base' and 'superstructure' were actively misleading. This idea was not, of course, foreign to non-Marxists familiar with Weber's famous argument that North European puritanism, for a variety of reasons, provided a particularly favourable climate for the development of industrial capitalism (Weber, 1964).

The *political culture* of a society, then, is that part of the dominant culture of that society which establishes the values and norms of political debate and decision-making. It was to ascertain whether or not the existence of democracy was related to the nature of what they called the 'civic culture' that Almond and Verba made their celebrated comparative study of political attitudes in five selected states (Almond and Verba, 1963), which has gained additional notoriety by being selected by the philosopher Alistair MacIntyre as an example with which to damn the whole comparative enterprise (MacIntyre, 1983). This study was based on a common questionnaire administered to a panel of respondents in each of the states in their own language. That technique has, of course, valuable possibilities. However, there are serious linguistic problems in administering a questionnaire in more than one language. Consequently unintended differences of meaning may, and some have argued do, arise, undermining confidence in the interpretation of the results. Certainly this sort of study is not what is meant here, or in political science generally, by the comparative study of politics, though it could in the proper circumstances become a useful part of it.

The dominant political culture is in part the product of the dominant *ideology* of the rulers of the society – and of their predecessors if, as is usually the case, they derive their legitimacy from them and want to make use of the cultural inheritance of the society for their own purposes. However, it is transmitted and hence shaped by many means. The family, the peer group, religious institutions, education, the mass media etc., all play their part. Almond and Verba argued that what they termed the 'civic culture' of Britain and the United States – a sense of general responsibility for others – facilitated the emergence and maintenance of democracy. Certainly the emphasis in both countries in the 1980s on 'possessive individualism' has been accompanied by a breakdown of this sense of civic responsibility and a steep increase in crime. These features were already characteristic of Italy and Mexico, two countries where Almond and Verba found the 'civic culture' relatively lacking.

IDEOLOGY

Ideology is a term which has caused much argument in political science. Karl Mannheim (1946) defined it as *'a pattern of beliefs that justifies a social order and which explains to man his historical and social setting'*. A more recent definition is *'a set of closely related beliefs or ideas, or even attitudes, characteristic of a group or community'* which is both *'descriptive and persuasive'* (Plamenatz, 1970).

The word was originally invented by a late-eighteenth-century French thinker, Count Antoine Destutt de Tracy (1754–1836), to designate the science or study of ideas which he had invented and which he was anxious to popularise. It was – surprisingly enough – Napoleon who first used it as a critical term to disparage as false systems of ideas held by his political opponents. In this respect he was followed by Marx, who used it to refer to the notions of his German rivals, which prevented them from seeing as he did the logically compelling nature of the real truths of politics.

Marx and Engels regarded logic and mathematics as being universally true. Law and morality, on the other hand, were determined by ideology. The remedy for this was to apply scientific standards of criticism to law and morality and to make the result, termed Marxism, *scientific* and therefore *true*. Marx never referred to his own system of thought as an 'ideology', but instead emphasised what he believed to be its unique status as truth by the phrase 'scientific socialism'. What distinguished scientific thought from ideology, for Marx, was that it could be and should be used as the basis for action (*praxis*). For him, ideology was 'false consciousness', an incorrect view of the world.

In this sense Marx was a positivist thinker, and those of his followers who believe political systems to be determined by their economic base have continued this tradition. More specifically, Marx and his followers see ideological thought as the product of a particular social structure, the dominance of a *class*. The dominant ideology of capitalist societies today is established by the ruling class, the bourgeoisie, and will be superseded only with the fall of the bourgeoisie following a socialist revolution which will bring an end to the class struggle and result in the abolition of all classes.

For a variety of reasons modern writers would no longer feel able, as Marx did, to draw a hard and fast line between 'scientific' and 'ideological' thought. Doubts first surfaced with Freud, who demonstrated that action could be, and frequently was, 'irrational'. Hence 'rational' explanations would give at best an incomplete and at worst a wholly misleading account of the reasons for a social action. Social 'reality', in the traditional sense, does not exist. Instead, what is accepted as social reality is itself a social construct (Berger and Luckmann, 1972). Other writers have suggested that 'science' itself is an ideological construct, and that the traditional picture of science as an orderly process of research should be replaced by a series of abrupt leaps when the existing *paradigm* which determines what is considered to be scientific thought becomes outmoded and is replaced by another (Kuhn, 1970).

Meanwhile, with familiarity, the word 'ideology' came gradually to lose its critical connotations and to be widely used simply as a handy term for designating *different systems of ideas, including Marxism itself*. The proponents of ideologies still tend to regard the term as pejorative when applied to their own system of beliefs which, in general, they prefer to term philosophies. No such imputation is here intended. The term is used simply to refer to the fact that different political systems, and within those systems different political structures (especially political parties), can be grouped according to the ideology within which they operate.

This broader view of ideology derives from the work of the Italian Marxist Antonio Gramsci, who while imprisoned by Mussolini left a record of his views in his *Prison Notebooks*. Gramsci had no doubt that ideology was the main means by which governments exercised political control, and that the use of force, which he termed *domination*, was an inadequate substitute, only to be used as a last resort. People, he observed, yielded freely to the appeal of ideology, especially in the form of religion or nationalism. From this he deduced that the ability (as he saw it) of a class to control a society came from the acceptance of its system of ideas as the ideas of the whole society, a situation which he termed *hegemony*. Alternatively, with Weber and Easton, it could be said that its system of values was seen as authoritative.

Gramsci, however, distinguishes between two different types of ideologies. *Historical organic ideologies* he sees as rooted in society and necessary to its structure at a given time. *Arbitrary or willed ideologies* are not. In other words, an old system of ideas can lose hegemony, or a new one achieve it, before the political changes consequent on the change take place. And at any one time, there will be competition between different systems of ideas for hegemony, the outcome of which has yet to be determined.

The distinction between organic and arbitrary ideologies goes further, however, by indicating that certain combinations of ideas are more likely to gain favour than others. Writers who prefer to use the term political culture would agree with this view, and say that those sets of ideas that are more likely to be accepted are those that are *congruent* with the prevailing political culture (Eckstein, 1960).

As a Marxist, of course, Gramsci himself believed that Marxism was a historical organic ideology. He believed, further, that it had already in his day achieved hegemony, and that it was only a matter of time, therefore, before its validity would be accepted and a socialist revolution take place in Italy. Meanwhile Mussolini's Fascism, being an arbitrary or willed ideology would, he believed, fail to take root and ultimately be swept away. In this respect, at least, he was right, though sadly he did not live to be freed, let alone to see Mussolini hanging upside down from a lamp-post outside a filling station in Milan.

The main *function* of ideology in politics, therefore, is to legitimise the existing order and permit the economy of the use of force. In other words, it enables governments to pursue unpopular policies, and for them to be accepted as authoritative. This it does both in authoritarian states and in liberal democracies, where its influence is the more significant for going largely unnoticed. It is therefore clearly a crucial factor in understanding why liberal democracy, despite its obvious weaknesses, has proved such a successful and adaptable form of government. The means by which this is done is by establishing within the dominant culture certain *values* (e.g. of class, religion or nation) from which are derived specific *norms of behaviour.*

The *vehicles* by which the ruling ideology is transmitted are numerous. They were collectively termed the *ideological state apparatus (ISA)* by the French Marxist philosopher Louis Althusser, but this suggests that they are more closely related to one another than, at least in some cases, they actually are. They include:

- the Church,
- the education system,
- the structure of politics, including the actions and ritual that surround it,
- political parties and their propaganda,
- the mass media.

Role of ideology in politics

Function: Legitimation, economy of force.
Means: Establishes VALUES (e.g. class, religion, nationalism) from which are derived NORMS (e.g. classless society).
Vehicles: Church, education system, political ritual, media, propaganda. Collectively (Althusser), the IDEOLOGICAL STATE APPARATUS (ISA).

Competitive party states

1 Establishes *dimensions* of party, e.g. Ulster Unionists and SDLP.
2 Restricts possibilities of *coalition*, e.g. Italian Communist Party.
3 Limits range of allowable policies, e.g. assassination of Hitler.
4 Justifies *administrative state*, e.g. European security co-operation.
5 Facilitates *co-optation*, and limits or deflects *criticism*.

Non-competitive states

1 Routinises *regulation* of population, e.g. 'classless society'.
2 Justifies *one-party state*, e.g. 'leading role'.
3 Rules out *alternative policies*, e.g. 'diamat'.
4 Facilitates *military intervention/revolution/the apparat*, e.g. 'historical materialism'.

Though the function of ideology will be similar, the values which are established and the vehicles by which they are conveyed will vary as between competitive and non-competitive systems.

Competitive systems

In liberal democratic systems the contest for hegemony takes place in public and is reflected in the competition of *political parties* (see Chapter 6) for public support.

1. Ideology above all establishes the *dimensions* of a party. It determines which members any given party can expect to be able to recruit, and whether it can continue to count on their support in changing political circumstances. A striking example is presented by Northern Ireland, where Catholics are scarcely likely to join either of the two main Unionist parties given their historic association with militant Protestantism, and conversely Protestants see the nationalist Social Democratic and Labour Party (SDLP) as a 'Catholic' party.
2. It channels and restricts the possibilities for *coalition* between parties. In Italy, for example, the Italian Communist Party (PCI) was excluded from all post-war coalitions on ideological grounds.
3. It limits the range of *policies* which a party can adopt in any given situation. The German Christian Democrats (CDU/CSU) have proved unwilling, despite the potential political risk to their dominance, to 'let sleeping dogs lie' and allow the Eastern German Länder to retain the right to abortion on demand.
4. By closing off options in this way it limits or deflects *criticism* and at the same time facilitates the *co-optation* of young politicians who see no possibility for their future advancement except within the system as already established. Closing off criticism in this way has undoubtedly been a strong factor in the growth in modern liberal democracies of the *administrative state.*

Non-competitive systems

Each of these aspects is even more clearly to be found in non-competitive states, but with certain crucial differences.

1. The justification for the *single-party state* is invariably ideological. *Nationalism* is most likely to be, as in post-colonial Africa, a justification where the state has been formed as a result of a successful struggle for independence. In some states (Angola, Congo, Guinea, Mozambique, Somalia, etc.) the rulers, either

before or after independence, aligned themselves with the former Soviet Union and adopted a form of *Marxist* ideology, and this remains the basis of legitimacy for the government of Cuba today.
2. In a true single-party state the possibility of coalition does not exist, of course. But in both Poland and the former East Germany (DDR) the basis of the governing 'coalition' was exclusionary. In other words, its purpose was to suggest a wider basis of public support than actually existed, while excluding the possibility of the emergence of a true opposition. Significantly the basis for the emergence of overt opposition in Poland was not a party but a trade union, for which Marxist theory offered no clear blueprint.
3. In both single-party states and military dictatorships a simplified, usually nationalist, ideology is used to underpin the *de facto* control of the public by force. Significantly, nationalism has emerged as the main organising principle in the former Soviet Union and Eastern Europe since the collapse of Communism there.
4. In consequence co-optation becomes the main (possibly the only) way in which the personnel of government can be renewed, and legitimacy becomes attached more closely than is safe to the survival in office of a specific individual or ruling group.

Classification of ideologies

Largely for ideological reasons, no satisfactory classification of ideologies has ever been achieved, and it is highly unlikely that one will be (see also Heywood, 1992; Vincent, 1991). There is, however, one with which most people in Europe are familiar: the division of political parties into parties of the *left* and parties of the *right*. This is so well established, in fact, that it is commonly used by people who have no idea at all what they mean by it.

This is not surprising, since the distinction between 'left' and 'right' is a historic one. Appropriately it dates from the time of the French Revolution, when those deputies who believed in change symbolised their allegiances by sitting on the left of the semicircular chamber of the French Assembly, leaving those who had more doubts about the wisdom of change to sit on the right. This distinction spread in due course from France to other European countries and from there to the rest of the world. The symbolism of the left as the seat of true progressive thinking, assiduously propagated in Europe in the inter-war period, dies hard, even in an age when there are parties to the left of the Communists, and the future of Communism is very uncertain. Yet only two decades ago the Gaullists in France strove hard to avoid being seated on the right because of the unfavourable image it held, even for them. Today it is perhaps best regarded as representing a progressive-conservative axis of classification.

But on the other hand the attempt to use other axes of classification for ideologies and their supporters is fraught with difficulties. Some stem from the indefinite nature of the enterprise since, in the nature of the case, ideologies cannot be weighed and measured scientifically. Others stem from the uncertain agreement between observers, as has been seen. But most stem from the determination of the participants themselves not to be labelled. A term such as *populism*, for example, which is very useful in studying political parties in Latin America, is bitterly resented by members of populist parties themselves (Canovan, 1981). Blondel's (fig. 3.1, p. 57) use of three axes should be sufficient to represent the principal distinctions between European parties and their ideologies (Blondel, 1973). In addition to a progressive/conservative dimension, he identifies a monarchical/republican dimension and a tough-minded/tender-minded dimension; the last-named deriving from the psychological distinction popularised by Hans Eysenck (1964). Such distinctions are helpful. They enable observers to identify, for example, within the stream of thought loosely termed 'Thatcherism' in the UK in the 1980s, and 'Reaganism' in the United States, two distinct but overlapping tendencies, which have been termed 'libertarian conservatism' and 'authoritarian conservatism' (Hoover and Plant, 1989). They also disclose streams of thought in the former USSR comparable to the 'New Right' in Western Europe or the United States (Yanov, 1978).

However, perhaps significantly, these dimensions do not include any qualities specific to either religious or nationalist ideologies. Yet even in Western Europe, the major cleavage between political parties has for many years been not between 'left' and 'right', but between different religious groupings.

In *The End of Ideology*, Daniel Bell (1961, reissued 1988) argued that ideological divisions were slowly disappearing in modern capitalist societies through the exhaustion of the ideas that had created them in the first place. Though his work dealt specifically with the United States, the decline of ideology was seen by him as the direct consequence of economic development leading to the creation of a *mass society*. Others, notably Herbert Marcuse (1972), lamented the disappearance of significance that this represented. Still others suggested that since technological imperatives could be expected to be the same for all societies at a similar stage of economic development, a degree of *convergence* could be expected between the ideological presuppositions even of the two superpowers, the United States and the USSR (Brzezinski and Huntington, 1964; cf. Hollander, 1973). Similar conclusions were arrived at independently in Eastern Europe itself (Bahro, 1978).

The collapse of Communism in Eastern Europe in 1989 would seem, at first sight, to have justified the predictions of the convergence theorists. However, much of their argument was based on the assumption that state intervention in Western economies, far from decreasing, was likely to increase, and certainly they did not predict (nor were they likely to have foreseen) the wholesale abandonment of Communist planning in favour of the principles of the so-called 'free market'. At the same time it is clearly of more than passing significance that the sudden void of ideology in Eastern Europe has been filled by two tendencies: religion and nationalism. Where these coincided, notably in Lithuania, Latvia, Estonia and Slovenia, and other conditions were favourable, a unified national movement was able to emerge and in favourable conditions to secure its objectives. Where they were in conflict, as in Armenia, Azerbaijan, Georgia, Croatia and Bosnia-Herzegovina, the consequences have been at best serious and at worst disastrous.

CLASS, STATUS AND PARTY

The notion of ideology is inseparable from the concept of *class*. By class is generally meant a large group of people with a relationship to political power determined by their economic position. Though people today associate the economic basis of class with Marx, it was in fact an association which was originally made by eighteenth-century economists (Calvert, 1982).

Marx saw the concentration of economic power in the hands of a few as leading ultimately to the impoverishment of the majority of the economically productive, leading to violent conflict and the displacement of class by class. By 'class' he meant a group of people with a common relationship to the factors of production, and for him classes, not individuals, were the major 'actors' in the process of social development.

> What I did was to prove 1) that the existence of classes is only bound up with particular historical phases in the development of production; 2) that the class struggle necessarily leads to the dictatorship of the proletariat; that this dictatorship itself only constitutes the transition to the abolition of all classes and to a classless society. (Marx to Weydemeyer, 1852)

Since the collapse of the Soviet Union it has been widely assumed that this is no longer the case. However, few things in politics are obvious and the empirical study of comparative politics should be able to ascertain exactly where and how far this process has advanced, if it has done so. In practice, however, it cannot. Again there are several reasons.

To begin with, Marx never actually defined class (he died leaving his definition incomplete) and though he frequently refers to classes he is inconsistent in his usage of the term. In some places in his work he writes of two classes, in others of three. It seems he was saying that though there were three classes that mattered, only two of them would eventually be left to come into confrontation: the owners of the factors of production, which he termed the bourgeoisie; and those who had nothing to sell but their labour power, the proletariat. Ultimately the proletariat would rise and overthrow their masters, the bourgeoisie, in a social revolution. The moment at which the triumph of the proletariat was at hand, however, would be heralded by the point at which a fourth stratum, that of the intelligentsia (namely the politically aware section of the intellectuals) would throw in their lot with the ultimately dominant proletariat. This last point has led to considerable uncertainty as to whether those movements led by the intelligentsia that claim to be acting in the name of the proletariat are actually representative of them or not.

Second, his use of the term 'class', though widely accepted by intellectuals, superseded an earlier popular definition of class as being what today, with Weber, writers would more accurately term *status* (Gerth and Mills, 1946: 186–7). By status is meant a perception of relative social standing, which may of course be due to hereditary factors or education, and so largely independent of economic factors. So when people are asked what *class* they consider themselves to be, in practice they answer in terms of *status*. Again we may attempt to combine empirical observation with questioning, but the standing of what we determine is very uncertain owing to the large social groupings involved. What is clear is that all societies of any degree of complexity are *socially stratified*; that is to say, they seem to be arranged in horizontal layers.

Societies may be stratified in a large number of ways. Gender, as noted above, forms the most basic distinction, but one which is always found in conjunction with others. Race has acted to stratify both traditional and modern societies. But in modern societies class, status and political power, though distinct from one another, are the main ways in which people determine their own social position and that of others, and each can be traded off against the other (Bendix and Lipset, 1967). And in both nineteenth-century Europe and in the twentieth-century Soviet Union, party, also, formed a basis for the organisation of political power.

Social class

Certainly in the United States, Western Europe and Japan, self-ascribed social position, which can be termed *social class*, is a major factor in determining individual political attitudes, though it is not the only one. Social position is always defined as relative to that of others and hence is crucially dependent on economic considerations (Parkin, 1971). In both the UK and the US, where religion is not at issue, the main factor determining the way in which people vote is their perception of the economic success or otherwise of the incumbent government, and in France the ruling Socialist Party was massively defeated in the assembly elections of March 1993 for that reason.

However, if social class is a key determinant of political behaviour in individual countries, the student of comparative politics is still going to encounter problems in looking at any two or more countries. The problem is a simple one, that government statistical services in different countries categorise their social structures differently. Thus in the United States social class is determined above all by income and conceived of as a sequence of bands ranging from lower lower class to upper upper class. In Britain, where it is extremely difficult to get people to answer questions about their income, the Registrar General's Classification (RGC) consists of a set of status categories based on the occupation of the male head of household. These categories do roughly correspond to income bands, but in no systematic way, and there is a significant division between 'non-manual' and 'manual' occupations, that does not correspond to any difference in wealth and/or income. In France, categories again follow occupational criteria. However, there are two additional criteria. All agricultural occupations are separately listed, and all urban occupations distinguish further between employers and employees.

Hence together wealth and occupation interact in a complex pattern which bears little or no resemblance to Marx's predicted antithesis between bourgeoisie and proletariat. The most striking difference between the three countries is the way in which education acts in each very differently to form the 'leading strata' of society, being apparently of greatest importance in France and of least in the United States. But in each case the significance of education is not so much that it does not help the rise of the 'lower classes' but that it helps to conserve the position of those already at the top (Calvert, 1982: 166–201).

Turning to the position in the former Soviet Union and Eastern Europe, the situation is different again, but not as much so as might have been expected. The society of the former USSR was in Communist theory free from antagonistic class divisions, though the 1936 constitution of the USSR recognised the continuing existence of two classes, workers and workers on collective farms ('peasants'), and one stratum, the intelligentsia. But Soviet sociologists themselves regarded four forms of inequality within Soviet society as resulting in 'contradictions': 'inequalities between the collective-farm peasantry and the working class, between town and country, between manual and non-manual labour, and finally those arising from the division of labour which transcends the groups of worker, intelligentsia and peasant' (Lane, 1971: 39).

In addition, Soviet society, although technically free from inequalities of *wealth*, was characterised by very sharp distinctions of inequality of *income* (Lane, 1971; M. Matthews, 1978). Cross-national studies showed that the inequalities of *esteem* that existed between occupations (status) were in fact very similar to those in Western Europe and the United States (Inkeles, 1968). Though there were also important differences, manual workers remained grouped firmly at the bottom of the status hierarchy (Lane, 1976: 182).

Most importantly, Soviet society was characterised by the dominance of an elite, which Djilas (1957) did not hesitate to characterise, in Marx's terms, as a 'class'. Though there was no private ownership of property, and it was impossible to employ and so exploit others, this special elite, the Communist Party, gained its power and status from the fact that it managed *and so controlled state property*. Significantly the existence of special privileges for the elite of the Party was identified as a major factor in undermining support for the regime well before the ultimate collapse of the system in 1991 (Zaslavsky, 1980). Among these privileges, it was apparent, was the ability to pass on status to their children through special access to educational privileges, so that although in the past it had been possible for people of poor origins (Khrushchev, Chernenko) to reach the very highest position in the Soviet political system, it was not clear that this exceptionally high range of social mobility would, in fact, continue (Parkin, 1971).

CONCLUSION

Communication is both the means by which politics operates and the way in which it can be undestood. Political socialisation enables members of a given society to understand the messages reaching them. In skilled hands, however, both formal and informal socialisation processes can be manipulated. One of the most important consequences of socialisation processes is the stratification of society, whether by class, status or party.

KEY CONCEPTS

class: a large group of people with a relationship to political power determined by their economic position.

code: economical statement conveying meaning.

communication: the transmission of a signal through a channel from a transmitter to a receiver.

culture: the entire pattern of behaviour of a given society.

hegemony: for Gramsci, the acceptance of the system of ideas specific to a class as the ideas of the whole society.

ideology: a set of closely related beliefs or ideas, or even attitudes, characteristic of a group or community, which is both descriptive and persuasive.

metacommunication: information conveyed unintentionally through signs.

status: perception of relative social standing.

SAMPLE QUESTIONS

Communication

Unless the syllabus specifically requires it, the general subject of communication is an unlikely subject for a question. However, understanding the basic principles of communication is absolutely vital in enabling students to interpret political information and to help them distinguish between evidence and opinion, especially in a cross-national context. A possible topic is:

How far has the growth of the mass media changed the fundamental postulates of liberal democratic politics?

Culture and ideology

Political culture and behaviour form a central theme of the study of individual states, and an awareness of the role of social stratification, and social class in particular, is of fundamental relevance to the structure of political parties and a basic requirement for questions on electoral systems. Possible themes are:

How far can the notion of the civic culture be applied to countries other than the United States?

What criteria are used in different societies to determine social class? How far can these criteria be used to make comparisons between different societies?

'Political power, properly so called, is merely the organised power of one class for oppressing another' (Karl Marx and Frederick Engels, The Communist Manifesto*). Discuss.*

'The flaw in the pluralist heaven is that probably 90 per cent of the people cannot even get into the system' (Schattschneider). Discuss.

Have we finally reached 'the end of ideology' in modern politics?

FURTHER READING

On the general principles of communication see Miller (1963). Easton's model of communication within the political system is discussed in Easton (1957, 1965a, b).

Almond and Verba (1963) has been much criticised, but remains an interesting starting point for the attempt to apply the notion of 'political culture' in a comparative context.

For an overview of the problems of ideology and a survey of current ideologies see Vincent (1991) and Heywood (1992). Mannheim's *Ideology and Utopia* (1946) is classic. The social construction of reality is discussed by Berger and Luckmann (1972). On populism see Canovan (1981). Brzezinski and Huntington (1964) came in for sharp criticism when first published, but merits rereading in the light of the events of 1989 and 1991.

Calvert (1982) is a useful introduction to the concept of class. The concept of social class most widely used (though one based essentially on Western Europe and the USA) is set in perspective by Bendix and Lipset (1967). Inkeles (1968) and M. Matthews (1978) discuss stratification in the former Soviet Union in a comparative context.

PART THREE
Structure and Function

5 The struggle for power

INTRODUCTION

All modern states derive their basic political structures from a period of violent disruption and reconstitution. Such a period of disruption may take the form either of an independence struggle, international war or revolution. The phenomenon of revolution is covered in detail in Chapter 11. Here the term is used in the usual sense to refer to political and social changes accompanied by violence, such as people associate particularly with England, the United States, France and Russia (Brinton, 1952), and in modern times with countries as diverse as Mexico, Turkey, China, Egypt (Leiden and Schmitt, 1968), Cuba, Iran and Nicaragua. In all of these instances an important feature of these changes has been the attempt to claim power by people claiming to act directly on behalf of the masses, and in the majority of cases this claim has momentarily led to direct rule by a convention (Verney, 1961; see also Brogan and Verney, 1963), a special type of *assembly* claiming complete control over every aspect of political and social life.

Executive and legislature

Convention theory. At the time of the French Revolution, all power was vested in the National Convention (assembly), and all other centres of authority were for a time destroyed, neutralised or subordinated. The chairman of the Convention was its servant, not its master. The execution of its policies was entrusted to committees created for that purpose. Thoughout its existence, including the period of the Terror (1793–4), the notorious Committee for Public Safety was re-elected monthly. In the parallel instance in England under the Commonwealth (1649–53) Parliament did not delegate even the ceremonial function of receiving ambassadors. Each was brought before the entire House to be formally introduced, and to bow and to be bowed to, rather in the way that to this day new peers are introduced to the House of Lords. Remnants of these and similar practices were still embedded in the earlier constitutions of Communist states, notably those of the USSR (1936), China (1949) and Cuba (1975). In practice, even in those instances, the system was substantially modified in certain well-defined ways.

A second characteristic of convention-theory government is a unifying political culture which seeks to make equal that which is not already equal. The consequence, therefore, is a conflict between centre and periphery, and more particularly, a conflict between two principles – the principle of *representation*, which favours having a big assembly so that representatives are as close to their constituency as possible, and the principle of *efficiency*, which favours small groups for taking day-to-day decisions. In practical terms this means that under the pressure of business the assembly sits for longer and longer hours, and in the end many of the representatives are tempted to hand the burden of work over to someone else. Popular pressure for them to do so may by then be very great, particularly where, as in the French case, the political system is threatened by attack and a speedy response is called for.

If an assembly is to survive for a long time as an effective and working instrument it must not only develop a system of committees, it must delegate effective power to them. Such a development is most strikingly illustrated by the United States Congress. However, in the United States the creation of a separate executive has created a *presidential* system. Where, on the other hand, one of the committees has come to assume the executive power while remaining within the assembly, as in Britain, the result is a *parliamentary* system. Both represent compromises by which a government, limited in its powers of decision, is in return guaranteed the right to extract a sufficient quantity of power resources from the society it governs. There are important differences, however, in the terms of the two compromises.

Parliamentary systems

In Britain, almost uniquely, the parliamentary system was not embodied in a single written constitution. Hence what became the prototype statement of the rules of the parliamentary system for most of the rest of the world was the Belgian constitution of 1831, which was, of course, specifically modelled on British practice. Present-day examples of working parliamentary systems include not only Britain and Belgium, but also Australia, Canada, India, Israel, Malaysia, the Netherlands, Jamaica, Germany and Japan. There is an independent origin for the parliamentary systems of the Nordic countries in Sweden in the eighteenth century (Verney, 1961: 18; cf. Hawgood, 1939, 145–6); and much earlier than that for the Althing of Iceland and the House of Keys in the Isle of Man. However, despite promising beginnings parliamentarism failed to develop in Poland (as, today, in the European

Community) because of the veto each of its individual members could exercise.

In a parliamentary system the functions of rule-application, nominally derived from a head of state, are in practice vested in a committee of the assembly, consisting of ministers appointed by the head of state, but responsible to the assembly for their political actions. In countries such as Britain or the Netherlands, where the head of state is a hereditary monarch, her functions are ceremonial only. In a state with an elected head, such as Iceland, Ireland or Italy, the president (as he or she is rather confusingly called), may have rather more power, though once elected he or she is expected to stand above the political struggle. In most states, exceptions being Japan and Sweden, the head of state has to sign documents giving effect to laws, and retains in this, and the choice of a first or prime minister, reserve powers which may be activated by some unexpected crisis, but which otherwise remain latent.

The executive committee, or ministry, must normally consist of elected members of the assembly, though this is not the case in the Netherlands, Luxembourg and Norway. It is the assembly, too, which normally elects the head of state, where this office is not vested in a hereditary monarch. Five countries that are exceptions are Austria, Finland, France, Iceland and Ireland. There the presidents are directly elected by the people, and in the case of Finland, as in the anomalous hybrid system of France, the president has an important independent sphere of authority in foreign affairs. However, even there, all power has in practice to be exercised through parliament, the collective entity formed by the head of state, the ministry and the assembly.

The fact that all power decisions pass through parliament has been confused in the past with the idea that power rests in it, or even, more misleadingly still, in the assembly itself. But, as for any other organisation, a parliament's effective power is limited, sometimes dramatically so, by the constraints of time and space. Hence the powers of the ministry, which is only indirectly responsible to the electorate, may well not be effectively checked by the assembly either (see Table 5.1).

Presidential systems

The other favoured compromise is the presidential system. This differs fundamentally from the parliamentary system. The prototype is the 1787 constitution of the United States. But not only has this been amended substantially over time (Neustadt, 1964) but as a model it has been taken up throughout the world only since 1946 and in a form which differs substantially from the original intentions of the framers of the American constitution.

Table 5.1 *Convention, parliamentary and presidential systems*

Attribute	*Convention*	*Parliamentary*	*Presidential*
Head of State	Chairman	Monarch or President	President
Head of Government	Chairman	Prime Minister	President
Executive	Committee elected by assembly	Appointed by PM from assembly	Secretaries of President
Executive members of assembly?	Yes	Yes	No
Executive can dissolve assembly?	Yes	Yes	No
Fixed term for executive?	No	No	Yes
Assembly checks executive?	Yes	Sometimes	No
Focus of power	Assembly	Parliament	None
Assembly controls own business?	Yes	No	Yes

Source: after Verney (1961)

It was perhaps natural that in the first three decades of the nineteenth century, presidential systems should have been adopted by most of the newly independent states of the Americas, with the exception of part of Haiti and of Brazil, which remained a parliamentary monarchy until 1889 (Needler, 1963). Only one other presidential state dates from this period: Liberia, a colony for freed American slaves, independent in 1847. After that there was a long gap, until the rising power of the United States created Hawaii (1892; annexed by the United States 1898) and Cuba (1901).

It was only after 1946 when the Philippines, under American tutelage from 1898 onwards, became independent, that the presidential system came to sweep the rest of the Third World, beginning with the Middle East and North Africa, and spreading throughout Africa south of the Sahara in the wake of the dissolution of the British, French and Portuguese colonial empires after 1960. So powerful was the urge to imitate it that even established parliamentary systems such as those of Pakistan and Sri Lanka were modified in the direction of presidentialism. But few of the systems that have resulted are true presidential systems in the constitutional sense.

In the prototype presidential system the assembly remains separate and distinct from the executive. Rule-making remains the function of the assembly; rule-application is entrusted to one person, the president, elected directly for a limited term, who appoints officials to assist him or her, which though they are also commonly called a cabinet, are not a committee of the assembly, and are not politically responsible to it. In the United States the potential conflict of function between president and legislature is met by a variety of devices, but most distinctively by the creation of an independent system of rule-adjudication with power to rule on the constitutionality of specific actions of either of the other two branches of government.

Since there is no focus of power, this system is dynamically unstable, and its invariable tendency has been for the president to destroy the compromise by assuming, often with the aid of force, control over all functions of government. To be a true presidential state, therefore, three conditions all have to be observed.

1. The president must be *elected directly by the people* according to agreed rules generally regarded as fair. The president must not be a hereditary ruler, be self-appointed, come to power by a military coup, or be nominated by the chiefs of a military regime.
2. He or she must be *elected for a definite term*. There is a subtle difference between being elected for a series of definite terms and being in power indefinitely, but in practice one tends to lead to the other. Consequently constitutional provisions limiting presidential terms are normal, though they are often abused, if necessary by the systematic rewriting of constitutional provisions, as with the Somozas in Nicaragua. Assumption of the presidential office for life invites the corollary that the shorter the life, the shorter the term. In practice, of the eight presidents of Haiti who have been elected for 'life', only Dr François Duvalier actually died in office; his predecessors and his successor were deposed. 'Papa Doc' did realise this might happen and one of the ways in which he ingeniously circumvented the restrictions on re-election was to hold municipal elections in 1961. At the top of each ballot paper was the President's name, and after the votes were counted Haitians were told that they had unwittingly given him an overwhelming vote of confidence (Rotberg, 1971: 232).
3. The president *must not be able to dissolve* (or suspend the powers of) *the assembly* during its fixed term of office. In practice this is often done, as in Uruguay in 1973, by the leaders of military or military-backed regimes, making use, in most if not all cases, of emergency powers, which will be considered further later (Weinstein, 1975: 132–3).

The balance is perhaps easier to attain when, as usually happens, the president is elected at the same time as the assembly. Even then, different political parties may, as in the United States since 1981 or in Brazil since 1990, be chosen to represent the people in each of the branches of government. In Chile after 1963 the timing of the respective terms was such that political conflict between the branches was actually made worse. Though the Christian Democratic majority in Congress in 1970 properly accepted the verdict of the popular vote and ratified the election of the Marxist President Salvador Allende, he in turn was unable to achieve a popular majority for his proposals for radical reform (Gil, 1965: 208).

Though there must, if government is to function at all, be a close relationship between the two areas of competence, executive and legislature, summed up in the American phrase 'checks and balances', they must be reciprocal and there must be limits on the president's ability to influence the assembly. This is not as easy as it seems. The executive president is both head of state and head of government; owns no superior, and can – and does – convert the duties of his or her ceremonial role into political power. Speaking on behalf of the government as a whole (particularly in foreign policy or in times of national crisis or disaster), making use of the resources of the media, and in particular being seen visibly associated with concrete evidence of achievement in the form of new roads, airports, dams or military installations, all can be used to generate or to strengthen existing support. And, as Montesquieu observed: 'It is an invariable experience that every man who has power is led to abuse it; he goes on until he finds limits' (Montesquieu, 1966: 151).

The executive president, unlike the head of government in a parliamentary system, is not limited in the power to recruit and to appoint heads of departments by the need to draw them from the ranks of the assembly. Once appointed, the heads of department are the president's subordinates; his secretaries, literally. They seldom have any independent power base. If the president's power to choose them is limited to an extent by the need to obtain congressional approval, the power to dismiss them is not, and there is a limit to how long any assembly, however powerful, can go on blocking presidential nominees.

The struggle for power

Research into ministerial careers suggests that there is less to choose between the parliamentary and presidential systems than this would suggest. Both are characterised by a very rapid turnover of ministers, some two-thirds of whom hold office for less than a year (Blondel, 1985). By reshuffling her Cabinet annually, Mrs Thatcher, Prime Minister of the United Kingdom 1979–90, was able to achieve an exceptional degree of ascendancy over her Cabinet. However, since she had to choose among her colleagues, who each had separate and distinct electoral bases, there came a time when this process brought retribution.

If, in a presidential state, secretaries are given the power to sit and vote in the assembly, they become to an extent responsible to it, and the result is a mixed system which is neither presidential nor truly parliamentary. Peru, before 1968 and after 1980, is an example which has had a long history (Bourricaud, 1970: 270). A more recent, and in other respects anomalous, example is France (Cerny, in Cerny and Schain, 1980: 32), where the constitution of 1958 was deliberately designed to weaken the powers of the Assembly as far as possible, while giving the President a substantial area of prerogative power in defence and foreign affairs. In both, the tendency is to make the president one of two foci of power, whereas in the true presidential system there is no focus of power.

Conversely, it has time and again been demonstrated, notably in two world wars, that in time of crisis the parliamentary system can manage an effective response to the challenge. Nor is there any truth in the suggestion that the parliamentary system is somehow unfitted to manage a programme of economic growth over a long period. In fact, Japan, currently the world's most successful state in the economic sense, has managed its economic growth since 1945 through a parliamentary system, and the German system is both parliamentary and federal.

In the Weberian sense, the parliamentary and presidential systems, as described here, therefore, are 'ideal types'. Even in its homeland, the United States, in the age of the 'Imperial Presidency' and in particular under President Richard M. Nixon, there were noticeable deviations from the strict constitutional assumptions of the presidential system. The parliamentary system does not depend on such a rigid set of criteria and, as the case of the United Kingdom shows, it can evolve within a relatively short period of time. But there must be limits to this process. The president of a republic in a parliamentary system such as France can be given more power. A monarch can be rendered virtually powerless, as occurred in Sweden in 1975 (*Annual Register*, 1975: 151). Yet such is the complexity of modern political systems that no one could deduce from these facts alone either that the French president or the Swedish Riksdag has become all-powerful. The visible constitutional structures are only a partial guide to the real structure of power and decision-making.

DECENTRALISATION AND DECONCENTRATION OF POWER

The effectiveness of power can be tested, in Dahl's terms, by the degree of subsystem autonomy and the number of subsystems within the political system as a whole (Dahl, 1964a: 35). It is clearly very relevant to any assessment of the power of central government to determine the extent to which the state is differentiated into subordinate units, or the extent to which it is centralised. The more centralised it is, the fewer opportunities the individual citizen has of making his or her views felt. But simple *deconcentration* of power – granting power to subordinate governments or agencies – has its limitations since the powers given can always be taken back again. On the other hand, few if any central governments are willing to *decentralise* power once they have discovered the advantages of being able to use it.

The majority of states, Britain and France among them, are strongly centralised. Some, but by no means all, have a considerable degree of regional autonomy, and Italy is an example where the central government has made effective concessions to competing regional loyalties and interests. Beyond these lie states in which a central government has been constructed by agreement between separate local governments, who with an independent power base continue to co-exist with central government, and power, as in Germany or the United States, is shared between them according to rules laid down in a written constitution. In a few states, such as Switzerland, the powers of central government extend to little more than the conduct of defence and foreign affairs – this form of government is known as a *confederation*. Often, as in the Swiss case, and as may well come in time to be true of Europe as a whole, the first step towards confederation is the formation of an alliance or league between states which retain full independence of one another.

Dahl's interest in this range of possibilities is natural enough, since, being an American, he lives in a federal state – one in which the balance between central power and regional autonomy is very carefully fixed. The United States emerged as a league of separate colonies in 1774 with the Association, and once war had broken out agreed (1777) Articles of Confederation. By 1786 the weakness of the confederation brought about a decisive shift of public opinion in favour of the creation of a federal state. However, federalism is the product of a political compromise, and so very unusual – a compromise between centripetal and centrifugal forces, the demands of central power and the demand for independence (Frankel, 1963: 17–19). This compromise is inherently unstable, with a tendency towards greater centralisation; and there are very few states in the world that are federal states at any one time. It just so happens that today most of them – Brazil, Canada,

Germany, India, the United States – happen to be rather important, and therefore federalism gets more attention than its historical existence might specifically warrant.

Although at national level the pressures of politics do not always allow for the degree of direct participation that one might perhaps hope for, in many states the conduct of local government is subject to noticeably less rigour and control. It is still possible for many societies, for example Italy, India, Tanzania and Brazil, to permit decisions at the local level to be made by the general gathering of citizens or by a locally elected assembly, subject to some kind of overall control from the centre, but with only a very generalised degree of control. In New England in the United States some townships still retain direct government through township meetings. More recently local cable television has enabled Californians to take part personally in the debates of the 'electronic town hall'.

In a British local authority there is an assembly in which, in theory, everybody is equal; again, the control of business is in its own hands, and it controls its own place of meeting. This is a relic of an old freedom which can operate at local level because there is a check in the overriding national interest. The recent history of local government in Britain and France shows just how tenuous that freedom is. In Britain, local authorities have been deprived of all significant autonomy and many are now threatened with individual abolition. They are no longer able to raise what money they like or to spend what money they like, subject only to the will of their electorates. Worse still, they have been ordered to do a great many new tasks for which they have been given no resources. In France, on the other hand, reforms in 1981 abolished the prefectoral *tutelle* and (until 1988) even the title of 'prefect' itself. At the departmental level many of the powers of the former prefects were transferred to the elected Conseil Général. At the communal level the traditional structure remains unaltered. However, despite this the central government clearly retains the right to alter or to abolish local government.

As will be seen later, the concept of total participation voiced at the time of the French Revolution is also embedded in the characteristic political structure of Communist states and a handful of other socialist states too, in a special way which varies significantly from the structure of liberal democratic states. Both the parliamentary system and the presidential system as compromises are, moreover, subject to certain types of mutations, and these types of mutation are most inclined to happen when governments fail to resist the pretensions of small groups within the state to assert authority over the majority. There are other circumstances, but these are the ones in which most differentiation in status has occurred.

This can be even more clearly seen in the case of India. As the very successful examples of Australia and Canada show, the parliamentary system is readily adapted to the special conditions of federal government. However, the Indian constitution of 1949 considerably modifies the traditional assumption of federalism: that both federal and 'state' governments will have clear and distinct areas of authority. It does so by providing for the federal government to impose 'President's Rule' (as in Uttar Pradesh in December 1992 following the destruction of the 16th century Babri mosque at Ayodhya by Hindu extremists) on a state which is regarded (by the federal government!) as being unable to govern itself responsibly. Direct rule from the centre, carried beyond a certain point, would destroy federalism and create a unitary state, though the point at which this might happen could be difficult to determine with certainty. But it is quite compatible with the overall sovereignty implicit in the concept of the parliamentary system, and it required the actual use of force, essentially a coup, by Mrs Gandhi to change the form of government radically (*Annual Register*, 1975: 253).

THE COLLAPSE OF CONSTITUTIONAL GOVERNMENT

The differences between parliamentary and presidential systems extend to the circumstances in which they collapse, or are so changed that they are no longer recognisable in their original form.

Parliamentary systems fail or mutate when the collective responsibility of the executive collapses. The problem with an executive that sits in parliament and is continuously responsible to parliament is that, whether for psychological, social, or political reasons, it finds it difficult to withstand the pretensions of the assembly, which are, after all, embodied in the constitution of the state, unless it can count on the collective loyalty of its members. This is possibly the only good argument against coalition government, namely that if people rush from Cabinet meetings to give press conferences saying they think their colleagues are swine, in a very short space of time the system ceases to work. It is necessary, therefore, if the very close and intimate interrelationship of the executive and the assembly is to continue, for the executive to remain collective. If one person becomes paramount, then the hostility of the assembly and of others becomes focused upon that one person, and he or she, in turn, is tempted to assume exceptional powers and even to rule as a dictator.

The tendency for the executive to assume additional powers has been a feature of those governments that have inherited the parliamentary system from a colonial country. States with parliamentary systems such as France and Britain, which had colonies early in the nineteenth century, have tended to implant parliamentarianism in them, and very successfully so. One need only look at Australia, the Bahamas, Barbados, Canada, India, Jamaica, Malaysia and New Zealand. In these states there has been relatively little tendency to move away from it, and in Pakistan and Sri Lanka there has recently been a significant desire to move back to the parliamentary system.

But a great many of the French and British colonies were acquired with great haste near the end of the last century, and the social systems, structures and decision-making processes of those states were subordinated without actually being removed. In other words, there is continuity between pre-colonial and post-colonial times, because the intervening period of colonial organisation has been relatively short. Furthermore, in protectorates such as Malaysia or Morocco, by definition, the existing social structure was left largely untouched and rule was indirect, leaving the existing decision-making mechanism substantially intact (Milne, 1967: 14–16). The tendency in many, but not all of these states has been away from parliamentarianism, because it has been felt uncongenial in view of the colonial associations it holds. The very natural, if perhaps misplaced, desire to get back to the state of affairs as it was before colonisation began, coupled with the habit of accepting authoritarian decisions engendered by the very nature of colonial rule, make the parliamentary system with its compromises temporarily unattractive. Faced with the burdens of development, the new executive is inclined to envy the apparent freedom of action of the presidential system and to urge its adoption, as in Ghana (Afrifa, 1966) and Nigeria, Zaire, Angola and Mozambique.

This is a reasonable, predictable and understandable development. It was to be expected that a new compromise would have to be reached in new states. What is improbable is that the presidential compromise, as at present understood, is going to last for a very long time. It necessarily involves the overt conflict of interests in public, and that seems, on the face of it, very unlikely beyond the next ten or twenty years.

The collapse of democratic governments

Parliamentary systems cease to exist in any meaningful sense when one of three things happens:

1. *When the head of state assumes power.* In Hitler's Germany with the Enabling Act in 1933, or France at Vichy with Pétain in 1940 (Carsten, 1967: 152–5), parliament yielded all its powers to the head of state and ceased to function. To secure such a result intimidation may be and in the first case was actually used, as also in the case of Mussolini's so-called March on Rome in 1922.

And, as in Czechoslovakia in 1948, the threat may be provided by foreign troops.

2. *When the assembly is dissolved.* Rulers can simply physically close the doors of parliament; barricade them; refuse to let the assembly meet. This does not always have the desired effect; in France in 1789 the delegates went off to a nearby tennis court and constituted themselves as a National Assembly.
3. *When some extra-parliamentary mechanism controls the choice of the assembly.* If there are not wholly 'free' elections and the choice of the assembly is controlled by the executive (Seton-Watson, 1956: 167–71) the system cannot be parliamentary. It is true, to some extent, that all choices for the assembly are always controlled by something. The very existence of political parties in their role of interest aggregation mechanism in most societies means that there is a degree of control of choice of the assembly. The only remedy against this, the pluralists would argue, is to invent more and varied political parties. But the control of the process of choice by the executive necessarily reduces the possibility of the parliamentary system of compromise functioning until it disappears altogether. Examples here might be the Falange in Spain after 1939 on the one hand (H. Matthews, 1957: 76–7), and in Eastern Europe before 1989, Czechoslovakia with its National Front, the former German Democratic Republic (DDR) with the Workers Unity Front (SED), Bulgaria with the Fatherland Front, and Poland with the United Workers Party.

Presidential systems, on the other hand, collapse when the delicate balance between executive and legislature is disrupted, and this happens most easily when the collective responsibility of the assembly weakens. In the clash between a single presidency and a multiple congress, if the congress fails to function as an efficient counter-balancing unit, then, necessarily, the system fails to work properly. It ceases to work at all when one of three things happens:

1. The system evolves into what, with the Venezuelan Vallenilla Lanz (1919), can be called *'democratic Caesarism'*. In this form of government the state continues to be ruled by a president, and regular elections may even be held, but the system is wholly dominated by the executive power through abdication of power by the legislature, either voluntarily or involuntarily, as has historically frequently been the case in the Latin American republics and is today in, for example, Iraq. So the democratic Caesar is the ruler of the presidential state, and the system is

characterised by 'omnipotent executive power and a subservient legislature' (Stokes, 1959: 302, 385). The reason is usually that the congress lacks a real basis of independent support, and so simply does not have enough political 'clout' to counter-balance the force of the presidency. The presidency can deliver all the possible goods, and as long as it can continue to deliver them there is no role for congress; congress merely signs blank cheques in advance by approving the presidential budget, and endorses them afterwards by approving the expenditure. A good test of this is the regular, unopposed passage of supplementary estimates for expenditure already incurred, a feature of the Mexican Congress under its one-party system.

2. *The military assume political power*, as in Chile in 1973 or in Argentina in 1976. Then clearly the presidential state does not really exist any more because the executive is not elected. In such circumstances Argentines speak of 'de facto' presidents, though the courts continue to give legality to their decrees and to treat their actions as legitimate (Calvert and Calvert, 1989; di Tella, 1983: 199–200). However, in 1992 when President Fujimori of Peru proclaimed a state of emergency and tried to dissolve Congress, the majority of deputies met in a secret location, deposed him and proclaimed the senior Vice President President in his place, though without much effect.
3. *The executive controls the choice of the assembly*. Means of coercion at his or her disposal may consist either of the armed forces, or of another personal armed force as with the formidable and much feared Tontons Macoutes under the elder Duvalier. Alternatively, choice may be in the hands of a ruling party, which can make use of the coercive power of the state to back up its decisions, though in practice these are unlikely to be challenged.

THE FORMER COMMUNIST STATES

In the former Communist states, use of this power was in the hands of the Party *apparat*, a centralistic organisation which uses part of the coercive power of the state to control the rest. What was distinctive about it was that its professed purpose was *changing* society. It is, thus, the exact opposite of a structure such as the army, whose task it is to preserve the status quo. Ghita Ionescu defines the *apparat* as a network of power which controls the formal structure of power. In Communist states this network consists essentially of the Communist Party and its appendages, with the interesting consequence that an individual's status is determined not by his formal position in the state, but by his standing in the Party. But Ionescu draws his net wider to embrace, in non-Communist states, 'any centralistic organisation which in an oppositionless state holds, in proportion to its share of responsibility in the running of the state, a smaller or larger part of the power of the state' (Ionescu, 1967: 16, 20).

Why did this happen? First, because of the contradiction in Communist theory between the theory of democracy and the commitment to change. In such circumstances there were a substantial number of people who did not like the idea of too much change. Second, as Milovan Djilas argues, the petrifaction of the ruling Party, which came to be composed of a 'new class' of officials who exercise their collective power to impede, and perhaps even reverse, the possibility of movement towards a more egalitarian state (Djilas, 1957).

Certainly one-party rule was not expressly stated in the 1936 Soviet constitution; it was merely assumed to follow from the claim made in Article 126 that the Party was the sole organisation representing the working people there (Hazard, 1964: 245). However, in the 1977 constitution the absolute position of the Party was made explicit. Whichever way one looks at it, therefore, the formal structures of Communist states cannot simply be ignored (Fejtö, 1974). Provided it is remembered that behind them the effective control of politics has for many years been in the hands of the Party, it becomes clearer why such a wide range of variance was in fact permitted.

The Soviet Union, Poland, Hungary, Romania, Bulgaria and Outer Mongolia had convention-theory-style governments, at least on paper. In theory, the system of government was based on a pyramid of soviets or some similar form of committee. In it responsibility ran from the bottom to the top of the society. Each level of the hierarchy elected delegates to the next highest level, with supreme control in theory vested in the vast assembly, supposed to be fully representative of the entire nation.

The influence of convention theory is especially evident in the Soviet constitution of 1936. Under it the Soviet Union did not have a designated head of government – Stalin was only chairman of a committee, as was Mao Tse-tung in China. The executive was, again in theory, only a committee of that assembly. Even more surprisingly, until 1977 there was not in the Soviet Union even a formally designated head of state, only a chairman of the executive committee of the Supreme Soviet (Hazard, 1964: 221). It is by no means the same thing to be a chairman as it is to be a president. A president has, or may have, executive power of his own; a chairman, notionally, acts only as a voice for the committee which he heads. It is hardly surprising that Leonid Brezhnev, as Chairman of the Praesidium of the Supreme Soviet, preferred not to be thought of as a chairman, though strictly speaking he was not quite a president. His real power, like that of all Soviet leaders from Stalin to Gorbachev, came from the combination of a formal office in the state apparatus with the real position of power held in the Party (Calvert, in Calvert, 1987: 250–3).

Second, a very characteristic feature of the Soviet system which has been slow to disappear was the idea of the collective responsibility of everyone, at any given level, for whatever others around them may be thinking or doing (Barghoorn, 1972: 148). Everybody was responsible for the deviation of a single individual; collective responsibility did not stop at the executive as against the legislature, or the legislature as against the executive, as in the parliamentary or true presidential systems. Collective responsibility ran throughout the society and involved collective responsibility of every group for every member of it. This again is no new phenomenon; it was no less characteristic of Spain in the time of the Inquisition or Geneva under the rule of the Saints, but it is no less coercive in its effect on the individual, since its corollary is that no deviation can be countenanced without endangering the logic of the entire structure.

What was new about the Soviet system was, third, the fact that the basis of control of the state was vested in a single party, and that this party claimed to have a special and unique ability to decide what was in the best interests of the community as a whole. This special knowledge is not an original idea; what is original is the fact that it is regarded as being vested in a political party, and not in a priesthood, as in the Islamic Republic of Iran. Political parties were, of course, well-established features of politics in Europe when in 1902 Lenin first enunciated in *What is to be Done?*, his view of the political party in its special role as a vehicle of continued agitation for revolutionary change (Lenin, 1967, I: 97ff.). It is from this role, and from the fact of his seizure of power in the name of the Party in 1917, that the characteristic notion of the Party as a permanent directing feature of government, carrying out a specific plan for change, derives. This role, moreover, was specifically written into the Soviet constitution of 1977 (Finer, 1979), only to collapse in 1991 in face of the clear evidence that it was unable to use it effectively.

This leads, fourth, to that distinguishing feature of Communist systems which made 1917 a second key turning point in modern political development, comparable only with 1789 and the emergence of the assembly. This is the assumption by the state of complete responsibility for economic matters. As it states in Article 4 of the 1936 constitution of the USSR:

> The economic foundation of the USSR is the socialist system of economy and the socialist ownership of the instruments and means

> of production, firmly established as a result of the liquidation of the capitalist system of economy, the abolition of private ownership of the instruments and means of production, and the elimination of the exploitation of man by man.

Aspirational as this inevitably is, it should be read in conjuction with Article 11:

> The economic life of the USSR is determined and directed by the state national economic plan, with the aim of increasing the public wealth, of steadily raising the material and cultural standards of the working people, of consolidating the independence of the USSR and strengthening its defensive capacity. (Hazard, 1964: 221–2, 223.)

Since the control of the state was in fact vested in the Party, it followed that, even though the USSR itself had chosen to demonstrate its democratic credentials by setting up political forms with a strongly convention-theory tinge, there was no reason why actual control by an *apparat* could not be combined with any other system of government generally regarded as democratic. This is, in fact, what did happen elsewhere in Eastern Europe.

Czechoslovakia after 1948 and the German Democratic Republic after 1949 continued to have formal parliamentary governments. The GDR adopted a constitution surprisingly similar to the old Weimar constitution. It has often been alleged that the Weimar constitution made stable government impossible in pre-war Germany, but it worked well enough if all political parties were abolished except one. At the top, moreover, after an experiment with 'collective leadership' in the early 1950s, power and the title of head of state were combined in the GDR in one man long before this idea had heen accepted in the Soviet Union itself (Heidenheimer, 1971: 265ff.). In 1974 an executive presidency was created for Ceausescu in Romania.

Yugoslavia had a more complicated history. Under Tito, it was a presidential state with an executive nominated by the assembly. It was also nominally a federal state, divided into six states according to old divisions between Serbs, Croats and Slovenes. Socially it was a state which provided for a high degree of workers' democracy, with characteristic structure of intensive participation in committees. But the control of the Party, the Yugoslav League of Communists, underneath the formal structures of the presidential state, was all-pervasive (Rubenstein, 1965, 1966: 202–3).

When Tito, who was a Croat, died in 1980, he left his successors a deliberately weakened state structure. Its formal head was not one person, but an executive council, originally created to help the executive function, and to prepare for the transition when Tito died. It survived until 1991, though only at the cost of failing to make many crucial decisions which helped accelerate the drift towards regional nationalism. What destroyed it in the end was the collapse of the Soviet Union, fear of which had helped hold it together, and the belief of the Serbs who controlled the Yugoslav National Army that their only remaining way of safeguarding Serbian interests was to resort to force.

The People's Republic of China was originally constituted on the Soviet model after the Communist seizure of power in 1949. In the 1960s it passed through the spectacular period of the Great Proletarian Cultural Revolution, when Chairman Mao attempted to renew the state by direct participation and self-criticism. During this period the formal institutions of government were not only disused but actually in disfavour, with the sole exception of the People's Liberation Army, which came to hold much of the effective power (Robinson, 1969: 32ff., 122–3). Then came a slow return towards constitutional order, culminating in the writing of the 1975 state constitution. Even this retained many of the revolutionary committees of the 1960s, a large number of which were eventually abolished and the authority of the Communist Party restored at the meeting of the fifth National People's Congress in February 1978 (*Sunday Times*, 19 February 1978). Despite this, the structure of Chinese government resembles the 1936 Soviet version rather than the 1977 one, except that the central organ is the Executive Committee of the Politburo, the body of which Chairman Mao was chairman.

Cuba, on the other hand, remained quite different from other Communist states until 1975 when, under pressure from the Soviet Union, it established a series of formal state structures culminating in a National People's Power Assembly chosen by regular elections, which had, in common with the 1940 constitution, been in suspension since 1959 (González, 1976). During this very long period Cuba resembled what in any other state in Latin America would be called 'democratic Caesarism' in that Fidel Castro, then nominally only Prime Minister, effectively controlled the government of his relatively small country by direct communication – through radio and television. Even the formal structure of the Communist Party, though older than the state structure, came into existence relatively late to conform with the doctrine of Marxism–Leninism that a true proletarian revolution could only be led by one (Goldenberg, 1965: 267–8). Here, too, the military influence has been growing until, with nine military members of the small Cabinet, Cuba began to embark on a series of overseas ventures in Africa which have interesting implications for the future role of smaller states.

CONCLUSION

The fact is that the formal structure of all states embodies the real feelings of their governments towards the participation of others, in that the most common reason that they do not work the way they are apparently supposed to do, is that they have been carefully designed not to do so. Some variation, fortunately, occurs as the art of designing political institutions is as yet by no means perfect, and so governments cannot always stop their people having an effective say. Modern states, therefore, can be divided into two categories according as the notion of participation is itself divided; and, as they exist to do at least two things – satisfy demands and generate supports – which are not compatible with one another, they all depend on some sort of compromise.

KEY CONCEPTS

apparat: a centralistic organisation which uses part of the coercive power of the state to control the rest.

assembly: group of people representing the society at large.

convention theory: belief that all power should be vested in the national assembly.

decentralisation of power: sharing of power by central government with other independently powerful bodies or agencies.

deconcentration of power: granting of powers by central government to subordinate bodies or agencies.

parliamentary system: governmental system characterised by the unification of powers, the executive power being vested in a committee of the legislative assembly and so responsible to the assembly.

presidential system: governmental system characterised by the separation of powers, the executive power being vested in a president and the legislative power in a separate assembly.

SAMPLE QUESTIONS

This chapter groups together a number of themes relating to the origin and use of *political power*.

What are the characteristics of presidential government in the United States? Why has it been so widely imitated in other countries since 1945?
How far is it true to regard parliamentary government as a European phenomenon quite unsuited to Third World conditions?
How far is the abuse of power in post-colonial states a product of the colonial past?
Is a substantial decentralisation of political power a necessary condition for democracy?
Has Djilas' thesis of the 'New Class' been justified by later events?
Is the 'one-party state' a contradiction in terms?

FURTHER READING

On democratic systems see Held (1988). Leadership in democratic systems is usually discussed on a county-by-country basis, but Weller (1985) deals with prime ministers in 'Westminster' systems and Rose and Suleiman (1980) compare presidents and prime ministers. Blondel (1985) is a comparative study of ministerial careers. Clapham (1985) discusses leadership in Third World states. On revolution, see Calvert (1990a), and Chapter 11, this volume.

On federalism, see Duchacek (1970), though Wheare (1963) remains useful.

An overview of communist and post-communist systems is given by Stephen White et al. (1990). Ionescu (1967) comments on the role of the *apparat* in Communist states. For the 'New Class' thesis, see Djilas (1957).

González (1976) discusses the Cuban system as reconstructed in the mid-1970s. Linz and Stepan (1978) discuss the breakdown of democracy in Latin America and O'Brien and Cammack (1985) the failure of the military regimes that replaced it.

6 How demands are presented

INTRODUCTION

Demands on the political system originate in the minds of individual citizens, often in a quite unformed state. They may well not be immediately recognised as political, and whether they are seen to be or not will depend on the nature of the society concerned. The citizen may, in virtually all societies, express demands *as an individual* by speaking or writing to a recognised outlet at some level of government. Historically, this right of petition applied in the Soviet Union as well as in non-Communist countries (Lane, 1978).

However, except in a very local sense, the voice of one individual in a modern society will normally carry little weight unless the demands which that individual *articulates* come from within the central elite and its decision-making body – what Easton (1957, 1965a, b) calls 'withinputs' or 'intraputs' – or until those concerned get together with others who share a common interest and *aggregate* their demands into a programme for action. In liberal democracies demands are typically articulated by *interest groups* and aggregated by *political parties*. However, this model is by no means always applicable elsewhere.

INTEREST GROUPS

It is now recognised that interest groups – people sharing a common interest – exist in all societies, though usually in a *latent* rather than an *active* state, waiting to be activated by a relevant issue. In a sense they cover the entire field of political interest articulation other than that of the individual, for the family itself can be regarded as an interest group. Many groups, especially those with better formal organisation, aggregate interests also into a common action programme. But the interest group differs from the political party, to which it is closely related, by not seeking political power for itself; it seeks merely, when it acts at all, to influence decisions taken by others.

For the purpose of comparative politics, the most useful system of classification of interest groups is still that of Almond, who divides

Table 6.1 *Institutionalised and anomic interest groups*

	Latent	*Institution*	*Anomic*
Non-associational	Sect	Church	Religious riot
Institutional	Occupation	Trade union	Strike
Associational		Pressure group	Demonstration

interest groups into four categories (Almond, in Almond and Coleman, 1960: 33ff.). These categories are non-associational, institutional, associational and anomic (see Table 6.1).

Almond's classification of interest groups

Non-associational	Born into, inherit membership
Institutional	By virtue of occupation
Associational	Voluntary choice
Anomic	Spontaneous, temporary

1. *Non-associational.* People do not join non-associational groups; they are born into them, and therefore as far as politics are concerned the groups may remain latent rather than active, often for many years. They include family and kin groups, castes, classes, religious sects (such as the Muslims of Bosnia-Herzegovina) and ethnic groups (such as the Serbs and Croats). Membership of such groups is, at least at the beginning of their politically interested life, a given in their environment. They are defined as non-associational, therefore, indicating that they have not joined together in the specific way, they just happen to be a member of this common bond of interest.
2. *Institutional.* Institutional interest groups include all groupings to which one belongs by virtue of economic necessity – the need to earn one's living. They include bodies like the armed forces, police, civil servants, teachers, professional groupings generally, and other occupational groups. However, although doctors (medical practitioners or physicians), for instance, form an institutional interest grouping, bound together by their common profession, in practice they can practice medicine only if they are members of a formal organisation, in the US the American Medical Association (AMA) or in the UK the British Medical Association (BMA). Each of these organisations speaks for the views of doctors whether the doctors like it or not, since all doctors have to belong to them. So at the institutional level

interest groups cease to be usually latent and shift to a more overt, participatory level.

3. *Associational.* As their name suggests, one is not born a member of an associational interest group, one chooses to join one. Straddling the boundary between institutional and associational groups are the trade unions. It is necessary for many purposes in many countries to belong to a trade union in order to earn one's living, but in Britain they are, at least, still considered to be in some sense voluntary bodies, as in the United States. They are therefore regarded, for most purposes, as being an associational interest group. The associational category also includes most of the various forms of pressure groups.

   Pressure groups can in turn be subdivided into two categories: those that are designed to defend interests on the one hand, and those that are formed to promote interests on the other. *Protectional groups*, such as the National Farmers' Union in Britain or the French Wine Growers' Association, consist of people who are actively engaged in a trade or profession whose interests they seek to defend. *Promotional groups*, on the other hand, do not necessarily consist of the people whose interests they seek to promote and, in the case of the British National Society for the Prevention of Cruelty to Children or the international pressure group Greenpeace, they could not in fact do so.
4. *Anomic.* 'Anomic' refers to a state of *alienation* from the normal processes of society, such as was originally described by Emile Durkheim in 1893 (Durkheim, 1964: ix). However, Almond does not define the word anomic in this sense, which is extremely confusing. Anomic *groups*, to Almond, have only a temporary existence and no formal organisation. They are 'spontaneous irruptions from the society into the polity' (Almond and Coleman, 1960: 34). Riots, demonstrations, strikes, walk-outs, and sit-ins form anomic interest groupings in this sense.

Protest and ungovernability

Now anomic interest groupings, considered as politically active entities, are in fact not distinct from non-associational, institutional and associational groups. Some are only actions performed by established groups and the rest can be regarded as a special type of associational group – a temporary one. There are some that are institutional, and there are some that are non-associational as well, so that it might, for some purposes, be more convenient to think of anomic interest groupings as a completely separate category of political action, one in which *protest* escapes from the normal channels of discussion (Calvert, 1967 – see also Chapter 11). Anomic interest group activity is generally regarded as an *indicator* of widespread alienation from the existing system and so of serious structural problems in a society which could in turn lead to significant political change.

In the 1970s there was considerable discussion as to whether various competitive states had lost the ability to process demands effectively and were becoming 'ungovernable'. As late as 1976 the British economist Samuel Brittan predicted that 'liberal representative democracy suffers from internal contradictions that are likely to increase in time, and that, on present indications, the system is likely to pass away within the lifetime of people now adult' (Brittan, 1976: 96). The 'ungovernability' thesis was supported by both left and right, though for very different reasons.

Anti-system violence. In many competitive states, despite their apparently open societies, the 1960s saw the emergence of violent movements dedicated to overthrowing the system: in West Germany the Baader-Meinhof gang, in Japan the Japanese Red Army, in Britain the Provisional IRA. To the left this represented 'the intensification of contradictions' which, they believed, would eventually lead to the break-up of capitalist states.

Limitations on resources. At the same time, the extension of the 'welfare state' in Western Europe after 1945 was consuming an increasing share of resources. In theory progressive systems of taxation were leading to a transfer of wealth from the richest to the poorest members of society. In practice, research showed that the redistributive effect of taxation was generally rather limited, and that both the contributors to and the beneficiaries of welfare-state systems were in the main the articulate middle classes. 'New Right' theorists like Brittan argued, therefore, that the limits of the system had been reduced. Hence not only would the state have to give up some of its responsibilities, but it was actually counter-productive for it not to do so. The 'Lafer curve', which suggested that a reduction in tax level would actually lead to an increase in tax revenues formed the basis for the economic strategy of President Reagan in the United States. 'Thatcherism' in Britain went further, in initiating after 1983 a far-reaching programme of 'privatisation' of state-owned industries and utilities, while at the same time cutting back the powers of trade unions and increasing the freedom of employers to resist wage demands. In the later 1980s privatisation came to be seen by the governments of many other countries as a method of escaping from the limitations of the 'weak state'.

For the purposes of comparative politics, therefore, what is interesting is not whether or not there are interest groups – because there are going to be interest groups, if only latent, in any given society selected for study – but the preponderance of one type rather than another. However, there is an implicit suggestion in Almond that the sophistication of the society is measured by the extent to which it manages to separate off political processes from the general social world. In other words the more complex the society, the more advanced it will be. And thus, for example, India is characterised as having 'poor boundary maintenance between the polity and the society'. That is to say, that the kind of social organisations which exist within Indian society also serve political purposes, and Almond considers this to be a sign of inadequate differentiation and therefore not sufficiently 'modern' (Almond and Coleman, 1960: 45).

Such a view reflects the contemporary obsession with 'modernisation', which views political development as closely analogous to economic development. Hence, since economic development can be measured and recorded in terms of simple indices of wealth and production, the same must be true of political development. The same notion of 'efficiency' gives rise to more, and more diverse, interest groups; specifically to a shift from non-associational or institutional interest groupings towards institutional and associational interest groupings.

The non-associational survivals, such as the religious base of Northern Ireland politics for example, struck Almond and Coleman as being archaic. This view is certainly correct, but it does not explain why one gets this curious obsession with religion, of all things, in the more developed and industrialised end of Ireland. This suggests that political and economic development are certainly not following parallel courses.

Pluralism

The *pluralists* see the ability to form groups as the *sine qua non* for a democratic society. However, a pluralist such as Robert A. Dahl goes much further than this. He recognises that a flaw in what he terms 'Madisonian' democracy, democracy based on the notion of one person one vote, with the emphasis on the role of the individual, is that in modern society there are so many individuals that any given one will carry little or no weight as such. The only way that the individual can successfully articulate interests, therefore, is in conjunction with others.

However, the existence of interest groups does not itself restore the capacity of the individual to affect policy. Indeed the existence very close to government of powerful interest groups is all too likely to have just the reverse effect. Dahl argues, therefore, that the only way individual interests can make themselves felt, and the balance of democracy be restored, is by multiplying the number of groups indefinitely, so that all possible interests are again represented. Pluralism, therefore, is not concerned merely with observing how things are; it is prescriptive, an argument in favour of liberal democracy.

However, there are others who argue that group action is not a substitute for individual action. Kornhauser, for example, agreed that the more associational interest grouping occurred, the more it downgraded individual action, and the less weight, therefore, the individual had within society. But he did not see the remedy for this as lying in the further multiplication of groups. In 'mass society' the individual could no longer hope to exert any real influence (Kornhauser, 1959: 92–3). Although the pluralist thesis cannot be wholly sustained from a conventional perspective, therefore, its testing undoubtedly remains one of the key tasks of present-day comparative politics.

Interest groups and policy-making

All these groupings are significant only in so far as they can be related to the political process. There has, in short, to be some kind of linkage. In theory at least, groups have a choice both of the *level* at which they extert their influence and the *manner* in which they do so.

Though the number of levels available will vary from one society to another, possible categories will include:

- the chief executive
- the cabinet
- the bureaucracy
- legislators
- political parties
- the general public.

The tactics to be used will obviously depend to a considerable extent on which of these levels is available for the exercise of influence. A private word with a member of the cabinet can obviously be very effective, but only if the government is receptive to the ideas being put forward. If the government is unreceptive, it may be necessary to apply indirect pressure and appeal directly to public opinion. In this case possible means will include petitions and demonstrations to obtain publicity through the media and a lobby of political organisations to use their influence on behalf of the cause. There is therefore a *general* relationship between the nature of the pressure group and the tactics employed, even though in practice there may be quite a lot of variation from one time and place to another. The methods used by a group depend on the kinds of aims it has and the acceptability of those aims to those involved in the decision-making process:

Clandestine/illegal. Some groups, such as ETA in Spain, the Provisional IRA in Britain or the Tamil Tigers in Sri Lanka, have aims which directly challenge the basis of the existing order and therefore operate largely in secret.

Ideological/open market. Other groups are entirely legal but challenge political norms *as defined by government.* Examples have been the Campaign for Nuclear Disarmament in Britain, various 'Black Power' movements in the United States, and (currently) the African National Congress (ANC) in South Africa. Governments may, therefore, refuse to deal with them, and in extremes, regard them as subversive and so to be excluded from decision-making. Hence they tend to use 'open market' tactics such as marches, lobbies of legislators, demonstrations, posters etc.

Pragmatic/'insider'. Others, especially protectional groups, have information and co-operation to offer government. They tend to have pragmatic approaches to their aims and are often given limited access to the decision-making process; hence they can negotiate on the inside of government, with a degree of privileged status (see Table 6.2).

For some groups, their influence begins at election time, when they try to secure the return of legislators favourable to their cause. In Britain a substantial group of Labour MPs are sponsored by trade unions – a custom which dates back to the days before MPs were paid. In the United States candidates of either party may be endorsed by unions and receive financial support for their campaigns. In both countries, and

Table 6.2 *How interest groups act to affect policy*

Operation	*Clandestine/ illegal*	*Ideological/ open market*	*Pragmatic/ 'insider'*
Promotional groups	ETA (Spain) Provisional IRA (GB/IRL)	CGT (F) CND (GB)	AFL/CIO (US) American Legion (US)
Protectional groups	Cosa Nostra (US)	AMA (US) CGT (F)	BMA (GB) TUC (GB)

in other liberal democracies, many legislators are effectively privileged lobbyists for special interests, while since the rest are not specialists on matters outside their own specialities, information from pressure groups has become an important part of the way in which they make up their minds.

To make the task of government easier, ministers often recognise the value of consulting with representatives of interests before formulating policy or embarking on legislation. They are not always pleased to be told that their ideas will not work or are unpopular, but in the event they may be glad they took the advice given them, even if they seldom have the grace to say so. As in the case of the British Medical Association and the Department of Health, some interest groups have won a legal right to be consulted, and when they are consulted they expect to have their views taken into account. The BMA is a particularly useful group to the British Government for two reasons. On the one hand medicine is a highly emotive subject which arouses strong feelings in the electorate, and the co-operation of Britain's doctors is essential. On the other hand it is an area in which 'expert' opinion is especially strongly valued. Hence the BMA, which was closely involved in the setting-up of the NHS, but none the less opposed it, has hitherto invariably been consulted over any changes involving it. On the other hand, its American equivalent, the American Medical Association (AMA), has long been one of the most formidably effective pressure groups in the United States, ensuring that any discussion of what it pejoratively terms 'socialised medicine' has no chance of getting to first base.

In a similar way, reflecting the close relationship that has grown up between government and some interest groups, many government committees contain representatives of interest groups as a matter of course. This situation appears to support the pluralist model of politics and to be desirable, in that a multiplicity of interests is being represented. But the process is highly selective and international comparisons make clear just how careful one has to be about accepting the pluralist position uncritically. In the words of Schattschneider (1961) 'the flaw in the pluralist heaven is that probably 90 per cent of the people cannot even get into the system'. On the other hand, the growth of special interest groups in the United States in the 1980s has increased concern about the effect of their negative impact on the process of choice. They may not have been able to secure victory for their chosen candidates, but they have been able to destroy the chances of their opponents. The systematic destruction of the Democratic candidate for the presidency in 1988, Michael Dukakis, by a combination of invective and innuendo, merely repeated what had already become the norm at state and local level.

POLITICAL PARTIES

Today the almost universally recognised mechanism for the articulation of interests, for the communication of articulate interests to the aggregative process, and indeed for the partial or general aggregation of interests, is the *political party*.

There is surprisingly widespread agreement that there are two main types of political party, but there are various terminologies used to describe them. Marxists distinguish between 'bourgeois' and 'proletarian' political parties, and this terminology is still used (by the Swedes) to classify the multi-party system of Sweden. However, this does not appear to accord with any well-defined differences in the origins of their members. American and European writers often distinguish, in another terminology, 'Western' political parties which compete with other political parties, and so-called 'non-Western' political parties that do not compete with other political parties (Almond and Coleman, 1960: 9–10, 17). Both perform the function of interest articulation as well as to a greater or lesser extent that of interest aggregation. But it is of course the differences that are significant, and this requires a much more rigorous reason for classification than mere geographical location. In any case there are cases in which it would be positively misleading to do so – in Japan, for example (Scalapino and Masumi, 1962). Hence here they will be termed *'competitive'* and *'non-competitive'* parties, in keeping with whether the system as a whole is competitive or non-competitive.

A 'non-competitive' party is in a sense a contradiction in terms, since the origin of party lies in competition. In the life of any community, at some stage, there emerges a cause of dispute which causes people to take sides and form *factions*. The reasons are obvious enough and they have recurred again and again in the history of new nations from the American Revolution down to the present day. For almost every practical task, and that includes *a fortiori* the task of government, there is a multitude of possible ways of doing it. And faction, therefore, is almost inevitable in political discussion. It is not wholly inevitable. It is possible for everyone to agree, at least for a time, on most things. But, generally speaking, the possibilities of disagreement increase rapidly in direct proportion to the number of people actually engaged in the political process. By the time there are as many people as there are in a modern industrial state the possibilities of disagreement are not only practically infinite, they are almost constantly exercised, which is even more important.

Competitive political parties emerged out of existing political *factions* in the late eighteenth and early nineteenth centuries in a number of European countries, and spread rapidly, coming to be recognised not only as existing but as having a right to exist (Sartori, 1976: 3–13). It is interesting to note that in the periods when political parties were still forming, in Sweden with the Hats and Caps, or in Britain with the Whigs and Tories, in each case the party's name was derived from disparaging epithets attached to them by their opponents. For example, though the etymology is disputed, 'Tory' means 'an Irish robber' and Whig seems to mean 'someone who drives a horse to look for corn' – presumably someone else's! So 'competitive' political parties in Europe, and even in the United States – though for a much shorter period – were shaped by the expansion of the franchise. They came into existence as relatively small groupings with an interest aggregation role to play, and they expanded outwards from this into mass organisations over a set of stages which gave them a particular kind of historical relationship to their societies.

Not surprisingly, where in the rest of the world the twentieth century has seen the emergence of political parties in the pursuit of independence from colonial rule, they too have emerged with the assumption of competitiveness already established. However, twentieth-century political parties have been created as mass organisations all in one go, and this gives these parties a very much more diffuse and less separable relationship to the interests. It means that whereas, on the one hand, the competitive political party in its traditional guise is much more intimately related to the interests that it is supposed to be articulating and therefore a better interest articulator on the whole, conversely, it is, of course, also much more under the domination of those interests.

The expansion of the franchise involved three main issues:

a) age – traditional societies varying in their concepts of physical maturity;
b) the necessity or otherwise for some kind of qualification, e.g. property, to indicate social maturity;
c) gender – whether women could vote as well as men and if so on what terms.

This process has effectively come to an end in most of Western Europe, where all adults of sound mind over the age of eighteen have access to the vote, except in Switzerland and Liechtenstein. In other parts of the world, the position varies more than is often realised. In the United States universal male suffrage as a principle was established by 1830. Women were first granted the vote in Wyoming in 1893 but had to wait until after the First World War (Nineteenth Amendment, 1920) for this to become universal. The minimum age of eighteen was established by the Twenty-sixth Amendment (1967), during the heady days of militant youth. The fact that the criteria for voting remain in some sense tied to a notion of social responsibility is reflected in the practice formerly followed in parts of Latin America of allowing a married man to vote at the age of eighteen, although an unmarried man, not being a responsible member of society, could not vote until he was twenty-one, while women, married or unmarried, could not vote until twenty-five or in extreme cases thirty (Pierson and Gil, 1967: 340ff.). Between 1860 and 1979 no one in Peru who was illiterate could vote anyway.

Second, parties are shaped by their *articulation*, as Duverger somewhat awkwardly calls it (Duverger, 1959: 64). They follow the configuration of the country in which they operate – physical, economic and demographic. They are shaped, above all, by its political structure, and in particular by the nature of the electoral system as a system of choice. Whether the tangible prizes are to be won locally or nationally – or, in a few federal states, regionally – determines the nature of the contest for which they gear themselves.

Third, the party may be limited in its possibilities on either of these counts by the nature of its *ideology* (see Chapter 4). Political parties thrive on ideas – within reason, and only so long as they remain or can be represented to be logically consistent with one another and with the traditional clientele of the party and their interests. Ideology thus limits the positions which a party can adopt in any given situation. At the same time it enables us to classify political parties into 'families' according to their intellectual ancestry.

Organisation of political parties

'Who says organisation says oligarchy,' wrote Robert Michels in 1911, and his observations on the German Social Democratic Party are equally applicable both to political parties today and to other bureaucratic organisations. Michels' thesis (the 'iron law of oligarchy') was that in any organisation the minority will come to dominate the majority. 'It is organisation which gives birth to the domination of the elected over the electors, of the mandataries over the mandators, of the delegates over the delegators' (Michels, 1959: 5).

There are three main reasons for this: the size of the organisation, the value of specialist information and the distance between the leaders and the led. Once an organisation has grown beyond a certain *size*, a division of labour becames necessary. This leads in turn to the delegation of power to specialists. As a result, these specialists take on the status of experts. Concentration of *expertise* leads to the concentration of both power and influence in their hands. The rank and file have not had the necessary training, are not specialists and therefore cannot participate. The size of the organisation also means that participation is limited by the sheer physical *distance* between the top and the rank and file.

Provisions for the leaders to remain in power include:

1. Superior knowledge because of specialisms, access to files, just being there when decisions are made. Knowledge gives the power to manipulate the organisation and win any debate.
2. Control of the organisational media (journals etc.) Views approved by the top are transmitted; others not.
3. Time, which, as highly-paid, full-time organisational workers, the leaders have (together with the incentive) to prepare debates, accumulate knowledge etc.
4. Political skill, needed by full-time organisational workers in order to attain power; once in power they develop this skill further and become full-time politicians.

There are also factors external to the organisation which contribute to oligarchy:

1. The general illegitimacy of opposition. Criticism is viewed as subversion.
2. The economic and social gap between leaders and followers. Leaders start developing a set of interests peculiar to their own group. These conflict with the interests of the organisation.
3. The need for leadership, the political gratitude of the masses and the cult of veneration among the masses. The masses are politically incompetent and apathetic. They are collectively grateful for having the chores of administration lifted from them.

Political parties are organised according to one of two structural types – direct and indirect (Duverger, 1959: 1).

Direct parties are those mass parties in which there are direct channels of communication from bottom to top. They can be based on either of two kinds of unit – the branch and the caucus. The caucus is a small group of people who meet for a common political purpose. In Britain the origins of Liberal and Conservative political organisation stem from such groups, both at the centre and at the periphery which, with the expansion of the franchise, found that they had a common cause for which to work. Organisation at the local level was necessary because parties at the centre were dependent on it for their survival.

The branch is much more common today – political parties are formed in new states as centralist organisations which try to set up branches (like the Abbey National Building Society in English High Streets, or HFC in every American Main Street), so that they can tap sources of interest articulation and, more importantly, finance (see also Randall, 1988). This for them means primarily support rather than demands, although they will then receive the demands from these various areas and deal with them accordingly. The distinction between the caucus and the branch is quite noticeable; the caucus has some kind of independent possibilities of survival. Caucuses can regroup themselves around another party grouping, for example, as in Northern Ireland where the Unionist Party every so often breaks up, selects a new leader who invents a new Unionist Party, writes a new constitution, and so on, yet all the same people all seem to be taking part in the same game all the time. The branch of the Labour Party in Britain which attempted to do the same kind of thing would be disowned, and a rival organisation would be set up in its place which would have the official cachet of being approved by Walworth Road (Lees and Kimber, 1972: 81).

The *indirect* political party, of course, may also have branches. If so, the branch will be under tight hierarchical control. But the branch is not the only possible form of organisation. It is also possible to organise on a cell or militia basis. The cell, numbering between three and five members, is particularly useful where the central government dislikes rival political parties and therefore the rival must be clandestine. This pattern was traditionally favoured by Communist parties in Western states such as Franco's Spain where open organisation was impossible. If the central government is weak, and unable or unwilling to exercise effective central control over the means of force, the other possibility is to organise like an army. This form has historically been favoured by the extreme right, as with the Afrikaner Resistance Movement in South Africa, which resembles the fascist parties of the 1930s. In a militia-based party everyone is subject to central control but there are a number of junior officers or NCOs whose duty it is to carry out central orders. The idea of organising a political party on a kind of quasi-military basis is very attractive to people of certain political persuasions, and it is also very effective for limited purposes. As Duverger points out, however, these two extreme forms, the cell and the militia, are related and tend to occur together (Duverger, 1959: 36–40).

This leads to the criterion of *membership*. In a competitive liberal democracy, political parties are normally *mass* parties. In other words, they seek to recruit all the members they can and there are no theoretical reasons why they should not do so. However, even in liberal democracies, there are (or may be) also *cadre* parties, and in single-party states such parties have a special significance. For in cadre parties membership is *not* open to all, but is limited to those cadres (hence the name) who have passed through a process of training and initiation. The existence of such tests is certainly not a sophisticated, modern idea; they are, it seems, one of the most primitive social rituals marking the stage of transition to full adult citizenship rights. The existence of tests of membership – other than the formal paying of dues – has significant implications for the nature of the political party. It cannot therefore be an associational body open to all, but must be more narrowly defined in terms of non-associational or institutional membership.

The best studied example of a cadre party was the Communist Party of the Soviet Union (CPSU). Members had to be nominated by two existing members, fulfil certain conditions, be accepted as members, and then undergo a period of candidate membership. In 1973 5.8 per cent of the Soviet population were members, which sounds rather restrictive. However, Hough points out that this figure represents 8.9 per cent of the eligible adult population (Hough, 1977: 126). Hence, though Party membership fell far short of that found in Austria, where a third of voters belong to a political party (Gerlich, 1987: 82), it compared favourably with Ireland (7 per cent – Mair, 1987: 103–5), the United Kingdom (5 per cent – Byrd, 1987: 210) or Spain (2 per cent – del Castillo, 1989: 187).

Ferdinand Tönnies (1955), whose distinction between community (*Gemeinschaft*) and company (*Gesellschaft*) is fundamentally the same as that between cadre and mass parties, wrote of a third type of organisation distinct from either. This was the order (*Bund*), a cadre organisation which unlike them does not serve a single purpose, but caters for all the needs of its members through a range of services which lock them firmly into membership. Before the First World War, membership of a political party such as the German Social Democratic Party did have something of this significance, in that membership of it became a complete way of life, with its own health insurance plan, journal and recreational and social facilities. However the fascist period in Europe discredited all such manifestations of total commitment, regardless of their actual ideological affiliation, and though more recently the Greens (Grünen) in Germany have tried to develop a similar model, the evidence is that a great many of the members remain inactive between elections (Kolinsky and Paterson, 1976: 174). Today, among the few survivals of this pattern are, in Europe, the Austrian Socialist Party (SPÖ), and, outside Europe, the Israeli Labour Party.

Political parties also differ by the criterion of *recruitment* – namely, how are their leaders chosen? There are some well-known cases in which the leader chose the party, and not the other way round: Hitler held party card no.7 in the National Socialist German Workers Party (NSDAP). Yet the position he held as Führer ('Leader') was unique. There could never have been, and could not be in logic, a training school for Führers. Even a man who rises to unusual eminence in an established party, such as Roosevelt, Stalin or Churchill, takes care not to provide for the succession of a man who could challenge him while he still holds power. Of their three successors, Truman, Malenkov and

Eden, only Truman, a man with the strongest institutional base and an independent fount of power in the American political system, managed to survive to become a political power in his own right.

It is, of course, the hallmark of a well-institutionalised party that it does not matter whether it has a good leader or not, the system survives despite him or her. Some leaders, such as Truman himself, or Attlee in the United Kingdom, seem to lack charisma, yet they grow in office and develop their own personalities in their years of power. But not all politicians do grow in office: some even shrink – Eden in Britain, Erhard in West Germany, and, more recently, Cresson in France and Bush in the United States. In a stable party with a strong organisational base continuity will be maintained until public support returns.

The question here is, do the leaders of political parties in a given country become leaders because they start their own parties? If so, one would expect to see a very large number of parties of very short life with little or no institutional continuity, and might well feel, with Sartori, that such bodies do not really deserve the name of party at all (Sartori, 1976: 254–5). Such parties do exist, and many have actually taken the name of their leaders for their designation, but have scarcely survived the death of their founders before either losing political support, as with the American Popular Revolutionary Alliance (APRA) in Peru in the 1980s, breaking up into factions, as with the National Revolutionary Movement in Bolivia or, as with the Justicialist Party in Argentina under Carlos Menem, changing their whole basis of appeal radically (Calvert and Calvert, 1990).

Parties, in the true sense of the word, therefore, are distinguished by permanence of structure, a deliberate attempt to win membership, and orderly procedures for recruitment of leaders at higher levels. Parties grew up in Western Europe in the nineteenth century, and to this day there, and in other parts of the world where similar views prevail, the ideal form of politics is seen as involving universal mass participation in universal militant parties free to operate in a highly aware population. General participation in universal militant parties is, in fact, to the people who live in these areas, the distinguishing feature of democracy, and the parties they have, therefore, are direct in structure, mass in membership, with institutionalised recruitment patterns, and are non-ideological in their appeal for votes.

PARTY SYSTEMS

The interesting thing is that despite this ideal, in a number of 'Western' states there are one-party systems to which no effective opposition is manifest, but where there do not appear to be any very good reasons why such an opposition might not develop. It cannot of course be assumed that all one-party states enjoy the support of all the people who live in them. However, some *hegemonic* parties (Sartori, 1976: 230) have achieved their position through their ability to convince the electorate of their merits and opposition parties enjoy some freedom to organise in a sufficiently aware population. A clear distinction has to be drawn, therefore, between *single-party* systems, which are non-competitive, and *one-party* systems, where competition is possible if not very effective.

Non-competitive systems

Non-competitive party systems are of two kinds. First of all, there are those states in which, often as a result of military intervention, all political activity has been prohibited and political parties are not allowed to operate at all. Second, there are those states in which only one political party is permitted (see Table 6.3).

In countries where the inhabitants perceive a constant external threat, the compulsion to form or to maintain a single party is overwhelming. For ideological reasons, namely the belief that the bourgeois world will stop at nothing to destroy them, Communist states experienced this compulsion. In the case of the Soviet Union it rested to some extent on a real historical foundation, the invasion of Russia by the Allies in 1919, and the experience of German attack in the Great Patriotic War (1941–5). But in other European Communist states it rested more on the fear that without the Soviet Union their regime could not survive, and as events since 1989 have shown, in this assumption they were correct. It was therefore for ideological reasons that the non-competitive, single-party states were created (Neumann, 1965: 158). Their rulers believed that their formula was the sole one for future success. They were future-directed in that they believed that their role was to modify society in a very specific way. Hence the party as a vehicle for what people want must give way to an instrument for compelling people to accept what they are supposed to need (Hill and Frank, 1983; see also Gehlen, 1969; Schapiro, 1970).

A number of countries in Asia and Africa adopted the single-party model after decolonisation, although many of them (Kenya, for example) are now returning to (or adopting for the first time) the

Table 6.3 *Non-competitive party systems*

No. of parties	*Country*
None	Ghana, Haiti, Kuwait, Myanmar (Burma), Saudi Arabia, Sierra Leone
Single	Armenia, China

multi-party model. Zimbabwe, where President Mugabe had repeatedly professed his enthusiasm for the one-party state, thought better of it. Certainly the nature and structure of the party system in these single-party states cannot be explained by internal factors alone, but must be sought in the wider context of world politics. For the argument often advanced in defence of these systems was that in the aftermath of colonisation the emerging state simply could not 'afford' the 'luxury' of competitive politics. Hence in these cases, too, the ideological justification of the monopoly of power by the single party was that total control of the economic system was essential for the planning of future development. The trouble was, as events showed, that the silencing of criticism by opposition, far from enhancing efficiency, allowed corruption to become rampant, and in an extreme case, Sierra Leone, the existing economic base of the country was virtually destroyed without any compensating advantage for the bulk of the population.

In Eastern Europe corruption came more slowly, and the system was tolerated for longer, mainly because of the rigidity introduced by superpower rivalry, which meant that in Hungary in 1956 and in Czechoslovakia in 1968 military intervention by the Soviet Union pre-empted possible change. However, Sartori's warning that no country had yet passed from a one-party to a multi-party system, or vice versa, without a fundamental discontinuity in its political process, namely, the use of force (Sartori, 1976: 280–2) proved excessively pessimistic. Since this prediction was made not only Spain, but more recently Poland, Czechoslovakia and other East European states have made the transition from a single-party state to a pluralist one without the use of force, though in other cases (Romania, Moldova etc.) the process has liberated ethnic conflicts which have involved significant levels of violence and have yet to be clearly resolved.

Competitive systems

All other systems are notionally competitive. However, as noted above, there are a significant number of countries in which opposition parties stand little or no chance of gaining power (see Table 6.4).

Though its hegemony has been broken following the breach in its dynastic leadership by the assassination of Rajiv Gandhi, the example of the Congress Party in India seems to illustrate both the reasons for this situation, and the limitations on it. There the party of Nehru enjoyed its initial hegemony as the combined effect of its leadership of the struggle for Indian independence coupled with the presence of Pakistan as a target for organisational and individual hostility. Nehru himself strengthened this position through the international goodwill and attention India obtained as the result of advocating, on behalf of

Table 6.4 *Competitive party systems*

No. of parties	*Country*
One	Bulgaria, Georgia, India, Japan, Kenya, Lithuania, Mexico, Mozambique, Paraguay, Romania, Singapore, South Africa, Zimbabwe
Two	Australia, Austria, Barbados, Canada, Colombia, Jamaica, Malaysia, New Zealand, Nicaragua, Nigeria, Portugal, Spain, Sri Lanka, United Kingdom, United States, Uruguay, Venezuela
Two and a half parties	Argentina, Chile?, Germany, Ireland
Multi	Belgium, Brazil, Belarus, Denmark, France, Italy, Luxembourg, Netherlands, Norway, Poland, Russia, Sweden, Switzerland, Ukraine

smaller and less influential countries, a theory of their place in the world which they found congenial. But basically the supremacy of the Congress Party was maintained as the result of its success in monopolising patronage and being able to 'deliver' on its political promises.

The importance of these rewards was such that, regardless of the intentions of the national leaders, local political activists had no reason whatsoever to see the monopoly challenged. As Turkey found previously, and Mexico is finding today, in these circumstances it is extremely difficult to develop a second competing party so long as a single ruling party controls national political life and with it the national economy. Effectively, the only real possibility of such rivalry developing will come from competition within the ruling party, which is most likely to occur as the result of changes within the social order precipitated by a crisis. Yet when such a major crisis did occur in Mexico in 1987–8, the ruling Revolutionary Institutional Party (PRI) was successful in retaining enough of its support, even in face of a major secession led by a charismatic personality, to make a convincing case for having won the elections of 1988. If, as often happens, the crisis arises from without, as when South African-backed forces attacked the Marxist Government of Angola in 1975, the effect may be the exact reverse – to unite rather than to divide the political community.

Is there then a similar explanation for two-party and multi-party systems? As regards two-party states, it seems significant that they grew up in the period before the control of the economy became an accepted part of the burdens of government. This being the case, the government of the day did not enjoy the ability to use these constraints to cut off opposition. It is the very sophistication of modern governmental control over banking, imports and economic production that enables a government to discriminate against its political opponents in a way so subtle that the necessary resources for opposition are hard to accumulate unless a base for them can be found on foreign territory. Two-party systems, also, seem to be associated most effectively with regional strongholds or bases as in Britain, the United States or Colombia, and are most often rooted in a conflict between centre and periphery as in Australia, or between two co-equal regional centres with pretensions to national leadership, as with the Liberals and Conservatives in Nicaragua. In such regional strongholds, economic resources and political strength go hand in hand.

All political parties, whatever the nature of their system, operate in a process of ultimate choice, which either directs their decisions or enforces them. Fundamental to this process of choice is the electoral system, which is susceptible of considerable elaboration, but may equally be very simple indeed. It is at this point of choice that the party changes from a body intended to present demands into one which is designed to mobilise support. This is done by permitting the public at large a carefully graded share of participation in the formal process of choosing representatives, provided that that share is compatible with the continued maintenance of the governmental system. If that is not possible other parts of the system come into play and the elections are nullified or rerun under conditions which will give the 'right' answer.

CONCLUSION

We can conclude, therefore, that interest groups are to be found in all societies, though possibly only in latent form. The number of active interest groups increases rapidly with the mobilisation of a politically-aware population. However, this does not mean that traditional forms of interest groups lose any of their power to influence events. The pluralist ideal may be hindered by the emergence of a strong hegemonic party backed by powerful interests. However, once the general principle of representation is conceded the emergence of competitive parties is very hard to resist.

KEY CONCEPTS

cadre party: political party with limited membership.

faction: informal group of people seeking a common policy within a political party, or where there are no political parties.

interest group: group of people joined together by a common interest; can be either latent or active (see pressure group).

political party: formal organisation of people seeking to achieve or to retain political power.

pressure group: formal organisation of people seeking to exercise influence over governmental decision-making.

SAMPLE QUESTIONS

Questions in this area focus on the themes of *representation* and of the way in which governments can be held *accountable* for their actions. They can be more specifically directed to one of the specific themes of public opinion, interest groups and political parties.

Do interests in society need to be represented by formally constituted groups or organisations?

Which categories of interests are most likely to gain representation in liberal-democratic states?

Can we arrive at a universal definition of a political party? How can we differentiate parties from other groupings?

Can we construct a useful typology of political systems based on differences in political parties?

Is political protest an inevitable and healthy feature of modern liberal democracies?

What devices help to ensure the political accountability of governments?

FURTHER READING

The 'mass society' thesis is presented by Kornhauser (1959) and Lipset (1960, repr. 1983). Michels (1959) contains the full statement of his 'iron law of oligarchy' and the reasons for it.

On political parties generally see Duverger (1959) and Sartori (1976). Political parties in competitive states are comparatively treated in von Beyme (1985). For the Soviet model see Hill and Frank (1983) and for the Third World, Randall (1988). Mezey (1979) discusses legislatures in the comparative context.

7 How support is shown

INTRODUCTION

How support is shown varies considerably from one society to another. In Saudi Arabia the successor to the King is chosen by family conclave. In the Vatican, cardinals have a choice of three methods: divine inspiration, selection by committee or ballot (the only method normally used). The electoral system used is one of the oldest still in use. But today most states either choose or ratify the choice of leader by elections.

ELECTIONS

There is nothing like taking part in elections to show the possibilities they offer for enjoyment, and otherwise. On the other hand, many people who do take part in elections become so keen on them that they come to believe that they are what politics is all about. That is not true, as is easily shown by the fact that some political systems have little or no place for them. And although at first sight the history of elections looks very complicated to the uninitiated, it merely reflects the fact that in every age the same problems recur (see *inter alia* Carstairs, 1980; Grofman and Lijphart, 1986; Mackie and Rose, 1991).

Elections are a process of choice. But they are not necessarily a choice between alternatives and, if they are, they are seldom if ever a simple process of choice. Most electoral systems are required to enable the electorate to do *at least* two different things at the same time. One is to choose *candidates*, the other is to register the approval of certain *policies* (Milnor, 1969: 3–4).

Now, it is not wholly possible to register approval or disapproval of any specific policy by the choice of candidate, because candidates do not necessarily agree with one another on specific policies, even where they regard themselves as being of the same party or holding very similar views. There are, moreover, numerous policies to be accounted for, many of which may seem relevant neither to an individual candidate, nor to the voters. All elections, therefore, involve some compromise between things as they ought to be and things as they are.

CONSENSUS AND CHOICE

The nature and importance of elections within any given society depends in the first instance on its concept of agreement, or *consensus* as it is often termed.

The *unanimity theory* holds that society must express Rousseau's *volonté générale* or general will of its inhabitants (Rousseau, 1958: 23; see also Partridge, 1971: 36). This will particularly be the case where elections are seen as the ratification of policies, since agreement on policies naturally involves the reaching of a common view by all concerned.

If agreement on policies is not essential, and the most important thing is to choose who is going to have to carry them out, then the *majority theory* will serve. It will be sufficient to count heads and give the decision to those who have the greater numbers. Indeed, to them may well be delegated all those day-to-day tasks with which the rest of society does not wish to be concerned.

Both assume that the question of choice is relevant. However, if one believes, as the Athenians did, that all citizens are equally well fitted to hold any office of state, then one might as well do as they did, and choose candidates by lot (Bury, 1956: 349). Arguably this is the most democratic way, and certainly it is the only way which is at least as fair as holding a vote.

In 1983 the present writer suggested (Calvert, 1983) that if the British House of Lords were ever to be reformed (which seems increasingly unlikely), it would be an excellent idea to replace it with a chamber selected by lot, by electronic means, from all adult citizens, to serve for a year at a time. Such a chamber could be a really effective check on the House of Commons, which would in itself probably be a very good thing. No doubt its members would not have the specialist knowledge of a professional body of representatives, but they would not share their prejudices, and in any case election is not a good way of choosing people with specialist knowledge, as those Greeks discovered who tried to choose their military commanders that way. It may or may not be a good idea to have a large number of lawyers in parliament, since parliament's job is to make laws, but if it is, then a better way of ensuring that members had the necessary legal knowledge would be to set them a competitive examination.

The question of choice can also be irrelevant because the office is powerless, and then the methods by which it is filled become quite meaningless. Heredity, for example, has in the past been an essentially random process, and it may do as well for selecting a formal head of state as any other. The Greeks themselves long retained it in the selection of priests, when secular offices had long since been made the subject of popular choice. But notwithstanding the aspirations of Jean-Bedel Bokassa, who created the short-lived Central African Empire (1976–8), or the example of brief spells of dynastic succession in republics like India under the Nehru/Gandhi dynasty, Nicaragua under the Somozas or Equatorial Guinea under Macías Nguema and his nephew Teodor Obiang Nguema, few people would be prepared to introduce heredity as a constitutional device today, and these examples hardly inspire enthusiasm.

Electoral systems
Elections offer choice between both *candidates* and *policies*

Unanimity systems
a Committees: 'the sense of the meeting'
b 'Method of marks': the problem of cyclical majorities
c Random choice
d Single party and *candidato unico*

Plurality systems
a Single member, single ballot

Majority systems
Not proportional
a Single member, second ballot
b Primary elections
c Alternative Vote (AV)

Proportional
a List systems
  1 Largest remainder
  2 Largest average
b Mixed systems
c Single Transferable Vote (STV)

UNANIMITY SYSTEMS

Unanimity systems claim attention first for three reasons. First, they are the ideal of political philosophers. Obviously, in an ideal world, nothing would be done except by universal agreement. Second, they appear to have come first in historical time, and to have formed the basis upon which all other systems of choice have been erected. And third, unanimity remains the basic daily principle of everyday choice in small communities everywhere, even where more complex systems have been developed for making choices of representatives or policies on a regional or national level.

Examples are all around us. Many forms of committee, from church organisations to university senates, will go to enormous lengths to avoid the divisive consequences of taking a vote, and will deliberate at enormous length in the hope that general agreement will be reached. Often there will be an expression, usually by the chair, of what the Quakers call 'the sense of the meeting'; that is to say, the policy which no one person has actually advocated but which combines the salient features of all those principal policies which have been advocated. Similar behaviour has been noticed in many other societies, whether it be the former Soviet Politburo, Indian *panchayats* or the *cofradias* or fraternities of Central American villages. Wherever it occurs, it is another example of the belief that reasonable people, discussing a range of policies, ought to be able to arrive at a just and fitting solution which is not necessarily likely to result from the mere counting of heads.

Indeed it is possible, as Duncan Black has shown, to prove mathematically that in many kinds of issue the mere counting of heads will not produce the answer that most people want (the Condorcet criterion). It can, and often does, produce a solution that is wanted by almost nobody (Black, 1958: 69–72, 218–19). The mathematical proof, moreover, is quite independent of the fact that the rationality of group decisions, however small the group, is limited by human nature. Discussion can be terminated by irrelevant factors long before the point of rational agreement is reached; such factors include the fatigue of the participants, their desire to get up and move around, to have a cup of tea, to go home and have dinner, or the fact that the bar opened ten minutes earlier. And with larger groups the problems are considerably worse, and no one can pretend that a hundred people sitting in a hot, overcrowded room for several hours of discussion really reach the most rational possible conclusion, unless it is to postpone the whole debate to a later and more suitable time.

At this point, too, come into play the many tricks by which individuals seek to steer the course of the decision in the direction they favour. These tricks, particularly those open to committee chairs, are indeed as lovingly described in that fundamental work *Microcosmographia Academica*, which remains of perennial importance to all students of committee behaviour everywhere, and not just in universities (Cornford, 1970: 14–16). No doubt it was the observation of them, a generation before Cornford, by Charles L. Dodgson (Lewis Carroll) which set that mathematician and logician to devise a system of choice by which policies could be selected by small groups on the basis of a mathematical procedure. This system, a modification of what he termed the 'Method of Marks' and which is more generally known as the Borda count, involved each member listing the policy options before him, including that of not doing anything; if a vote on the agreed list failed to produce a majority for any single proposal, then each issue would be voted on in turn against every other, and if this produced a cyclical majority (A beat B, B beat C, C beat A) there should be no decision, this evidently being the favoured option. Significantly enough, on the most important occasion on which this method is known to have been used, the choice of a design for a new belfry, the Fellows of Christ Church agreed to combine two proposed designs, rather than to accept any one of them (Black, 1958: 206–7).

Obviously this is not something that can be done when choosing candidates, rather than policies. It is impossible to combine two or more candidates. A candidate who is not on the original list can, of course, be chosen by way of compromise (a 'dark horse'), but by definition such candidates are seldom the first choice of anyone. How then, otherwise, to choose candidates who command the unanimous consent of the electors?

The obvious way is the simplest: to offer them a single slate of candidates which they have only to ratify or to reject. The classic instance of this practice was seen in the former Soviet Union, where the elector could either drop an unmarked ballot paper into the box, thus voting automatically for the single name on it, or enter a polling booth and cross the name off. Consequently, to avoid the imputation of disloyalty it was, well into the 1980s, 'not done' for anyone other than a very high Party dignitary to vote in secret. Hence the 'right' to cross names off was a dead letter, at least as far as elections to the Supreme Soviets of the Union Republics and of the USSR itself was concerned.

If the right was exercised at city or province level, then it was ineffective. At elections to village, settlement or district soviets, however, the right was exercised and a limited number of candidates did fail to get majorities: in June 1973 eighty candidates were rejected in this way. A second election was then held with a fresh official candidate, nominated, as before, by a section of the CPSU or of a recognised social organisation, such as a trade union, factory or farmers' collective, Komsomol or cultural society, often one recognised as having the right to nominate to that particular seat. Candidates, even for the Supreme Soviet of the USSR, did not have to be members of the CPSU, with the curious result that in the 1970–4 Supreme Soviet, for example, 421 of the 1,517 deputies (27.8 per cent) were non-Party members (Churchward, 1975: 103ff.).

In Poland under Communist rule the Sejm officially contained a coalition of parties, and elections were held by a party list system. Only one list, however, was nominated for the seats to be filled, though as in the USSR this allowed for the possibility of crossing off some names rather than others. As early as 1958 this facility was used, though not to any great extent, and certainly not to the extent that any one candidate was actually defeated. It has been suggested, nevertheless, that the ruling party was keenly alert to any evidence from the electors that particular candidates were unpopular. They might then take care to see that such candidates were given a less prominent task to do in the future, thus preserving the principle of unanimity, but at least taking note of the electorate's views (Butler, 1959: 170–1).

There are other parts of the world in which the fact that only one candidate is presented for election is not regarded by many people, and particularly perhaps not by Russians or Poles, as a sign of unanimity. The single-candidate election (*candidato unico*), which was rediscovered in Eastern Europe after the Second World War and more recently has been adopted by many African states, has in fact been a feature of Latin American systems since the early years of the last century (Stokes, 1959: 344–6). As noted above (Chapter 6), the tendentious argument that political competition was 'wasteful' of energies that otherwise should have been used in national development has long since been discredited by the examples of states such as Ghana and Nigeria. Kenya has recently returned to multi-party competition and Zimbabwe has thought better of eliminating opposition. Another name for the same device is the plebiscite, much copied since Louis Napoleon seized power in France in 1851, ratified his *coup d'état* by a plebiscite that year and in 1852 confirmed his self-appointment as Emperor by a second plebiscite. There are varying degrees of subtlety possible. Sometimes the candidate does not allow anyone else to stand, but perhaps more frequently no one else seriously thinks there is much point in trying. Occasionally, even in more open systems, opposition parties fail to agree on a candidate, as in Mexico in 1976, when the official candidate, Gustavo López Portillo, was unopposed.

These are not meaningless offices. In presidential elections, where one person, however chosen, will in the end represent an entire nation with all its cross-currents of opinion, it is an impossible task to give free rein to all shades of opinion. We can scarcely be surprised, therefore, that it is seldom well performed. However, legislative seats may be keenly contested in the very states where the president holds absolute power, as in Brazil under a succession of military governments after 1968.

PLURALITY SYSTEMS

Next to the principle of unanimity in order of age comes the idea of a plurality, as it is termed in the United States, or, as it is known in Britain, a simple majority. In the United States a majority means one more than

50 per cent of all the votes cast, and so the American terminology offers less possibility of confusion.

The first attempts to reach a mathematical approximation to the views of the people in a given area were certainly not devised by political scientists, and they were not devised by people of much mathematical skill, so the concept of a plurality, being the simplest, was easily adopted. The fact is, it did not really matter that such a simple method was used until political parties came to be accepted features of the political landscape, since the majority of elections went uncontested. It was only towards the end of the eighteenth century that the French Encyclopedists, and in particular the scholar and mathematician Condorcet, began first to study possible alternatives which gave less peculiar results (Black, 1958: 156–85).

The only plurality system still used is the 'first past the post' system; more correctly, the single-member, single-ballot system (*scrutin unique a un tour*), used in the United Kingdom, the United States, Canada, New Zealand and South Africa. Under it the country is divided into geographical constituencies, each of which will return one representative. On the appointed day the electors vote for one candidate by marking a cross on a ballot paper; the candidate who has a plurality of the votes, even if he or she lacks a majority, is declared elected. If a tie occurs, as it frequently has done at English municipal elections, and recounts fail to disclose an error of counting, the tie is broken by the drawing of lots.

The system, then, is exceptionally simple, but it does have disadvantages. Locally these are well illustrated by the example of the constituency of Caithness and Sutherland in Scotland in 1945, where in a three-way contest only some sixty votes separated the winner from the the bottom of the poll. The subsequent history of the constituency, one of the few in Britain whose boundaries remained unaltered during that time, shows an even more remarkable sequence of anomalies (see Table 7.1). Nationally the system merely generalises such anomalies, so that

Table 7.1 *'First past the post' – Caithness and Sutherland, 1945–70*

Party	*1945*	*1950*	*1951*	*1955*	*1959*	*1964*	*1966*	*1970*
Con	5,564	6,969	9,418	10,453		4,550	4,662	5,334
Lab	5,558	5,767	6,799	5,364	6,438	6,619	8,308	8,768
Lib	5,503	6,700	3,299	2,674		7,894	8,244	6,063
Ind C					12,163	2,795		
SNP								3,690
Maj	6	269	3,015	5,089	5,725	1,275	64	2,705
Result	C gain	C	C	C	Ind C gain	Lib gain	Lab gain	Lab

in the general election in Britain in February 1974 the Conservatives obtained the most votes, but the Labour Party got the most seats. Hence Labour formed the new Government despite the fact that in a three-party election the overwhelming majority of the electorate had voted against them (*The Times*, 1974: 266). This position was reversed for the four elections between 1979 and 1992, in which the Conservative vote remained remarkably constant at some 42 per cent.

In fact at no election in the United Kingdom since 1935 has the winning party obtained an overall majority of the votes cast. The same was true of the American presidential elections of 1960, 1968 and 1976 (Pulzer, 1975: 4, 97, 98). And in South Africa in 1948 the Nationalists obtained 51.6 per cent of the seats, with only 40 per cent of the votes cast and, having once obtained power, proceeded to disfranchise voters of non-European descent and to impose punitive laws on the majority of their society so that they could not be deprived of power by legal means (Butler, 1959: 232–4; Carter, 1958: Chapter 5). An even more telling criticism is that if the system had been used in Weimar Germany, the Nazis, with only 37.4 per cent of the votes cast in July 1932, would have won 60 per cent of the seats and so found themselves in power a year early (Pulzer, 1975).

This is the necessary consequence of two effects of plurality systems that are usually praised by their supporters.

1. They produce a *majority government*. This is true in one sense: in very few countries does one party actually command a majority of the votes, but a plurality system will usually give *some* party a majority of the seats. But it does not give them a majority; it only makes it *look* as if they had a majority.
2. As a result, plurality systems do, as their advocates suggest, lead to stability. Since the winning party does not have to fulfil the onerous condition of achieving a genuine majority, with all the advantages of incumbency, it can ensure its own re-election.

Milnor argues that the use of the single-member, single-ballot system results in 'the blatant punishment of parties of limited appeal and the reward of pragmatic competitors' (Milnor, 1969: 43). In the United Kingdom this means that in February 1974 the Liberal Party got six million votes but only a handful of seats. On the other hand, Nationalist parties, hitherto even more unfairly treated, were suddenly given a quite disproportionate importance in the balance of seats in Parliament (*The Times*, 1974: 266), which they subsequently lost.

Of course, the fact that the British Liberal Party survived so long proves that 'first past the post' does not eliminate all variety of opinion. It would hardly have been acceptable for so long if it did, and even in white South Africa a small though wholly powerless opposition was able to survive. Nor did the system prevent the rise of the British Labour Party as a third party at the beginning of the twentieth century. What it did do was to accelerate its arrival as the second party, just as it did with the Republicans in the United States between 1854 and 1860. Since then no third party has gained more than ephemeral success in the United States. Anderson's vote in 1980 was barely sufficient to qualify for federal funding and in 1992, though Ross Perot won some 20 per cent of the popular vote for president (despite having at one stage withdrawn from the contest), no new party emerged with him and the ultimate beneficiaries were the Democrats.

The fact is that under this system the big rewards are allocated as the result of the capture of a small group of so-called 'floating voters', whose votes in relatively few constituencies determine the outcome. Since 1945 these key constituencies in the UK numbered approximately eighty, or some 12.5 per cent of the total (Milnor, 1969: 41–2), but with continued population movement the number has been declining steeply since 1979. For rather similar reasons relating to the movement of population out of the big cities and into the suburbs, and southwards to the 'Sun Belt', in the United States some two-thirds of the states are dominated by a single party for all or most of the time and the big Northern industrialised states (with the idiosyncratic exception of California) have been slowly losing their key balancing role in the maintenance of the two-party system.

Hence, if there is a really serious criticism of the 'first past the post' system it is not so much that minorities have very little say, but that the vast majority have very little either. Their massive votes, piled up in so-called 'safe seats' for one or another party, contribute very little to the result, and so can virtually be taken for granted by the party managers in determining party policy and strategy. In other words, though nationally the balance in both Britain and the United States may come out about 'right' in terms of the two main parties, it is the result of good luck, not good management. The argument that the anomalies of the system can therefore be disregarded is specious.

For the problem with good luck is that it is always liable to run out when most needed. Composing a legislature, such as the British House of Commons or the American Congress, is not in itself critical; the real problem is to choose a government. Under the parliamentary system this is done indirectly by the choice of individual members of parliament of the majority party or parties, and they have to live with the result, which makes them appropriately cautious. It is not surprising, therefore, that when drafters of constitutions have sought to impose some check on the choice of an executive president (or governor of a state, or mayor of a city), they have usually chosen to have the selection of the people ratified by the legislature. This, it should be emphasised, does not make the plurality system a majority one, but in theory it should make the president more generally acceptable.

In practice, however, it merely introduces new complications. Thus in 1970 in Chile, Salvador Allende, candidate of the Popular Unity (UP) coalition, secured 35 per cent of the popular vote between three candidates and so a narrow plurality. Congress had therefore to ratify the election, but the majority of his opponents, being committed to the principle of popular choice, felt impelled to accept the plurality as the expression of the popular will (Feinberg, 1972: 162–3). Instead, however, of accepting the limitations of his position, Allende then proceeded to carry out a very far-reaching programme of social change, culminating in the formation of large-scale armed movements forcibly seizing and redistributing land without any form of legal sanction, and ultimately the army stepped in, deposed Allende, seized power, and having once seized it refused to give it up, leaving Chile with a totally unconstitutional regime.

MAJORITY SYSTEMS

Leaving aside the question of the numerous other factors that contributed to this unhappy result, what could the Chileans have done to their constitution which might have helped to ensure a presidential majority? They could have adopted a *majority* system, as indeed their neighbours the Argentines had done on the other side of the Andes. There they have a second ballot, or 'run off' election as it is known in the American states, between the leading contestants. A number of countries use the same system in the choice of their legislatures.

As applied to presidential systems, the second ballot merely means that the top two candidates have to fight it out at a second round, thus ensuring that one must have a majority of the votes cast. This certainly does not guarantee that there will be no argument, and the history of Argentina since 1955 demonstrates that even the best constitutional arrangements are useless if key people are determined to disregard them. But given goodwill it is a simple and effective device.

In France since 1958 (except in 1986) elections to the National Assembly have been conducted on the same system (*scrutin unique a deux tours*) (Butler, 1959: 33ff.). The country is currently divided into 555 constituencies, each returning one deputy (an additional twenty-two members are elected by the overseas departments (Départements d'Outre-Mer – DOM)). Two ballots are held on successive Sundays. On the first ballot only those candidates who achieve a majority of the votes cast in the constituency are elected, provided also that they are the choice of at least 25 per cent of the registered electors. In the remaining constituencies all candidates who have achieved in the first ballot at least 12½ per cent of the votes enter the second ballot, in which a simple plurality suffices to elect. In 1978 only sixty-eight of 491 metropolitan seats were filled on the first ballot (*The Times*, 13 March 1978).

Though this is a proper majority system it still has its faults. As applied to a single constituency, it gives a reasonably fair result; but applied to France as a whole the result is by no means proportional. In 1978 the parties of the left, for example, obtained 49 per cent of the votes on the second ballot but still received only 40 per cent of the seats (182). This is because the population size of the constituencies varies very considerably, and this variation in size leads in France, as in Britain, to the piling up of useless majorities in many seats which happen not to return members which support the government (*The Times*, 20 March 1978). The same phenomenon used also to be true of the United States, but as the result of a Supreme Court decision there the 1960s saw a thorough reapportionment of the congressional districts and other electoral districts in the search for more exact proportionality (Baker, 1966). In the United Kingdom where the advantage of the present system to the Conservative Party in 1991 is of the order of 3 per cent, boundary changes due to be implemented in the immediate future are expected to *increase* this advantage. In Brazil the over-representation of the rural north east gives an even greater advantage to right-wing parties.

A second type of majority system involves holding the second ballot *before* the main election. This is the system, invented in the United States, of the 'primary election'. Electors who register as members of one or another political party may take part in an official ballot to select the candidates of that party in their area or district. Where there is not more than one party likely, in normal circumstances, to win – and that means in about two-thirds of the United States – this system will not guarantee a majority, but it will at least ensure there is some kind of election. This situation, from the region with which it is most often associated, is often termed 'the southern primary', and in states such as Florida, where a large number of party factions might otherwise result in the election of a candidate with very little popular support, a second primary election is required if a majority is not achieved on the first round (Milnor, 1969: 49–52).

The third type of majority system is the most logical of the three, since there is no second ballot at all, the process of forming a majority being combined in one act of choice. This is the *alternative vote* (AV), as used in Australia for elections to the Federal House of Representatives. Here the country is divided into single-member constituencies as before, but the voters, instead of making a single mark on their ballot paper, number their candidates in order of preference. If no one candidate secures a majority on first preferences, the second preferences of the bottom candidate are added to them, and so on until a majority is achieved.

Unhappily, though the alternative vote looks an attractive idea, and works very well in the choice of officers for small organisations such as student unions, it is disproportional and it does not even seem to be very effective at reconciling choices. Between 1900 and 1951 some 77 per cent of successful candidates for the Australian House of Representatives achieved a majority without it, and in only a handful of cases, it seems, would the result have been different under the 'first past the post' system (Rydon, 1956). It is not necessary to stop either at two ballots or at a simple majority. In papal elections there are an indefinite number of ballots, though the fact that the cardinals are walled up with no access to the outside world is designed to hasten the process of agreement. The winner is the first candidate to secure two-thirds of the votes cast.

PROPORTIONAL SYSTEMS

Before truly proportional electoral systems became generally known, there were a number of attempts to improve older systems. A few of these semi-proportional systems are still used.

The *limited vote*, by which the elector has fewer votes than there are seats to be filled, was used for a few constituencies in Britain between 1867 and 1885, and ensures at least some representation of minorities. It is still used in Gibraltar. The extreme form of this system, the *single non-transferable vote* in a multi-member constituency, has been used in Japan in election to the Diet since 1900. Another variant, the *cumulative vote*, where the elector has as many votes as seats but can give any or all of them to any candidate, was used in Cape Colony from 1850 to 1909, and after 1870 in school board elections in the United Kingdom. In the United States it was still in use in the state of Illinois in 1976 (Hansard Society, 1976).

Each of these systems in different ways lessens to some extent the importance of party membership to the candidate. It is, accordingly, ironic that the first truly proportional systems to be devised, and those still most widely used, not only in Europe but in the Middle East (Israel, Lebanon), Latin America (Argentina, Bolivia, Guatemala etc.) and the Caribbean (Guyana), are the *list systems* (*scrutin de liste*), which have exactly the opposite effect.

List systems

Under list systems optimum proportionality would be secured by treating the country as one vast constituency, as in Israel or the Netherlands.

In Israel there are two problems which arise as a result. One is that there are a very large number of very small parties represented in the Knesset, and this has given them disproportionate influence in the choice of a government. The other is a certain isolation of the elector from the representative, made evident by the fact that over half the members of the Knesset live in Tel Aviv (Akzin, 1967: 79).

Normally a country is divided into multi-member constituencies, which may be simply the existing departments, provinces or regions. The elector casts a vote not for an individual candidate, but for the party list of his or her choice. The votes are then counted and seats allocated to each party in proportion to their respective totals. In the simplest form of the system the candidates are chosen in the order simply in which their names appear on the list. Under this system, used for example in France in 1945 and 1946, great power is given to the parties and within them to the local general secretaries, who tend to put their own names at the top of the lists.

There are two ways of making the allocation. The simpler is also the earlier: the *largest remainder* system (*le plus fort reste*). Here the number of votes cast is divided by the number of seats to be filled to give a quota. Seats are then allocated to parties for each complete quota they have received, and the one not allocated by this method goes to the party with the largest remainder – hence the name. As in other list systems, the remainders may alternatively be credited to a national pool, from which additional seats may be allocated. Unhappily, this system, which favours small parties and for just this reason was retained in Paris in the 1951 and 1956 Assembly elections, is also open to manipulation by any large party that has the ingenuity or courage to divide itself into two or more parts. In Europe it is used in Denmark, Greece and Italy, as well as for the allocation of additional seats in Germany.

Under the Imperiali system used in Italy, the country is divided into electoral regions. Within each region, the quota is obtained by dividing the total number of votes cast by *two* less than the number of seats to be filled. Seats are then assigned to each party according to the number of quotas obtained. Remainders are then carried over to a national pool, from which additional seats may be assigned to a district on the basis of that district's quota. Any further remainders are then disregarded (see Table 7.2).

Elsewhere, the largest remainder system has been superseded by one or other version of the *largest average* system (*la plus forte moyenne*) (Lakeman, 1970: 90ff.). The principle is the same in each case: that seats should be allocated to each party in such a way that each party has as near as possible the same average number of votes per seat. There are two main variants of the formula by which this is done: the d'Hondt system, which tends to favour large parties, and the Saint-Laguë system,

Table 7.2 *The Imperiali largest remainder formula*
1976 Chamber of Deputies election: Como-Sondrio-Varese district Quota = 54,073

Party	*Popular vote*	*Seats at district*	*Remainders to national pool*	*Pool seats*	*TOTAL SEATS*
Christian Democrats	516,128	9	29,471	0	9
Communists	308,661	5	38,296	0	5
Socialists	134,574	2	26,428	0	2
Social Democrats	42,563	0	42,563	0	0
Republicans	37,860	0	37,860	1	1
Liberals	20,040	0	20,040	0	0
Italian Social Movement	41,237	0	41,237	1	1
Proletarian Democracy	23,138	0	23,138	1	1
Radicals	11,398	0	11,398	0	0

which favours small ones, though not as much as the largest remainder system.

The arithmetic in each case is quite simple if on the face of it the reasoning behind it is inscrutable. The totals cast for each party are set out in order of magnitude, and below them the results of successive divisions by whole integers (2, 3, 4,. . . etc.), of each of the larger values to the last value *before* that achieved by the smallest party. The figures thus produced are then arranged in rank order, and that one corresponding to the number of seats to be filled, the 'electoral quotient', is used in the same fashion as the quota in the largest remainder system to determine the allocation of seats. Any remainders are then disregarded (Lakeman, 1970: 93–7; see also Rae, 1967: 31–4) – though they may, alternatively, be assigned to a national pool. The Saint-Laguë system, used in Sweden and Norway since 1952, is similar, but uses the divisors 1.4, 3, 5, 7,. . . etc.

This system is used unmodified in Israel and Turkey. Since it favours large rather than small parties, it was used in France in 1951 and 1956 for all constituencies outside Paris. But it was not intended to have its usual effect, which in this case would have been the over-representation of the extremes of the Communists on the left, as well as the Gaullist RPF on the right. It was therefore used only with the ingenious addition of the *apparentement*, a provision that any party *or coalition* obtaining a majority of the votes in a *département* would receive all the seats of that *département*. This blatantly unproportional feature of an otherwise apparently proportional system did not work perfectly, but it worked well enough in 1951 for the centre parties to get 60 per cent of the seats in the Assembly for only 51 per cent of the votes, and for the Communists to get only 16 per cent of the seats for 24.8 per cent of the votes (Campbell, 1951; Cole and Campbell, 1989). When the

Socialist Government reintroduced the system for the 1986 elections, the *apparentement* was not used, but the relatively small size of the constituencies used gave a markedly disproportionate result.

In Spain the constituencies are even smaller. As a result, party representation in the Cortés is almost as disproportional as it is under the British system. More proportional results are obtained in Finland, Luxembourg and Portugal, where constituencies average some twelve members.

Other modifications of list systems have generally been made to give the voter greater choice of individual representatives. They have been modified to enable the elector to choose one candidate within one list in Belgium, the Netherlands and Denmark; more than one candidate within one list in Italy, Norway, Sweden and Greece; and candidates from more than one list in Finland, Luxembourg and Switzerland (National Council).

The 'additional member' system

At first sight the system devised by the Allies for West Germany, and retained since reunification for the whole country, looks very different. It combines territorial representation by single-member constituencies with a party list system to give a proportional result overall. It is therefore often called a 'mixed' system. However, it is in fact a fully proportional system utilising a single national pool, and the Hansard Society's term the *additional member system* seems more accurate (Hansard Society, 1976).

In Germany since December 1990 the country has been divided into 328 single-member constituencies for elections to the Bundestag. There are an equal number of seats allocated by region (*Land*) to the political parties to make the overall balance of parties in that *Land* proportional. Hence the voter has two votes, one for a candidate and one for a party.

Counting begins by totalling all second (party) votes on a national basis. Then all parties to have achieved at least 5 per cent of the national vote, or three elected seats, are allocated a total number of seats in proportion to their national vote. These seats are then divided by *Länder*. Meanwhile, as will already be evident, the first (candidate) votes will have been counted by constituency and the results declared. The number of directly elected seats achieved by each party in each *Land* is then deducted from their proportional total, and the balance made up by allocating additional seats to additional members from the party list of that *Land* according to the largest remainder system. In the rather rare eventuality that a party has won more directly elected seats in any given *Land* than its national share would give it, it is allowed to keep them, and the overall number of seats in the Bundestag is increased by that number (*Überhangsmandaten*). In the first all-German elections of 1990 there were six of these, making a total of 662 members in all (Keesings, 37904–5). Hence, as used in Germany, the system is not perfectly proportional. A by-product of the system is that, as is usual with list systems, there are no by-elections; in the event of a vacancy occurring, the next name is selected from the regional list (Hansard Society, 1976: 49–51; Appendix 1).

The West German system was of course the product of a compromise between the three rather different electoral traditions of the Allies, and was designed to avoid the multipartism of the pre-war Weimar Republic (1919–33), which had used the unmodified d'Hondt system, though with the curious and significant difference that it was the number of votes per seat and not the total number of deputies in the Reichstag that was fixed by the Weimar constitution. As Lakeman points out, the same number of parties had in fact existed under the single-member, second-ballot system used before 1918. Hence it is reasonable to believe that the causes for their number lay in the nature and complexity of German society and not in the electoral system (Lakeman, 1970: 196).

A similar system is now used in Mexico for the Chamber of Deputies, where in 1963 the basic single-member, single-ballot system was modified by the addition of extra members to increase opposition representation, and in 1977 this was extended into a fully proportional system.

One of the two favourite arguments against proportional systems is that they will act to create a multiplicity of small parties. The other is that this will give rise to political instability, caused by a succession of weak coalition governments unable to take decisive action. The French political scientist Maurice Duverger states, however, that, though proportional systems tend to preserve a multi-party system, they do not appear to act very strongly to create one (Duverger, 1959: 245–52). Though Duverger himself has not been very consistent in this view, the facts seem to bear it out. On the one hand, in the UK since 1951, the number of political parties represented in the assembly has increased in number even under the 'first past the post' system. And under the German system the exact opposite has happened. The number of parties represented in West Germany dropped sharply during the 1950s and in 1961 only 'two and a half' parties were left, creating a stable system giving an overall majority in the Bundestag regardless of which party or combination of parties was in power. And, despite this, the results, considered nationally, have continued to be strikingly proportional, while to

Table 7.3 *Constituency and list seats in the West German Bundestag 1949–87*

	CDU const	*CDU list*	*CDU total*	*SPD const*	*SPD list*	*SPD total*	*FDP const*	*FDP list*	*FDP total*	*Other const*	*Other list*	*Other total*	*Surplus*
1949	115	24	139	96	35	131	12	40	52	19	42	61	CDU1 SPD1
1953	172	71	243	45	196	151	14	34	48	11	23	34	CDU2 DP1
1957	194	76	270	46	123	169	1	40	41	6	5	11	CDU3
1961	158	86	244	91	99	190		67	67				
1965	154	91	245	94	108	202		49	49				
1969	121	121	242	127	97	224		30	30				
1972	96	129	225	152	78	224		41	41				
1976	134	109	243	114	100	214		39	39				
1980	121	105	226	127	91	218		53	53				SPD1
1983			244			193			34				G27
1987			223			186			46				G42

date the ability of the parties to manipulate the lists has been used with reasonable restraint (Lakeman, 1970: 103, 265; Hansard Society, 1976; see Table 7.3).

Single transferable vote

Under the third proportional system, however, party influence is reduced to a minimum, for the simple reason that it is the only system which enables the individual elector to choose between individual candidates regardless of party which still gives an accurate overall balance of party representation. This is the system known in the United Kingdom as the single transferable vote (STV). It is known in the United States and Australia as the Hare System, after Thomas Hare who invented it in 1857, but it had in fact been devised independently two years earlier by C.C.G. Andrae in Denmark. It is used in Australia for the Federal Senate, for the Upper House in New South Wales and the Lower in Tasmania, for the Senate in South Africa, and in Ireland and Malta for both Houses. In Britain it was used from 1917 to 1949 for the election of university representatives, and in Northern Ireland from 1920 to 1929 for the Stormont Parliament and since 1973 for local government. It seems that in London it is considered the best system for the Northern Irish and the Scots, but not so far for the English or Welsh, or at least not for those who have not had a university education (Lakeman, 1970: 105ff.).

It is not necessary to have a university education to understand STV, however, and one need not be more than literate to use it. All the elector has to do is to mark on the ballot paper an order of preference

(1, 2, 3, 4 etc.) for the listed candidates, and drop the paper into a box. Such arithmetical problems as then arise are handled entirely by the returning officer.

Under STV the country (or area) concerned is divided into multi-member constituencies which should, for the maximum degree of proportionality, be as large as possible. In a multi-party system the minimum requirement, broadly speaking, is that each return five or more representatives. In Ireland between 1935 and 1980 a large proportion of the constituencies returned only three members of the Dáil, the balance of which was in consequence distorted markedly in favour of the dominant Fianna Fáil party. In 1947 and again in 1969 the proportion of small constituencies was increased, while in 1959 and 1968 constitutional amendments proposed by Fianna Fáil to replace it by the British system (and so entrench themselves in power) were rejected by the voters. The official reason, the desire to keep constituencies as small as possible in a predominantly rural country, points to the only theoretical disadvantage of STV. It is very well adapted to a heavily urbanised area, like England, though in a multi-party situation it would probably be difficult for voters to exercise effective choice for more than about ten seats.

In each constituency counting begins by ascertaining the total number of votes cast. This determines the quota, which in this case is called the Droop Quota, after H.R. Droop who proposed it in 1869. The Droop Quota is the minimum number of votes a candidate must have to be certain of being elected, that is the total number of votes divided by one more than the number of seats to be filled, plus one, or:

$$\text{quota} = \frac{\text{votes}}{\text{seats} + 1} + 1$$

While the quota is being determined, the first preference votes (1s) for each candidate are being added up, and any candidate who has achieved or exceeded the quota is declared elected.

If a candidate has got more votes than the quota, however, his or her surplus votes are 'wasted', and it is one of the basic principles of STV that no one's votes can be wasted. The second count, therefore, involves the distribution of any surpluses from the first count, in order of magnitude if there is more than one. Now, obviously, the surplus votes are not just taken off the top of the pile – that would be ridiculous. What happens is that all the fortunate candidate's ballot papers are counted a second time, this time by the second preferences (2s). Then the number of each, reduced to a proportion corresponding to the size of the surplus, is credited to the account of each remaining candidate. Any candidate who has now received the quota is elected.

The next step is to eliminate the bottom candidate. None of this unfortunate's votes has yet had a chance to elect anybody, so they are all redistributed to the second preference candidates at full value. If the eliminated candidate has received any second preferences from the candidates who have already achieved the quota, they are transferred on to the next (third) preference candidate marked on them, if any, but only at the reduced value at which they were received.

If at the conclusion of this second count there remain any further seats to be filled the process will be repeated until the final result is achieved, which occurs *either* when the necessary number of candidates has reached the quota, *or* when the number of candidates left in the running is equal to the number of remaining seats, *or* when only one seat remains to be filled, and one candidate has a majority over all the other candidates left in the race, whichever is the sooner.

The following example from the 1992 Irish general election illustrates the process (Table 7.4). Two candidates, David Andrews (Fianna Fáil) and Niamh Breathnach (Labour) reached the quota and were elected on the first count, though in the latter case with such a small surplus that it was not distributed until count seven, when four minor candidates had already been eliminated without much effect on the totals. Sean Barrett (Fine Gael) was elected on count eleven and Liz Keogh (Progressive Democrat) and Eamonn Gilmore (Democratic Left) on count twelve; the latter without achieving the quota, when only one other candidate remained in the race.

Of course it is quite a valid criticism of STV that even if its mathematics is not particularly obscure, the fact that it does involve the element of trust makes it unsuitable for general use. However, the interim report of the Labour Party Commission on Electoral Systems, which considered this argument, did recommend the adoption of the system for the Scottish Assembly they had planned to set up after the British general election of 1992 (Plant, 1991b). The reason was that any other system applied to Scotland was likely to give rise to a permanent one-party domination, which, as the example of the Stormont period in Northern Ireland demonstrates, is unhealthy for the continued survival of liberal democracy.

Certainly proportional systems do not tend to favour stability in this sense. But do they lead to unstable government? In one sense, of course, it does not matter if they do. If that is what the people want, they should be allowed to have it. The mathematicians give an awkward answer from the point of view of the practical politician. Their models of electoral behaviour suggest that electoral choice should be much less stable than it actually seems to be in practice (Riker, 1982). Further research has tended to confirm that electoral systems are unstable *but* that this does not matter since no one actually knows what is happening (Nurmi, in Calvert, 1987: 220).

Table 7.4 *Dun Laoghaire, Irish general election, November 1992*

Electorate: 87,495 Total Poll: 60,049 68.6% Valid Poll: 59,370 Quota: 9,896
Elected: *D Andrews (FF) N Breathnach (Lab) *S Barrett (FG) H Keogh (PD) *E Gilmore (DL)

Surplus/Votes of Votes distributed	*Count 1*	*Count 2 Surplus Andrews*	*Count 3 Votes McAneny (49)*	*Count 4 Votes Murdock (115)*	*Count 5 Votes F'Ptrk (849)*	*Count 6 Votes Quinn (1,823)*	*Count 7 Surplus Brat. (178)*	*Count 8 Votes McDowell (2,337)*	*Count 9 Votes Coffey (3,688)*	*Count 10 Votes Cosgrave (4,422)*	*Count 11 Votes Barnes (6,068)*	*Count 12 Surplus Barrett (1,694)*
*D Andrews	13,418											
N Breathnach	10,074											
*E Gilmore (DL)	7,045	+218 7,263	+6 7,269	+35 7,304	+254 7,558	+173 7,731	+68 7,799	+681 8,480	+281 8,761	+251 9,012	+417 9,429	+359 9,788
H Keogh (PD)	6,497	+211 6,708	+1 6,709	+10 6,719	+16 6,735	+93 6,828	+28 6,856	+379 7,235	+181 7,416	+344 7,760	+1,096 8,856	+1,182 10,038
*S Barrett (FG)	4,852	+243 5,095	+2 5,097	+5 5,102	+36 5,138	+101 5,239	+17 5,256	+120 5,376	+147 5,523	+2,044 7,567	+4,023 11,590	
*M Barnes (FG)	4,261	+195 4,456	+5 4,461	+4 4,465	+14 4,479	+35 4,514	+31 4,545	+234 4,779	+192 4,971	+1,097 6,068		
L Cosgrave (FG)	3,683	+119 3,802	+1 3,803	+1 3,804	+15 3,819	+377 4,196	+11 4,207	+109 4,316	+106 4,422			
*B Hillery (FF)	2,973	+1,173 4,146	+5 4,151	+2 4,153	+84 4,237	+388 4,625	+4 4,629	+143 4,772	+2,482 7,254	+348 7,602	+155 7,757	+153 7,910
B Coffey (FF)	2,119	+1,227 3,346	+4 3,350	+5 3,355	+91 3,446	+87 3,533	+5 3,538	+150 3,688				
V McDowell (G)	1,784	+65 1,849	+14 1,863	+19 1,882	+153 2,035	+288 2,323	+14 2,337					
M Quinn (Ind)	1,705	+35 1,740	+9 1,749	+7 1,756	+67 1,823							
K Fitzpatrick (SF)	801	+30 831	+1 832	+17 849								
E Murdock (WP)	110	+5 115										
M McAneny (Ind)	48	+1 49										
Non-transferable			1	10	119	281		521	299	338	377	

As we have now seen, there is much truth in the view that for any given desired result, an electoral system can be devised. And in consequence, proportional systems, paradoxically, occur in two quite different situations; one, where this condition of general trust manifestly exists, as in the countries of Europe, and one, where the condition manifestly does not, as in Latin America, where one is forced to the regrettable conclusion that it does not matter anyway, since the vote is free in inverse proportion to the importance of the result. Electoral systems are determined by governments and not governments by electoral systems. It is therefore governments that have both the inclination and the opportunity to interfere with freedom of choice.

ELECTION RIGGING

If a government feels that, for the sake of its national and international reputation, it must hold elections, but wishes to guarantee that it does not lose power as a result, it frequently happens that it arranges for the elections to be 'rigged'. In fact election rigging is a widespread practice in ostensibly 'democratic' countries with allegedly 'free' elections, and governments in those countries are frequently charged with it in the speeches of their political opponents. Unfortunately, rigging is also found locally in elections in countries where the government does not exercise any direct control of them, so individual cases are often very difficult to judge. The reason is quite simple. Although a government may be quite confident that a free election will return it to power, or accept an arrangement by which its tenure of power is shared from time to time with its political opposition, local officials with their political careers at stake may not take the possibility of personal defeat so calmly. Hence, unless central control is strong, paradoxically, elections may be marred by a greater or lesser degree of interference in the freedom of choice.

The weakest point in any electoral system is the candidate. If candidates are unwilling or afraid to present themselves for election then no free choice can take place.

In all countries, candidates for election have to fulfil certain basic legal requirements. They must be citizens of the country, of full age and of sound mind, and not have a criminal record. 'Frivolous' candidates are discouraged by a formal process of nomination and in the United States candidates may be required to secure a substantial number of signatures in a number of different areas to demonstrate that they have sufficient support to warrant a contest.

Candidature may be discouraged simply by social pressures. Would-be candidates may discover that their position at work is threatened either by their colleagues or by their employers. If they are professionals or self-employed they may find that their livelihood is threatened by the refusal of others to supply them, to work with them, or to consult them. Where membership of a trade organisation or of a trade union is obligatory in order to work in a particular occupation, fear of having this membership withdrawn may be more than enough to discourage political activism. Then it is possible to construe the basic criteria of fitness more or less strictly, applying a legal prohibition to candidature. In the USSR political opponents of the regime have been certified as mentally ill, and detained as such; in Brazil and Uruguay they have been deprived of their political rights, but allowed to retain their liberty; while in South Africa restrictions can be and are placed on their freedom of movement, speech and assembly by the Minister of Justice.

In many countries, people are imprisoned for their political views, sometimes, as in Cuba and Paraguay, for very long periods, sometimes, as in Argentina, Chile or Iran, in response to specific challenges, though it is impossible to draw a hard and fast line between these. The political nature of the imprisonment, too, is normally disguised by presenting charges of involvement in conspiracy, charges which, by the nature of the secrecy surrounding state security, are usually very difficult altogether to refute.

In extreme cases, political figures who presented a threat have been murdered. The instigators of the death of Jorge Eliecer Gaitán in Colombia in 1948 are still unknown, but the belief that his assassination was intended to preclude political reform was sufficient to touch off a major civil war which, sadly, in the end resulted in the imposition of a dictatorship (Fluharty, 1957: 99–101). Assassination has been an increasingly prominent feature of Colombian politics since the rise of the drug cartels, and in the lead-up to the election campaign of 1990 two leading candidates who had promised to tackle the problem were murdered. It is less commonly used by governments, though the assassination of Pedro Joaquín Chamorro in Nicaragua in 1978 is generally regarded as having been the work of agents of President Anastasio Somoza (who was himself in turn assassinated in Paraguay in 1980 by an Argentine group).

Fortunately, such tactics sometimes provoke a public reaction. In Guatemala in 1966 the assassination of Mario Méndez Montenegro, the principal opposition presidential candidate, created such anger that his brother stepped into his place and was carried into office on a tide of public sympathy which neither the government nor the army could resist (Gott, 1970: 67; Melville and Melville, 1971: 204–6). A more familiar example is that of Cory (Corazón) Aquino, whose husband, the opposition leader Ninoy (Benigno) Aquino, was shot in the back in August 1983 at Manila on the steps of an aircraft closely guarded by the security forces of the dictator Ferdinand Marcos. Deprived of electoral victory in 1986 by a blatantly rigged election, she was swept into power by a popular insurrection.

Restraint on candidature is imposed less dramatically but more effectively by institutional means, by restraining the freedom and scope of action of political parties, which in many countries serve as the sole legal vehicle for nomination. Parties may be dissolved altogether, as in Chile or in Peru after 1968. Only official parties may be recognised as having legal status, as in Syria or Egypt. Or 'extremist' political parties may be singled out for special treatment, as with the banning of the German Communist Party (KPD) in West Germany, where the rise of fascist parties has been similarly guarded against.

Even where candidature and political organisation are both officially free, the electoral process itself may be subject to several kinds of manipulation. In the United Kingdom party nomination is not required but independent candidates are discouraged by the requirement that the candidate must lodge a deposit, which is returned only if he or she secures more than 5 per cent of the votes cast. Fortunately as a result of inflation rather than of goodwill, the deposit, currently £500, is sufficiently small not to act as much of a restraint, bearing in mind that it represents about £10 in 1918, when the deposit was originally set at £150 and the limit at 12.5 per cent.

Electoral districting is subject to two sorts of manipulation. Varying the number of electors can enable more members to be returned for one party than another. However, given the propensity of human beings to group together in certain areas rather than others, it may be necessary to tolerate a degree of variation rather than have some constituencies unreasonably large in geographical terms. Varying the boundaries of electoral districts to secure a desired result is at least as old as Governor Elbridge Gerry of Massachusetts, who in 1820 devised a district shaped like a salamander – or 'gerrymander'.

In Britain voting in public, ended by the Ballot Act of 1870, displayed evident abuses in the form of intimidation of electors, which led to its abolition. But there are two ways in which the same effect can be achieved by different means. In the USSR and other Communist countries, as noted above, it was simply socially 'not done' to make use of the secret voting facilities which were available. To do so was to attract unfavourable attention. This is the exact opposite of the system in the United States, where to use the voting machine the voter has first to pull a handle which ensures that curtains are drawn tightly round the booth, ensuring complete privacy.

Alternatively, facilities may be provided that are not in fact secret although they profess to be so. An ingenious example was the French referendum in Algeria in 1958 on the adoption of the constitution of the Fifth Republic: for the convenience of the largely illiterate population, the authorities had thoughtfully provided them with two voting slips: one white which said '*Oui*', and one purple which said '*Non*'. It was, of course, the aim of the exercise to secure the largest possible number of votes that said '*Oui*', and the colour purple for the '*Non*' slips was deliberately chosen because it was regarded as being unlucky. However, this was not all. When Muslim voters, clad in long flowing robes with no pockets in them, went into the booths to vote and went to fold up their slips and put them into the box, they discovered that no repository had been provided for the slip they did not use. They could either drop it on the floor, in full view of the soldier stationed outside, or they could walk out holding it in full view.

In the same election other artistic touches included the careful distribution of polling stations so as to keep them well away from centres of opposition – one was even stationed on an island in the middle of a river, where the only boat was operated by the army. Where all else failed, the army supplied the necessary number of voting papers to make up the balance.

'Ballot stuffing' is perhaps the most common, and almost certainly the tidiest way, of rigging elections, but it has to be carefully done. In the Bolivian elections of 1978 votes cast were found to exceed the number of live electors by an astonishing amount. Even in the United States, where the control of elections is in the hands of the state governments and local interests, maladministration still occurs and may indeed have important consequences. In the presidential election of 1960, the very narrow margin in favour of President Kennedy could be accounted for by rather dubious totals from Cook County, Illinois, and from Texas, both areas notorious for electoral malpractice, characterised by long counts in which earlier returns are reversed by a sudden disclosure of late totals from the more remote areas. And in Northern Ireland personation continues to be a problem, symbolised by the well-known slogan 'Vote early and vote often!'

CONCLUSION

To sum up, therefore, the problem of securing a genuinely free electoral choice is not an easy one. Fortunately, even where there is extensive local or national interference in the outcome of elections, they continue to be of great political significance as evidence of the real balance of political power within the society.

KEY CONCEPTS

additional member system: list system (q.v.) with single national pool.

Borda count: choice of policies by a group assigning marks to each and then totalling the results.

Condorcet criterion: the choice of a candidate who is preferred by the most voters.

cyclical majority: when in a series of pairwise choices, each candidate achieves a majority over the next candidate.

dark horse: candidate not on the original list who is chosen by way of compromise.

Droop Quota: the minimum number of votes that a candidate must have to be elected.

election rigging: illegitimate interference with the freedom of electoral choice.

'first past the post': in Britain, common, if incorrect, nickname for the single-member, single-ballot system.

gerrymander: drawing of electoral boundaries in such a way as to give an advantage to one party rather than another.

list system: fully proportional electoral system assigning seats in proportion to voters' choices between rival party lists in a multi-member constituency.

majority systems: electoral systems in which a candidate does have to achieve an overall majority.

plurality systems: electoral systems in which a candidate does not have to achieve an overall majority.

proportional systems: electoral systems which give a distribution of seats in proportion to the number of votes cast for each party.

single transferable vote: fully proportional electoral system utilising voters' rank order of preferences for individual candidates in multi-member constituencies.

slate: list of candidates for various offices.

SAMPLE QUESTIONS

The main concern of this area of the syllabus is with electoral systems and their effects, with reference both to the choice of leaders and of assemblies. Understanding of these processes is essential information for a question on a recent election in a specific country, e.g. France, Germany, while electoral reform is a traditional topic and remains a strong possibility on a paper on British government.

Does it matter which political leader is chosen and which is not?
What are the minimum requirements that must be fulfilled for an election to be fair?
If a 'free' election were held in Eastern Europe, how could we tell?
How far is it possible to devise an electoral system that gives an accurate representation of popular preferences?
In what sense, if any, is coalition government weak government?

FURTHER READING

On elections generally see Carstairs (1980), Grofman and Lijphart (1986), Mackie and Rose (1991). Since Black (1958) there has been an extensive debate on the mathematical foundations of choice – see, for example, Nurmi (1987). For British readers, the Hansard Society (1976) summed up the advantages and disadvantages of the different systems. Lakeman (1970) argues the particular merits of proportionality, but Plant (1991b) argues a wide range of other factors need also to be taken into account.

Research on the impact of corruption and electoral malpractice has until recently been relatively neglected, and there is as yet no accessible introduction to the subject.

8 Inside the black box

INTRODUCTION

At the centre of government, where the ultimate decisions are taken and inputs converted into outputs, sit the *decision-makers*. It is here, inside what has been playfully termed the 'black box', that the popular imagination places unimaginable mysteries. It does so, moreover, despite the many memoirs by leading politicians and statesmen, which tend on the whole to show that the business of government is very much like any other managerial job, the main difference being the scope of the decisions taken. As a result it is possible to interpret the way in which decisions are made according to a number of different interpretations or *models*.

The fact is that people in all countries look to their political leaders for something called *leadership*. They do this whether or not they have chosen them to do the job, and the surest sign of the legitimacy they attach to their leaders is the ease with which they accept their right to lead, even if they do not agree with what they are doing. Generally, however, they set some distance between themselves and their leaders, indicating that they belong to a distinct political group. Such groups, forming a relatively small part of a society as a whole, are often termed *elites* – a term invented by the Italian sociologist Vilfredo Pareto (Pareto, 1965). Traditionally, the ability to lead, and hence the right to membership of a ruling elite, has been attributed to the outstanding qualities of the individual or individuals concerned. Weber, as noted above, regarded this kind of claim to political authority, which he termed 'charismatic' authority, as being the earliest or original form of authority, seeing it being 'routinised' in modern societies into the more advanced form of 'legal-rational' authority.

LEADERSHIP

Quite a lot of work on leadership has been done in laboratory conditions by psychologists. They work with small groups, but this in itself presents students of politics with no problems, because most councils, cabinets, committees, boards and the like, are rather small. True, such groups certainly cannot be studied under clinical conditions and, in the absence of the responsibilities they have, their reactions to stress can only be partially simulated. What can and should be done, however, is to use all available information to deduce the way in which such groups should behave, checking these deductions against the information about their actual behaviour which subsequently becomes public.

Such deductions are much more likely to be accurate if it is remembered that psychologists now regard *individual personality* as only one of four factors of leadership (Gibb, 1969; Stodgill, 1948: 45). The other factors are:

- the nature of the *group*
- the *situation* with which it is confronted
- the *task* to be performed.

Hence different personalities will be effective leaders in different situations or when confronted with different tasks. The political leader plays a crucial role in keeping the ruling elite or party together, by maintaining what is termed group *syntality*, that is to say, the will to work together to perform the task in hand. In open-ended experiments with small groups, usually of soldiers or student volunteers, where leadership is not necessarily predetermined, it appears that there are four main ways in which leaders may emerge (Cattell and Stice, 1954: 493):

- The *problem-solving* leader is the person who knows how to deal with the problem in hand, and shows the others how to do so.
- The *salient* leader assumes leadership in all situations by a combination of the inadequacy of the others or the adequacy of the leader.
- The *sociometric* leader is the one whom the others say they would choose to lead them if they were given a chance to do so.
- The *elected* leader is the person whom they actually do choose. S/he may not be the same person as the 'sociometric' leader, the person who is most popular; and, indeed, given the characteristics of most electoral systems, there are structural reasons why s/he will often not be.

These then are the four types of leadership that have been identified in small-group situations. Clearly, these findings must in some way be relevant to the problem of leadership in politics, and in comparing aspects of leadership between different countries, it will be useful to use these categories. First, however, some general principle or principles have to be identified which explain how the differences between leaders can be expected to vary.

A key to this can be found in the psychologists' overall conclusion that, in any given situation, it is easier to suit the task to the leader, than to find a leader to undertake the task. It is the understanding – or misunderstanding – of this principle that determines the development of structures of government, for the two problems cannot in fact be separated from one another. A particular leader long in office alters the job to suit his or her approach to it. The initial response of successors is usually, but not always, to try to continue with the same methods, in which in any case they have a vested interest. But when they find that they cannot effectively operate within the same structures, they set to work to alter them. Hence, over a period of time *leaders* change the nature of the *offices* they hold, downgrading some which have previously been powerful and increasing the strength of others (Calvert, 1987). This is why, generally, rapid periods of institutional change follow long periods of stable succession. The prediction of such periods of rapid change, and determining whether or not they are likely to follow a given course, is one of the fundamental questions of political science (see Chapter 11).

Although in primitive societies the form of monarch was not universally adopted, it was nevertheless widely used, and historically lies behind the formation of most modern states (Chapter 1). Monarchy, replicating the primitive structure of the extended family, took root in small societies where the monarch was approachable and so to a considerable extent accountable, and was effective because it was efficient.

As states grew, the monarch was no longer able to oversee all the business of government. Simply ordering individuals to carry out tasks ad hoc without any long-term responsibility for them lightened the load only slightly. The remedy was delegation. The most frequent form seems to have been the delegation of all the tasks of government by a hereditary leader to a single figure, the vizier responsible for all the tasks of government, but this form positively encourages the palace coup (replacement of the leader at the hands of the strongest subordinate). Hence, though as in the case of France under the reign of Louis XIII and the minority of Louis XIV or – an extreme case – the Japanese Shogunate, such first ministers can give strong and capable rule despite a succession of weak rulers, the first strong ruler to emerge will wish to curtail their powers, as in France in 1660 or in Japan at the Meiji Restoration (1867).

Delegation of the powers of government to those territorial magnates who wanted it, on a geographical basis, similarly proved to have its weakness. In this case the great danger was that the state would be split up altogether, as nearly happened to France with the rise of late-medieval Burgundy, temporarily happened in China under the 'warlords' of the 1920s and 1930s, and has finally happened in former Yugoslavia today. In each case the danger to centralised control was the alienation of the balance of military power. Once lost, it could seldom be recovered, and then only by good fortune coupled, perhaps, with external aid, as in China during the Second World War. Afghanistan and Somalia both form recent examples where central government has effectively ceased to exist as a result of the multiplication of regional armed forces.

The solution was found by developing the structures, not of the family itself, but of the household in the wider sense. The separation of functions, already familiar from the organisation of large bodies of servants in a great house, was modified to make use of its distinctive feature, the division of responsibilities among a large number of people by the subject, and not the geographical area, of their responsibility. Out of this developed, ultimately, the concept first of a *council*, or assembly of the principal officers responsible for carrying out the orders of the monarch, which form the apex of a *staff* for maintaining them. As noted above, however absolute a ruler, or however feared a modern dictator, neither would have any power were it not for the existence of people prepared to carry out their orders and to act on their behalf.

BUREAUCRACY

The permanent staff of government are known as *civil servants*, or, less happily, as *bureaucrats*, and the state of affairs in which they take the principal decisions of government as *bureaucracy*. Bureaucracy is used even more loosely to designate decisions which the speaker regards as unsatisfactory, and this in turn reflects the fact that most ordinary citizens do not understand just how complex the network of governmental decision-making really is. Hence, if they do not get what they want from it they attack 'bureaucracy', in the same way that if their television set does not work they give it a good thump.

This is unfortunate, because one of the major characteristics of the modern state is the fact that it possesses a permanent bureaucratic structure. In fact the word 'bureaucracy' (a hybrid word, from French *bureau* – a desk, and Greek *kratein* – to rule) was coined in the mid-eighteenth century by Vicomte de Gournay to designate a new and he believed previously unknown type of state, one in which power itself had passed into the hands of salaried officials (Albrow, 1970).

In fact, historically, he was wrong; bureaucratic systems had been devised independently in several of the historical bureaucratic states, for example, Egypt and the Byzantine Empire; while the Chinese, who developed in pyramidical administration the foundation for a remarkably stable social as well as administrative structure, were in due course, through the Northcote–Trevelyan reforms, to influence the formalisation of bureaucracy in the British Empire (Bridges, in Robson, 1956: 25).

But de Gournay lived at a time when in Europe there was much concern about an individual's right of recourse against the state. There were, then, three possibilities. In the *Rechtstaat* a clearly formulated system of administrative law set out precisely what the citizen's rights were, and provided a remedy through special administrative courts. (This is the position today in France and other countries of the Code Napoléon.) In the *Justizstaat* there was no separate system of law or courts, but the citizen had recourse through the ordinary courts to the remedies afforded by common law. (This is the case today in Britain, the United States, Ireland and most Commonwealth countries.) In the *Polizeistaat* the state assumed the right to 'police' every citizen for the common good, and there was no recourse. This general power, found also in other states, is still known rather misleadingly as the 'police power' in the United States (Chapman, 1970: 16).

The bureaucratic state differed from all three types. There, though the formal recourse through law existed in theory, in practice it was denied by the secrecy attached to the bureaucratic process. This is a complaint which has had new life in the twentieth century. What then is bureaucracy, and why has it spread so widely?

Weber on bureaucracy

Weber, analysing the characteristics of bureaucracy, found ten aspects that he considered of particular importance in defining the position of bureaucratic staff in its purest form. We can summarise his position, however, by saying that for Weber bureaucracy is *a system of administration by paid officials chosen by merit and arranged in a hierarchy by which the higher officials supervise the work of the lower ones.*

Three themes run through these distinguishing characteristics.

1. The importance of strict *legal* criteria delimiting the sphere within which the official operates, which in turn depends on a strong accepted concept of legality.
2. The clear separation of the private from the public aspect of the official's life; s/he is fully *accountable* to his or her superiors, but only for the job s/he is paid to do, and s/he is not accountable in any way to the general public.
3. The way in which *rational* criteria determine both the nature of

the job and his or her fitness to perform it. As an 'ideal type' the picture of the legal, rational and accountable bureaucrat is obviously attractive to those who wish to see such principles operate in government.

The Weberian criteria of bureaucracy

1 They are personally free and subject to authority only with respect to their impersonal official obligations.
2 They are organised in a clearly defined hierarchy of offices.
3 Each office has a clearly defined sphere of competence in the legal sense.
4 The office is filled by a free contractual relationship. Thus, in principle, there is free selection.
5 Candidates are selected on the basis of technical qualifications. In the most rational case, this is tested by examination or guaranteed by diplomas certifying technical training, or both. They are *appointed*, not elected.
6 They are remunerated by fixed salaries in money, for the most part with a right to pensions... primarily graded according to rank.
7 The office is treated as the sole, or at least the primary, occupation of the incumbent.
8 It constitutes a career. There is a system of 'promotion' according to seniority or to achievement, or both. Promotion is dependent on the judgement of superiors.
9 The official works entirely separated from ownership of the means of administration and without appropriation of his position.
10. He is subject to strict and systematic discipline and control in the conduct of his office.

Source: Weber (1964: 333–4)

It therefore appealed both to governments, as in Europe, and to their citizens, as in the United States, as a systematic solution to the problem of reconciling their divergent interests more closely. Its continued extension in the twentieth century is the clearest proof that this reconciliation has been seen as a success, even if it is at the same time attended by steady criticism.

The critique of bureaucracy

The greatest attraction of bureaucracy is also one of its most frequent grounds for criticism by citizens: it operates, as Weber noted, by implementing common instructions impersonally without regard to the power or position of the individual suppliant (Gerth and Mills,

1946: 198, 215). If efficiently maintained (but cf. Blau and Duncan, 1967), this can be an admirable feature (LaPalombara, 1963; Marx, 1967), and it is certainly much preferable to any older system where the will of the prince is law. In modern times, however, it has increasingly been found necessary to mitigate the apparently harsh effects of impersonal decision-making by strengthening the process of appeal against administrative decisions. Britain, France (Ridley and Blondel, 1964: 24–7, 31) and Germany have each found very different solutions to this problem, but the fact that so much has been done in each country since 1950 indicates the felt need for change. A major problem is that administrative tribunals themselves tend to be suspect as part of the bureaucratic structure (Allen, 1947: 76ff.; Keeton, 1960). Hence the Scandinavian countries were the first to appoint an independent officer, the *ombudsman*, to review administrative decisions with the power to quash or vary them, and in Britain the Parliamentary Commissioner for Administration and in France the Médiateur have been given a similar responsibility, though with lesser powers (Stacey, 1978).

An additional problem of administration in many developing countries is that the bureaucracy there is seen as having been invented not for the sake of the local inhabitants (although their interests have not necessarily been infringed), but for the sake of the colonising power. Civil servants in post at independence may well have been regarded as collaborationists, and their great powers make them an easy target for nationalist criticism.

Riggs' (1964) classification of bureaucratic systems was designed to reflect this developmental perspective. Riggs seeks to distinguish between three stages in the development of post-colonial states, using an analogy drawn from optics, namely the passage of light through a prism (see Figure 8.1).

- Traditionally, in the conciliar state, decision-making was 'fused', the decisions in different areas being incorporated in the same body in the way that white light contains all the colours.

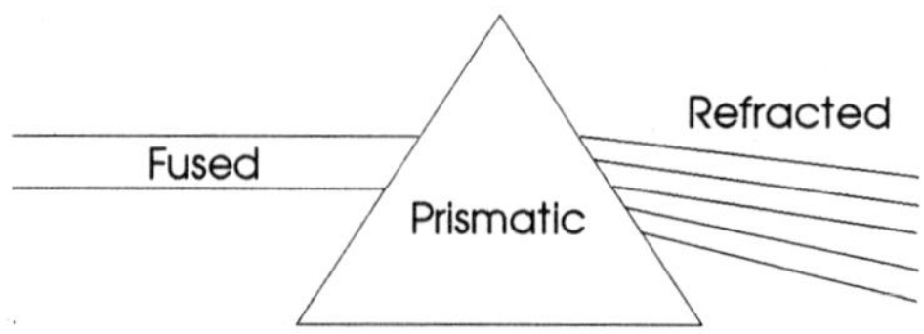

Source: Based on Riggs (1964)

Figure 8.1 *The 'prismatic' society*

– In a modern government, on the other hand, the areas of competence of government are split into functional areas, each the responsibility of a different government department. Decision-making, therefore, is 'refracted', just as white light leaving the prism is refracted into different colours.

However, most developing countries have mixed institutions in which functions are incompletely separated. The analogy is with light actually passing through a prism; hence Riggs' term, 'prismatic' society.

This model, Riggs suggests, is characterised by what he terms the *Sala* system of administration: an over-centralised system in which every decision has to be taken several times over, and people still hanker after the multi-functional model. They speak to a friend of a friend, they write to the President of the Republic, or they take his private secretary to lunch, trying to find a single point at which all decisions that interest them can be decided.

There are three consequences: decision-making becomes, or remains, over-centralised, every decision is taken several levels higher up than is really necessary, and the top level in particular is both over-worked and over-powerful; there is serious waste in public spending because money is spent two or three times over; and no one knows exactly how much is being spent, and in such an atmosphere administrative and political corruption flourishes (Wraith and Simkins, 1965). Many of the military coups that have deposed governments in Africa (e.g. those that brought to power Ibrahim Babangida in Nigeria, Jerry Rawlings in Ghana and Valentine Strasser in Sierra Leone) have had as one of their two or three principal avowed aims the ending of corruption. The bitter irony is that within months the new military regimes are usually at least as corrupt as the civilian governments they replaced or supplanted – and often much more so.

However tempting it is to blame this state of affairs on bureaucracy itself, a word of caution is needed about the alternatives, the most important of which is the conciliar system that preceded it. The basic unit of this system was not the individual official, but the ruler in *council*. A council consisted of a group of men each of whom was an expert on one aspect of affairs of state. Collectively they were not specialists; yet because of the need for the ruler to authorise all decisions they had to discuss and resolve all matters brought before them, regardless of subject. The process was thus tedious, time-wasting and highly inefficient. A viceroy of New Spain in the eighteenth century is said to have said of the Council of the Indies at Seville: 'If death came from Spain we should all be immortal.'

Conciliar government has been retained at the highest level, the Cabinet, in the British parliamentary system, but there too its inefficiencies have had noticeable effects: the Privy Council gave way to the Great Cabinet, the Great Cabinet to the Cabinet proper, and in time of war the Cabinet to an Inner Cabinet, a War Cabinet, or a system of 'overlords' (Jennings, 1951: 297, 306). Despite the inefficiencies of the Cabinet system, however, it supplies something that the hierarchy of bureaucracy cannot do, a forum in which decisions can be taken that affect the work of several or of all departments. Ironically, it is bureaucracy that has enabled the Cabinet as such to survive at all, since it provides the individual ministers with the capacity to do their jobs, and keeps the lesser decisions off their desks (Cohen, 1941: 37). Even then it has been calculated that the average British Cabinet member spends only about half an hour a week actually running his or her department. Not surprisingly the majority of them speedily become 'house-trained', acting as mere spokespersons for the departmental point of view rather than agents of government bringing about change.

Bureaucracy is criticised for another obvious success, the increase in government employment that it brings with it; a theme taken up in C. Northcote Parkinson's *Parkinson's Law* (1958: 5–14). In Britain, the Thatcher Government inherited in 1979 a governmental payroll of some 540,000; in the United States today civil service covers more than 2.5 million employees, 90 per cent of whom work outside Washington. In Nigeria the combination of weak civilian government and military intervention has created a stratum of 'Perm. Secs' with hugely inflated salaries, and lesser bureaucratic offices multiply at great cost to the public purse. One of the attractions of privatisation, therefore, is that it promises to replace whole squadrons of civil servants by taking away their functions and giving them over to external contractors.

DECISION-MAKING

Leadership is therefore inevitably influenced by the nature of this staff, this body of people who implement decisions. And this involves, second, the question of how far the members of the staff share in the exercise of power, in the making of decisions. For if they do, deductions about the behaviour of the central ruling group drawn from experience of small groups may well not be applicable. When one has identified the leaders and their staff, however, one has done no more than lay the essential foundation for assessing how they actually make decisions. It is easy to assume that those taking the decisions are rational persons freely operating in conditions of full information and unlimited time. Yet such is not the case.

It was dissatisfaction with the obvious weaknesses of what he terms the 'Rational Actor' model of decision-making, particularly in foreign affairs, that led Graham Allison critically to compare it with two rival models of the decision-making process, using the Cuban Missile Crisis of 1962 as the subject of analysis (Allison, 1971).

The *Rational Actor* model assumes the rationality of the decision-making process as a whole: it will have clearly formulated goals, and make decisions so as to maximise its objectives in attaining those goals. In doing so it chooses among a range of rational alternative policies so that, by examining the action taken, the observer can deduce the reasons that led to the adoption of that policy option. Such a model is inherently satisfying on logical grounds, but it leaves much unexplained. The two alternative models which Allison offers, however, seek not only to explain what the first model does not, but to do so in a way which is itself coherent and meaningful.

The *Organisational Process* model sees government as a constellation of organisations grouped in parallel and in hierarchy, each with different tasks and different procedures (Allison, 1971: 78–95; drawing *inter alia* on Barnard, 1938; March and Simon, 1958). There is no one set of goals but, for each level of disaggregation, the goals are the maintenance of the organisation itself in terms of budget, manpower, job satisfaction and esteem. All problems therefore are 'factored', different parts of the problem being handled by different organisations in terms of their perceived goals. Such is the volume of routine work, moreover, that each organisation develops routines, or standard operating procedures, by which the majority of its work is handled. The 'answer' to a new problem, therefore, involves, not a complete *search* through all possible policy alternatives, but what has been termed *satisficing*, the acceptance of the first routine that comes to hand that will handle the task in terms of the organisation's perceived goals at that moment. Such routines, and even more the complex *programmes* of routines of large, complex organisations, are inflexible and unlikely ever to be wholly appropriate to any specific task. Moreover there is a general tendency to avoid uncertainty about the future by constructing responses to likely *scenarios* which are thought particularly likely to happen, though such long-term plans are likely to be ignored thereafter in the construction of lesser plans and routines used also for day-to-day action. Change therefore proceeds *incrementally*, and major changes in policy within the organisation can proceed only from deliberate intervention from a higher level aimed in such a way as to prevent attempts to circumvent or forestall it by standard operating procedures.

Such processes, however, are no less characteristic of the highest level of decision-making than of its subordinate organisations, and there, in Cabinet or Politburo, where disagreements from time to time come into the open, it becomes clear that policy outcomes are themselves the product of the competing individuals of which the organisation as a whole is composed. Allison therefore offers us what he terms a *Governmental Politics* model (Allison, 1971: 162–80; see also Neustadt, 1964). Others have preferred to call it the *Bureaucratic Politics* model, though its usefulness is not limited to examination of the workings of the bureaucracy.

The *Governmental Politics* model sees individuals as players in a game, whose output is the sum total of all their decisions. The player's power to influence decisions depends on his or her job; his or her possession of that job in turn determines how s/he will look at every issue ('Where you stand depends on where you sit') (Allison, 1971: 176, quoting Don K. Price). The game proceeds along action channels structured by *rules* and *deadlines* that have to be met, by a process of *bargaining* in which action on one issue is traded off against action or inaction on another, and this bargaining is vertical as well as horizontal in its implications, as between those who have much power ('Chiefs') and those who have little ('Indians'). Since the noise level is high and time short, decisions taken to meet deadlines tend to be based on the minimum of evidence and defended much more strongly than a rational examination might suggest desirable, and decisions are both misperceived by the participants and mis-communicated to others. But because of the importance of hierarchy to each individual, gains may be maximised by *reticence* such that major objections are not voiced despite being seen or felt.

Table 8.1 illustrates the main points of comparison between these three models.

Table 8.1 *Models of decision-making*

Rational actor	*Organisational process*	*Governmental politics*
One organisation	Constellation of organisations	Individual players in a game
Hierarchy of goals	Goal is maintenance of organisation	Job determines issue
Goals clearly formulated	Problems 'factored'	Rules and deadlines channel action
Problems analysed	Standard operating procedures	Bargaining
Search of all alternatives	Programmes of routines	Chiefs and Indians
Rational choice of best alternative	Satisficing	Win some lose some

Source: Allison (1971)

ASSEMBLIES

Though the governmental politics model comes closest to the position adopted in the organisation of this book, it is, as will be seen, not in any way an exclusive *explanation* of the way in which government works. The fact is that the governmental politics game is 'played' by members of organisations, who as part of their working beliefs about the game *as a whole* hold that their actions, in some not wholly clear way, contribute to the 'national interest' and must therefore be 'rational' in overall terms. This is particularly true of members of *assemblies*.

Assemblies form the last stage of interest aggregation in both parliamentary and presidential systems. In both, therefore, even where they have little visible effect on policy outcomes, they play a significant role in the structure of party rule, pressing the claims of constituents and of special interests, and acting as a conduit for grievances. They are, in short, significant, if subordinate, members of the political elite. As such they form an important part of the structure of patronage by which the government is maintained (see Chapter 9).

However, in presidential systems they are substantially more likely to play a significant role in decision-making, since in parliamentary systems the presence of the executive in parliament, and its ability to control the outcome as long as it can maintain majority support, severely curtails the assembly's independence of action. Thus Mezey's (1979) classification of assemblies according to the degree of their impact on policy is critically dependent on the context in which they have to operate. Only in presidential states, and under unusually favourable conditions, can assemblies be categorised in his terms as *active* makers of policy. The United States is the only example which has operated in this way consistently over many years, and even there it has been subjected to substantial pressure from the executive in the era of the 'Imperial Presidency'.

The sad fact, however, is that presidential states, because of the separation of executive and legislature, are much more commonly prone to intense and debilitating conflicts between the two. Conflict of this kind has frequently in the past led to one of two outcomes: either military intervention accompanied by the deposition of the executive and the suspension of the assembly, as in Chile in 1973, or a 'self coup' (*autogolpe*) in which the President uses force to close the assembly and to rule by decree, as in Peru at present.

In Britain and Germany parliament as an assembly is dominated by the executive of the day and can be categorised as *reactive*. Both influence government policy but seldom control it. In 1982 in Germany Chancellor Kohl demonstrated the subordination of the Bundestag when he was able to engineer the 'constructive vote of no confidence' by which his government was overturned by its own supporters and so received a new mandate from the electorate. The French Parliament, shackled by the constraints of the 1958 constitution, is even weaker. Though its individual members may well exercise an even greater influence over policy through the effect of the *cumul des mandats*, they have little power to influence legislation and government business takes absolute priority. At an individual level the Italian deputy has much more power, and collectively can make and unmake governments, but the prolonged dominance of the system by the Christian Democrats has made much of this activity rather superficial.

The most powerful parliamentary assemblies are those of the 'consociational democracies', where multi-party government requires negotiation between coalition partners on a wide range of issues, and collectively the assemblies exercise a significant influence on policy outcomes.

The existence of extra-parliamentary controls, whether wielded by the military, a party militia or a 'secret' police, adds an external dimension to the restraint under which many assemblies have to operate. In many newly-independent countries since the 1960s assemblies have been speedily marginalised, though in differing degrees those of India and Sri Lanka, for example, have retained intermittent influence, despite executive dominance. However, in the former Communist countries assemblies were *minimal*, the Supreme Soviet of the USSR meeting for only a handful of days a year to acclaim the reports of government ministers and committees. The future of assemblies in Eastern Europe, other than in the Czech lands, must by virtue of this tradition be regarded as at best *marginal*. And any categorisation must allow for the fact that there are a significant number of states, such as those of the Gulf region with the problematic exception of Kuwait, in which assemblies do not operate at all, or in which, as in Myanmar or Peru, they have been suspended and the country placed under martial law (see Chapter 10).

ELITES

Outside the ranks of the political leadership and the bureaucracy in most – if not all – societies a number of people can be identified who, together with the political leaders and the senior bureaucrats, monopolise a disproportionate share of political power. In so far as this forms a self-conscious group of men and women aware of their special position it is commonly termed an *elite* (Parry, 1969: 31). It is a term, however, which defies easy handling in the comparative context because of its indefinability. Although everyone knows what an elite is when they see one, they seem to have a great deal of difficulty deciding what exactly an elite is not.

Pareto's original concept of an elite as a group conscious of its own existence was straightforward enough. But relatively few people have read Pareto, and for most English-speaking readers the concept has been fundamentally transformed by C. Wright Mills in his book *The Power Elite* (1956). The 'power elite' for Mills is not an elite in the older sense, in that the members of the power elite – if there is such an entity – do not necessarily know each other, and indeed they may not be sure that each other exists; in the United States, his argument runs, key people in business, the armed forces, and in government will act together in a certain kind of way without having common links between them, or indeed without really knowing that they are acting together. The British equivalent is still sometimes referred to as 'the Establishment' (Thomas, 1959). The power elite seems much too diffuse to be useful in a comparative context, and for that reason is best abandoned.

What then of the elite proper? This is probably best considered as a phenomenon, not of societies, as Pareto originally envisaged it, but of organisations, as Michels suggested in the context of political parties, and the political decision-makers do form such an organisation. As such they can be identified, labelled and studied. When this is done, some trends are immediately obvious. In the small group of key decision-makers women are scarce; minors are excluded altogether. And not all males of adult age can take part, because they lack some or all of the necessary qualifications. Hence though individual members of the elite are not necessarily easily identified by their social characteristics, the elite *as a whole* has a very different social composition from the social strata from which it is drawn.

So much is obvious enough. What is not so obvious is the astonishing number of these qualifications, and the extent to which the possession of a sufficient number is restricted to a very few. So much is this the case that even in the most 'democratic' state the access to political power is broadened, if at all, not by widening the circle of eligibles, but by limiting the time that any one person can stay in a position of power. This may be done by formal as well as informal limitations on the duration of office. When all the necessary exclusions have been made, there remains a small group of about a hundred people who appear to be the most influential people in the society. But this method predetermines the result. To say that the country is run by an elite is to accept that these people really run it, and that their identities are known. Neither may in practice be the case.

Elites can be divided into two distinct but overlapping types. Traditional elites are rigid, and the distinctions by which they define themselves are absolute. If to be a member of the elite it is 'necessary' to be male, it is no use being female; if of a majority ethnic group, minorities need not apply.

But how relevant is this today? In Western European states, certainly, there is no formal barrier against any citizen becoming a member of parliament, a minister or even prime minister. But in practically all presidential states there is a constitutional requirement that the president must be a 'natural born' citizen of the republic. So Dr Henry Kissinger, President Nixon's Secretary of State, could not become President of the United States under its constitution (Wolf-Philips, 1968: 210), because he was born in Germany as a German subject.

As this rather special case shows, it is not necessary to be able, even in the United States, to become president in order to be a member of the political elite. But to be a member of a political elite does *not* imply equal possibilities of access to all levels of it, and Nixon could appoint Kissinger Secretary of State without any danger to his own political position, since he could not become, by that fact, a rival candidate. Had he not been fortunate to live when he did, the same problem might have befallen Alexander Hamilton, who made the mistake of being born in the West Indies, but he was covered in the transitional provision of being a citizen when the constitution came into effect.

In some other countries the restrictions on access to the highest office are even more constraining. In Mexico, the president must not only be a natural born citizen, but the son of natural born citizens (Wolf-Philips, 1968: 153). A similar restriction would have excluded Woodrow Wilson from becoming President of the United States, or Winston Churchill from being Prime Minister of the United Kingdom.

Transitional elites are relatively flexible. These are groups which use acquired characteristics in their strategies of 'social closure' – excluding the non-elite. Such a characteristic *par excellence* is education. In both Britain and France, though in very different ways, the nature of the educational process is crucial to access to the higher reaches of political power. Religion is another characteristic which may be acquired; so too, historically, is race, for there is no biological basis for racial discrimination, and the interpretation of what constitutes a 'race' has varied historically so much that its role as a strategy of 'social closure' is shown very clearly. Other, perhaps even less definable criteria are often lumped together into a generalised notion of 'social class', based loosely on income, wealth or occupation. Again, there is no way of assuredly separating individuals into distinct groups by such criteria, partly because there is not meant to be. Last, occupation itself may serve as a criterion on its own, as in the case of the military profession. Flexibility here is limited to an extent depending on the degree of skill involved. An ancient Spartan would not get far without being skilled in the arts of war, whatever the arts of war may be.

Two points about these criteria are of particular importance. Many of them are interrelated, or may be interrelated, such that deficiency on one account may be made up for by proficiency on another. All of them tend in practice to be related to wealth, itself a measure of power resources. Wealth, status and political power can be traded off against one another, and inherited wealth, in particular, implies early advantages in education and training which predispose an individual to leadership. And, historically, two types or aspects of training have been of particular importance: military and legal.

At one time soldiers, perhaps, actually were the strongest members of society, though skill must always have been very important too. But the introduction of firearms has been a great leveller in this respect. Lawyers come from the intellectuals, but have a specialised training.

CONCLUSION

The views of political thinkers on elites can be categorised according to three criteria: whether they believe that they are inevitable or not; whether they believe they are desirable or not; and whether they think they are part of them themselves or not. Among those who considered they were inevitable were Pareto, who invented the word, and Michels, the sociologist who demonstrated that they were a feature of all types of organisations and not just of government (Michels, 1959: 390). It was Pareto who regarded the ultimate determinant of political change as being the possibility of the 'circulation of elites', that is to say, the replacement of a spent elite by a new one (Michels, 1959: 378). But as we have already seen, this tells us little that we do not know already, particularly since the replacement of members of an elite will happen anyway through the ineluctable processes of mortality. And it is perhaps more rewarding to regard, as Michels does, elites as being in a perpetual state of competition, and to try to identify their characteristics more precisely.

The sort of questions that need to be asked before accepting the assumption of a ruling elite uncritically, are these: Is there really just one ruling elite, or do different elites control different organs of government? Does the army, for example, come under the same sort of control as civilian organisations? Are there different answers for different regions? What do we mean by *ruling elite*? How many of the so-called elite actually rule, and how often can they expect to get their own way? These are difficult questions to which we may expect to get different answers from personal observation and from asking others in the society what they think, and we may well agree with Geraint Parry that some combination of the two methods alone can give any satisfactory answer for it is doubtful if the word elite will ever be anything more than a vague collective noun for the government of the day and its friends (Parry, 1969: 115, 139).

KEY CONCEPTS

bureaucracy: system of administration by paid officials chosen by merit and arranged in a hierarchy by which the higher officials supervise the work of the lower ones.

Cabinet: in UK collective body of ministers (secretaries of state) forming the highest executive organ of government.

circulation of elites: for Pareto the replacement of a spent elite by a new one.

conciliar system: system of administration by a ruler in council.

***cumul des mandats*:** in France, holding several elective offices at the same time.

elite: in any society those who, together with the political leaders and the senior bureaucrats, monopolise a disproportionate share of political power.

office: each formal position held by a decision-maker, whether elective or appointive.

ombudsman: in Scandinavia permanent official with special powers to rectify administrative error; by extension, popular term in UK for the Parliamentary Commissioner for Administration, cf. in France the Médiateur.

Parkinson's Law: for C. Northcote Parkinson 'Work expands to fill the time available for its completion'.

police power: in USA general power of government to regulate matters for the public good.

power elite: for C. Wright Mills the most powerful and influential people in American society, whether or not they know it or each other.

prismatic society: for Riggs a society characterised by governmental system with incomplete functional separation of powers.

'Rational Actor' model: for Allison pattern of decision-making characterised by total information and a search of all available alternatives.

satisficing: the acceptance of the first routine that comes to hand that will handle the task in terms of the organisation's perceived goals at that moment.

social class: stratification of society based loosely on income, wealth or occupation.

social closure: reinforcing the elite by excluding would-be entrants.

staff: group of officials responsible for carrying out the will of a leader.

syntality: the will to work together to perform the task in hand.

SAMPLE QUESTIONS

Questions on decision-making will expect some knowledge of administrative theory, the ability to relate some or all of public opinion, interest groups, party interests etc. to a specific decision or set of decisions. In the comparative context, to concentrate on a single-issue area where a range of information exists would be helpful. Alternatively, a question may expect the application of a range of theoretical ideas in a single-country context.

'Not what is to be done but how it is to be done is the main difficulty facing politicians and administrators alike.' Comment.

Why are policy and administration in developing countries frequently criticised as elitist, centralised and remote from people's real needs?

Outline your preferred model of decision-making within British central government. Give reasons for your choice.

Using recent examples, show how public opinion has affected a specific governmental decision in a country of your choice.

What is an elite?

FURTHER READING

Beetham (1987) is an interesting and accessible introduction to bureaucracy. Albrow (1970) contains a well-argued critique of Weber (Gerth and Mills, 1946), as does Page (1992). The arguments of Riggs (1964) can only really be fully appreciated in the original.

On the policy process in general see Ham and Hill (3rd edition, 1993). Allison (1971) systematised concepts of decision-making which had already attained recognition by specialists such as March and Simon (1958) on the 'organisational process' model or Neustadt (1964) on 'governmental politics'. On the concept of the elite see especially Parry (1969). Pareto's views on the 'circulation of elites' are expounded in Pareto (1965). On political succession see Calvert (1987).

PART FOUR
System Maintenance and Political Change

9 Maintaining the system

INTRODUCTION

Once in power, the major task of any government is to stay in power. Constitutionally, this is done through the government responding to the demands made upon it, the administrative apparatus functioning efficiently to meet these demands, and the courts impartially deciding the law, regulating disputes and averting the development of potential trouble in the social system. In practice, the main effect of such institutions is felt indirectly, through the process of *political socialisation*, which ensures that the great majority of people regard the system as more or less legitimate.

Regardless of the means employed for the regulation or suppression of force in general, it is of course inevitable in human societies that there will also be some sort of unregulated or unsuppressed minimum. This minimum can conveniently be referred to as 'violence'. The definition of violence as the unregulated use of force is normal, though in popular usage force and violence may be – and often are – considered as interchangeable terms.

In liberal democracies, violence in society is controlled through the use of the *legal system*, but even there behind the legitimate authority of the government lies a very wide range of powers to control and to coerce, all backed by the sanction of force (see, *inter alia*, Hewitt, 1982; Hillyard and Percy-Smith, 1988). More or less prominently displayed according to the nature of the system, the resources available to government include as a matter of course a substantial army, an extensive police system, and some kind of paramilitary reserve or militia that can be called upon in emergencies.

The maintenance of a stable government is the fundamental assurance of the political control of a ruling elite. Losing control of government means at the least that their power will be severely curtailed, at most that it will be lost for good. But maintenance of a government is only part of political control, since it can operate effectively only if the system of relationships around it is also maintained. For this reason the need of a government or regime to maintain itself is usually referred to as 'system maintenance'.

POLITICAL SOCIALISATION

The process of control by the state begins with the *socialisation* of youth.

The *family* is the earliest vehicle of socialisation, though from an early age the influence of the child's *peer group* modifies its effects. The family is the most effective agency in transmitting the traditional *values* of the society embodied in stories, proverbs, legends and nursery rhymes. These can be translated into *norms* which people expect to obey as a matter of social custom. In turn such norms are often enshrined in specific *rules* of behaviour. Collectively values, norms and rules form the political culture of a given society.

It is interesting and significant how far the material for early socialisation differs between states, forming the basis of nationalism and other value-systems in the process. As between Britain and the United States, there is a shared basis of language and legend, and many of the basic social virtues are perhaps not so very different. Both societies tend to undervalue intellectual achievement as compared with, for example, French, German or Japanese society. However, the US system tends to place a much higher value on social conformity and 'getting along' than the British. The US self-image of a tough frontier society which has made good has, however, considerable influence throughout the rest of the world, through the agency of Hollywood, and against the diet of modern cowboy stories the American child seems to have relatively few patterns of civic (as opposed to legal or police) authority. This is associated with the very low esteem for the police in the American community, and the high emphasis on force as a means of settling disputes in the folk mythology of its members. Both are replicated in the influence of the peer group.

Political socialisation not only involves the inculcation of certain values, more or less unconsciously, but also the code by which aggressive behaviour is ritualised and sublimated. The more elaborate the ritualisation, the more the members of the society can be incorporated into it, and the less likely force becomes in actual fact. Stable societies tend to be those in which *social cleavages* are either relatively faint or occur at different points in the social fabric (Rae and Taylor, 1970).

The role of the *educational system* therefore becomes the major vehicle by which the state can influence the socialisation process at a stage early enough for it to make any difference. It has been understood since ancient times that a democratic society must educate its citizens in the ways of democracy. But even within liberal-democratic states there are considerable differences in emphasis. The French school system has long been distinguished both by its uniformity and by the extent of its elitism. Reforms in the 1980s loosened the control of Paris over the curriculum at just the same time as in Britain increasingly rigorous controls were being introduced by central government. In Germany, on the other hand, education is primarily a matter for state (*Land*) governments, and the *Länder* accordingly compete with one another to offer a high-quality education, and one which lays great emphasis on practical skills. The educational system of Japan, which is modelled on the old Prussian system, is also highly elitist. In the United States, on the other hand, control of the curriculum is a matter for the local community, and primary education lays considerable emphasis on awareness of one's democratic rights and obligations.

A major contrast between Britain, on the one hand, and the United States and France, on the other, is in the formal role of *religion*, though there can be little doubt that in each case religious belief has tended on the whole to be a stabilising and indeed conservative force. In England, with its established (official) Church, religious instruction has for many years been one of the only two subjects required by law to be taught to all children. But in the United States the constitution prohibits the teaching of religion in public schools. In France, the Republic was traditionally anti-clerical and in French schools even the wearing of articles showing one's religious affiliation is forbidden with school uniform. In Ireland the Catholic Church has a special place, but freedom of religious belief is a constitutional right and the first President of Ireland was a Protestant. But in Northern Ireland social cleavages all lie along the fault-line between the two communities. Even then, as the case of Belgium and the Netherlands shows, such societies can develop stable democratic institutions, but in Northern Ireland, sadly, this has not been allowed to happen.

SYSTEM MAINTENANCE

The term *system maintenance* conjures up a misleading picture of a rigid, static framework, like a historic house preserved from decay, but not capable of adaptation to meet new needs and circumstances. Yet the definition of the ruling elite (Chapter 8) is imprecise and vague simply because it is in a necessary state of constant change. The same is equally true of governments themselves. Certainly there may be few if any differences, as far as most citizens are concerned, between one government and the next, for the administrative structure around it changes more slowly than it does. But on the other hand no government, even a dictatorship, remains the same for very many years at a time. In the case of a very long-lasting regime, such as that of General Franco (1939–75) in Spain, the mere combination of ageing in office with the blockage of promotion for younger elements may postpone change. However, this is not in itself sufficient to prevent change in the system overall, even during the ruler's lifetime, as has been demonstrated by the wholesale transformation of Spanish politics since 1975. Similarly the rapid moves towards a market economy in Eastern Europe since 1989 were preceded by limited reforms under Gorbachev's policy of *perestroika,* allowing the creation of co-operatives and permitting a limited amount of market activity. Whether or not this means that the changes will be accepted without widespread social unrest remains to be seen, however.

Analytically, system maintenance requires four things. *Power resource extraction* involves a certain proportion of power resources available to government being used to generate further resources. For this purpose governments maintain a national bank, a finance ministry, and a range of departments concerned with taxation. Other resources will be used for *input control,* to block demands on the political system. The maintenance of governments is ensured in this way most easily by a judicious combination of rewards and punishments. Rewards are available both for members and would-be members of the elite, and no less significantly for potentially useful people who might otherwise be political opponents, who may be *co-opted* into the system. As well as co-option (co-optation), rewards include promotion, pensions and honours. Punishments include demotion, dismissal, fines, banishment, imprisonment and even execution. There is a significant difference between the two. Rewards are wholly within the control of the government, provided always that they can extract the necessary power resources from the population to pay them. Punishments, however, can be freely used only where their impact is wholly political, for the fear of citizens of the arbitrary use of power by a government is such that the use of the more extreme forms of punishment, without clear legal sanction, will destabilise the social system.

Use of rewards and punishments in this way is concerned specifically with the maintenance of the *political system.* System maintenance, however, also involves the use of both positive and negative sanctions on the *social system* as a whole, which have here been termed *positive and negative interest arbitration.*

REWARDS

Maintenance of a government depends in the first instance on rewarding those within it, who form, as Machiavelli pointed out, the most dangerous rival claimants to political power (Machiavelli, 1950: 414–15). Making war on another state is a reward to some and a useful opportunity to punish others without fear of retribution. It is therefore useful for the coercion of reluctant supporters; as is the threat of it, as Hitler seems to have understood very well.

Anticipation is the key to reward. The reward that one gets is seldom as good as the reward one thinks one is going to get, as every child has speedily found. Hence a well-organised, stable political system places great emphasis on an elaborate system of ranks, and promotion within it. This is not as easy as it sounds, as the higher offices are necessarily fewer in number than the lower ones, and fewest where they become most desirable. Perhaps the most efficient such structure, and certainly the longest-lived, was that of the mandarinate in the Chinese Empire. All modern civil services are organised on much the same lines, with fixed rules of retirement and rotation in office (as with ambassadorships) to ensure the constant expectation of vacancies to be filled.

In the United States from the time of President Andrew Jackson (1829–37) civil service positions were filled with political appointees on the 'spoils system', which rewarded the supporters of the victorious political party with jobs. Even today the highest positions in the various departments continue to be filled by political appointees. This calls attention to the value of a career structure in political office, which is very conspicuous in the United States, where experience in a lower elective office is almost indispensable to be taken seriously as a candidate for a higher one. At first sight, this would seem to be quite independent of the wishes or needs of the government. But in practice the administration may also confer a period of appointive office, to make someone a possible candidate for a much higher post (Anderson, 1968: 474–5).

In Mexico, rotation in elective office is guaranteed by a complete prohibition on re-election. Consequently, candidate office-holders alternate spells of elective and appointive office in a pattern in which service within the ruling party forms the main criterion in political advancement (Grindle, 1977: 46–7; Needler, 1990: 81–2). An awkward by-product is that all positions are changed every six years, leading to marked bureaucratic inertia, since it is much more dangerous to make the wrong decision than to make no decision at all.

In the former Soviet Union both formal governmental offices and posts in the Party hierarchy were elaborately graded, allowing 'Kremlinologists' and journalists to play the fascinating game of assessing the relative standing of members of the praesidium by the places in which they stood on Lenin's tomb on May Day, and the order in which they were listed on the occasion of state visits (Barghoorn, 1972: 1977). The corresponding process of assessment in Washington, London, Brasília or New Delhi could only be a matter of rumour and gossip, though leaked information might well anticipate important changes in the composition of a future government.

Co-option (co-optation)

When a vacancy occurs in an appointive office, that vacancy has to be filled. Apart from promotion, this is also an opportunity for *co-option* (*co-optation* in the United States) – the bringing of new members into the political elite by appointing them to formal governmental positions. Co-option is the basic mechanism from which all other forms of choice have been derived (Calvert, in Calvert, 1987). It serves four principal purposes, apart, of course, from its basic purpose of choosing new members of the elite to undertake specific tasks which need performing.

First, it can be used to reward supporters for their loyalty and so consolidate the power of the ruling group. The British Cabinet in this way habitually includes representatives of all major factions within the ruling party, and in fact it was Margaret Thatcher's policy of excluding those who thought differently from her that was in the end to lead to her downfall. In the United States system it was traditional before 1960 for a successful presidential candidate to appoint his defeated rivals of his own party to Cabinet posts. Though he did not wish to do this, Kennedy appointed Adlai Stevenson as Ambassador to the United Nations and gave his job Cabinet status.

Second, therefore, it may be used to maintain an existing regime in power as far as possible unchanged despite the inevitable processes of ageing and mortality. This has two major disadvantages: any government left to its own devices tends to appoint safe, dull and uninteresting people who will not form a threat to their political control, and no one else can get a chance of access to power. This process is unlikely to be challenged as long as the senior leaders remain capable of discharging their duties, since there are few people who will take the risk of offending them. Those within government have got used to them and refuse to believe that they will ever go. Those outside console themselves with the thought that they cannot last for ever, and this is of course true.

An interesting feature of politics since 1945 has been the number of men who have been able to retain political power to an age far beyond that which would be permitted in most other occupations. Churchill in the UK, Franco in Spain (Matthews, 1958), Salazar in Portugal (Figueiredo, 1975), Adenauer in West Germany, De Gaulle in France (Werth, 1965: 9), Tito in Yugoslavia (Auty, 1970), Mao in China (Fitzgerald, 1976), Brezhnev in the Soviet Union and Reagan in the United States, all remained in office long beyond the normal retiring age. An extreme example is Taiwan, where Chiang Kai-shek remained President until his death, surrounded by the people who had supported him at the time of his flight in 1949, on the assumption that they formed the legitimate government of something called the Republic of China. Since no by-elections could be held on the mainland, for obvious reasons, vacancies in its parliament as well as its government were filled by co-option (Lumley, 1976: 63). Long periods of government of this kind are distrusted by many political observers on the grounds that the pressures for change that build up under them may prove, when they are released, to be uncontrollable.

Third, co-option may, on the other hand, be used much more subtly to bring in and to advance young and active members of society who, from their political connections, charisma or ability, might otherwise come to form dangerous political opponents. Their talents, harnessed to the service of the government, can then be of positive value in ensuring that adaptability which enables a system to survive even serious crises. The example of Mexico has already been mentioned. France is another, where the institution of the *cabinet du ministre*, or small group of personal advisers surrounding a ministerial hopeful (not to be confused with the British or American Cabinet), makes an institution of the process of gaining experience in the inner circles of government before launching out on one's own (Marceau, in Cerny and Schain, 1980: 53). In the United States each presidential hopeful carries along with him a team of advisers which, as with the men from Georgia surrounding President Carter will, if required, follow him to Washington as the key figures in setting up a new administration. Some of these 'President's men' have thus begun an independent political career, notably Clark Clifford, who began his career in the White House under Franklin Roosevelt (Anderson, 1968: 134ff.) and ended it in disgrace under indictment for involvement in the collapse of the Bank of Credit and Commerce International.

Last, subtly used, it can be used to bring rival leaders of other parties into the governing circle. Again Roosevelt is an excellent example of a president who appointed political opponents, valuing the conflict of ideas and advice that they brought him. Other more recent presidents have systematically used the same device to disarm important sections of political opposition. Richard Nixon appointed Governor Connally, a Democrat from Texas, to his Cabinet, and Ronald Reagan Jeane Kirkpatrick, then a Democrat, to the high-profile post of Ambassador to the United Nations. The custom in many European states of creating a ruling coalition larger than is actually required to ensure a majority in the assembly, as in Italy under recent 'Pentepartito' governments, is only an extension of the same idea.

Patronage and clientelism

Patronage is a loose word which covers not only appointment to jobs of office-seekers, but also appointments on their behalf which act to strengthen their political position or to reward their family, friends or supporters.

In many countries it is accepted that political office brings with it the duty, as well as the opportunity, to use patronage on behalf of one's family. This phenomenon, which is termed *clientelism*, is often found in connection with the illegal making of personal gain out of one's office (Clapham, 1982). Such appointments can be embarrassing, as when Carlos Menem of Argentina appointed to office a number of relatives of his wife, and then, after an all too public estrangement from her, found that her sister, Amira Yoma, his appointments secretary, had been charged by the Spanish police for complicity in drug-smuggling. More recently President Collor of Brazil, on the eve of presiding over the Earth Summit at Rio, was accused of corruption by his own brother and subsequently resigned under the imminent threat of impeachment (December 1992).

Well-chosen personal connections can, however, be of most value if they ensure sensitive offices are in 'safe' hands. Thus Anastasio Somoza Debayle of Nicaragua placed his half-brother in command of the National Guard on which he relied for his ultimate support (Diedrich, 1982: 83, 107, 139). In Cuba, when Fidel Castro assumed the title of President, his brother Raúl received the titles of Lieutenant General, Second Secretary of the Communist Party and Minister for the Revolutionary Armed Forces (*Annual Register*, 1976: 91), and has since been formally designated as his brother's successor. In Communist North Korea Great Leader Kim Il-sung has designated his son as his successor.

Outside the family circle stand the clients who are bound to their patrons by a set of reciprocal though unequal obligations. As the patron is advanced through the system, it is their duty to see that their clients are cared for, and hence at each change of government there is a fierce and undignified scramble for jobs (Grindle, 1977). Clientelism is often seen as being the distinctive feature of Third World politics, and certainly it is inevitable that under a clientelistic system there will be no hard and fast distinction between public and private and corruption will be endemic. What seems clear is that the effects of clientelism are much more serious in authoritarian or one-party states than they are in competitive systems. Though it is probably impossible to eliminate corruption entirely, the threat of public scrutiny forms an effective brake on the more outrageous forms of corruption, and may well be more significant than the possibility of legal charges, which are themselves subject to the influence of patronage.

The importance of patronage is not by any means confined to the allocation of jobs. Pensions and retainers ease the task of getting rid of members of the government who otherwise would impede necessary or desired changes by softening the financial shock of retirement or dismissal (sometimes so successfully that they end up very much better off than they would have been in office). For the sake of appearances they may be combined with some kind of office which though honorific is more or less a sinecure. Many are (fairly) content with the honour rather than the reward. Others are not.

Honours

Honours are the most insubstantial and the most versatile of all forms of reward. In Britain an elaborate system of badges of distinction, conferring the right to use certain titles or letters after one's name, serves to recognise by enhanced status the long service of many people who have worked for many years in the routine tasks of government (Mr Major has promised to end this), or who by their efforts have achieved distinction in fields of endeavour which the government wishes particularly to commend. It is a system which uses practically no financial resources beyond the slight cost of the badges and ribbons conferred, and for elaboration it probably has no parallel.

But though it derives from the system of real rewards conferred by medieval monarchs, the use of honours is not by any means confined to monarchies. In France the Légion d'Honneur, in numerous gradations, has been democratised in a fashion appropriate to a republic, but is no less valued for being widely conferred. In the United States, the constitution prohibits the creation of titles of nobility. But it does not prohibit the creation of exclusive distinctions such as the Presidential Medal of Honor. Elsewhere in the republics of the Americas honours flourish too. Argentina has the Order of the Liberator General San Martín, Peru the Order of the Golden Condor, Mexico the Order of the Aztec Eagle, and even tiny Guatemala the Order of the Quetzal, in five categories. In the former Soviet Union and the East European countries honours and medals were conferred in profusion. One of the more unusual of these distinctions was the title of Hero of Soviet Motherhood instituted in 1944 for women who had had five or more children (Inkeles, 1968: 217).

Such honours, which involve an advancement in status without necessarily a change of class or rank, are only the formal aspect of a much more widespread phenomenon. The term 'cordon bleu' refers to the fact that Louis XIV conferred the Order of the Saint Esprit, whose ribbon was blue, on his chief cook. At the same time for the whole court, as for other European courts of the day, physical proximity to the king served to denote status, and every action of the monarch was invested with political significance (Mitford, 1966: 63). Eating in public, for example, ceased to be a method of ingesting food and became a demonstration of power, with the inconvenient result that royalty seldom if ever enjoyed a hot meal. Invitations to formal banquets remain to this day symbols of status in most societies, while in presidential states generally the opportunity to gain the ear of the president, even for only a brief moment, marks out political standing as much as it ever did in the old monarchies of decadent Europe.

In the former Soviet Union before Gorbachev the leaders avoided contact with the people so that the make and size of their official cars became the chief sign of their status to the outside world. But although the official car is equally a sign of status in the United States, candidates for office are required to undergo the gruelling initiation of a campaign in the course of which they are expected to shake as many hands as possible. Even then, the day after his inauguration, President Clinton opened the doors of the White House and shook the hands of 2,500 more visitors. It was a bold decision, since even the most superficial handshake, as Edward, Prince of Wales discovered on the course of his Australian tour in 1921, can leave one's hand so bruised that it can become entirely unusable, and he caused concern at home by having to shake hands with the left hand; something which is completely contrary to the symbolic meaning of a handshake as a sign of friendly intent (Windsor, 1951: 42–3). Hence honours, whatever they are, have to be maintained at a manageable level. They have not got to involve too much wear and tear on the system – or the hands.

PUNISHMENTS

Down to the time of President Kennedy (1961), the American eagle, which appears on the Great Seal of the United States holding an olive branch in one claw and a sheaf of arrows in the other, used to face towards the arrows. The President, feeling that this suggested aggressive intentions inappropriate to the modern world, had the eagle reversed to face the olive branch (Sorenson, 1965: 517) – and the Vietnam War followed.

Obviously, there is no direct connection between these two events, but the story does symbolise the great importance attached in all ages to a government's ability to punish transgressors, in this case from outside. The ability to punish people who break the internal laws of a government is symbolised in the House of Representatives by two great reliefs, one on either side of the Speaker's chair, of the ancient Roman symbol of authority, the *fasces*, a bunch of sticks bound round an axe. Symbolically the rods are for beating people and the axe for cutting their heads off.

In modern governments the sanctions for internal opposition within the elite are seldom as drastic as this, and the power to punish is, in its more severe manifestation, reserved for criminals (negative interest arbitration). But the government does still use sanctions to retain control of the political process.

The simplest and most effective punishment for prominent figures, where available, is dismissal from office. In Britain in 1962 the Prime Minister, Harold Macmillan, dismissed seven members of his Cabinet in what came to be known as 'The Night of the Long Knives'. One of those dismissed, the Foreign Secretary, Selwyn Lloyd (later Speaker of the House of Commons), went simply because he seemed to be unpopular (*The Times*, 14 July 1962). In the United States, President Nixon dismissed his Acting Attorney-General when he refused to carry out his orders to dismiss the Special Prosecutor appointed to investigate the Watergate affair (*Congressional Quarterly Weekly Report*, 21, 43, 27 October 1973). The orders, which he had believed to be illegal, were carried out by the Solicitor-General Robert Bork, who was later nominated for a place on the Supreme Court by Ronald Reagan, happily unsuccessfully. In the Soviet Union Marshal Zhukov was dismissed from the Politburo in 1957 when it was feared he might be becoming too powerful. There is a great deal of power to sack in most political systems.

Demotion, either real or symbolic, may be less severe in its consequences, but it is no less real. It can either take the physical form of transfer to a less significant office, or the symbolic one of exclusion from the centres of power and decision-making. No specific action is needed to qualify for such treatment. The failure to support sufficiently vocally or consistently the power of the decision-makers may in itself qualify for sanctions, though the possession of a strong independent power base or other useful qualities may protect to some extent. In Britain under Margaret Thatcher Sir Geoffrey Howe was ostracised in this way, before being transferred to a job in which he had little or no interest.

Exclusion from prospective rewards may in itself be sufficient punishment. This is particularly the case where the ruling elite is rigid in its criteria for admission and can control access, as with the Broederbond in South Africa. Failure to be admitted to the 'club' of the powerful is not subject to appeal. But the position in society of a political opponent may be made absolutely untenable by being subject to mass denunciation and abuse, as was the case in China during the Cultural Revolution (Robinson, 1969).

The treatment of suspected opponents in Communist states was particularly disagreeable since the individuals subjected to such treatment, or, worse, to physical detention or molestation, had to secure permission from the state to leave the country, and such permission was often denied, evidently in the belief that a desire to leave the country would be a bad advertisement for the country they left behind. Fidel Castro, tried for insurrection in 1953, was released under amnesty by Fulgencio Batista in 1955, went into exile, and returned to overthrow the government that had given him clemency. Castro did not repeat his predecessor's mistake. When his old friend Huber Matos was arrested for expressing opposition, he was sentenced to twenty-five years in prison and made to serve every minute of his sentence. The Berlin Wall stood until 1989 as a memorial to the fact that, prosperous as life might have been in East Germany compared to other Communist states, politically it was so restrictive that thousands were willing to risk death to escape from it, and 217 were actually killed in the attempt. However, such restrictions are not confined to Communist states. At the time of writing, Aung San Suu Kyi remains under house arrest in Myanmar (formerly Burma), despite the fact that as leader of the opposition she successfully won a democratic election organised by the military regime which is still holding her captive.

Only towards the end of the Brezhnev period did the leaders of the former Soviet Union show signs of realising that banishment may have its uses. By releasing Alexander Solzhenitsyn, they succeeded in calming opinion abroad while removing the embarrassment at home. And at the other end of the scale of tolerance, the practice of voluntary or forced exile as a treatment for political opponents is so much part of the Latin American tradition that it has given rise to important initiatives to recognise the right of political asylum in international law. Many Latin American politicians spend a noticeable proportion of their lives in exile. Victor Raúl Haya de la Torre of Peru founded its most important political party, APRA, while in exile in Mexico. Having during one dictatorship spent six years in the Colombian embassy in Lima (Alexander, 1973: 13–14), he was elected President in 1962 but a military coup deprived him of victory. He died in 1980 as President of the Constitutional Convention which helped return Peru to democratic government. In a different way, Hugo Banzer of Bolivia, overthrown in a military coup and retired from direct involvement in politics by diplomatic exile as Bolivian Ambassador to Argentina (*Annual Register*, 1978: 74), later returned to Bolivian politics as a successful leader of a right-wing party. The importance of political exiles in other parts of the world, however, is no less. Ex-King Norodom Sihanouk of Cambodia, who gave up his throne to act as Prime Minister, fled from the Khmers Rouges to exile in China, only to be returned by international agreement to the position of head of state in a coalition government. Even more dramatically, Ayatollah Khomeini returned from exile in France in 1978 to act as focus for the Iranian Revolution of 1979 which overthrew the Shah and led in time to the Islamic Republic of which he became symbolic head.

Though the arrest, detention and execution of political figures is all too common, the government cannot necessarily act wholly arbitrarily, though it has much more freedom to do so if it has first assumed emergency powers. Arrests in themselves may have no custodial intent, but merely be used to break up foci of political activity. Since, though, they are often used as an opportunity to beat up or torture captives regarded as opponents of the regime, their mere possibility acts as a deterrent to political opposition. Detention of political opponents for longer periods is in any case so commonplace that it was a feature of decolonisation by Britain in places as far apart as India (Nehru), Kenya (Kenyatta) and Cyprus (Makarios). Detention differs from imprisonment in being an arbitrary act of administration rather than a judicial procedure, but the conditions and consequences need not be any different.

Execution of political opponents is seldom practised openly by established governments for fear of international repercussions. Covert and disguised examples are, unhappily, far from rare. Since the restoration of democratic government in Chile the bodies have been located of many of the hundreds killed by military and/or police after the coup of 1973, as earlier of many of the more than 9,000 killed in the 'dirty war' in Argentina (1976–9). There are many reports of executions from Iran after 1979 following at best only a nominal trial by the religious authorities, though similar reports from Iraq under the dictatorship of Saddam Hussein were long ignored by the Western powers. In Africa thousands died under the dictatorship of Macias in Equatorial Guinea, while under his first government, Jerry Rawlings in Ghana executed four of his predecessors as head of state and head of government. In Guatemala and El Salvador in Central America ruling elites have used 'death squads' closely linked to the armed services to assassinate political opponents. A Serbian armed secret society ('the Black Hand') which had killed King Alexander and Queen Draga of Serbia in June 1903 (Goodspeed, 1962: 24–5) was responsible for the assassination of the Archduke Franz Ferdinand in Sarajevo which sparked off the First World War. At the time of writing Serbian irregulars are engaged in 'ethnic cleansing' in the secessionist states of Croatia and Bosnia-Herzegovina as well as of ethnic Hungarians in the Vojvodina. Such activities, however, go well beyond the bounds of morality, to say nothing of the relatively limited needs of system maintenance.

INTEREST ARBITRATION

When sanctions of reward and punishment are applied not to political control of members of the government and of the elite but to the social control of the society at large, the economy of force dictates that the principal agency of the government will be the *law* and the structures particularly associated with it.

Because of the technical nature of the subject, knowledge of the law in most societies is the especial property of a guild of men and women who regulate admission to their profession collectively through examinations or similar means. Even in the former Soviet Union lawyers were self-employed persons (M. Matthews, 1978), and where their guilds are well established and strong, as in the United States, France or Britain, they can attain a high degree of autonomy within the political system.

Since it is from the ranks of those people that those who have to judge cases are drawn, a high degree of conservatism in legal systems could be predicted, and in fact they appear particularly resistant to change, retaining their formal structures even in times of revolution or civil war, unless superseded by martial law or revolutionary tribunals made up of lay people.

There are, therefore, two different forms of legal systems.

The earlier system requires judges to interpret traditional law based on precedent and hence wholly or partly uncodified. This form was once universal, for, as noted earlier, the belief in a system of law seems in most early societies to have come before the development of distinct structures to interpret it. Today its best-known forms are found in the United States and the Commonwealth countries. However, traditional law is also found in many other parts of the world. The world's oldest university was founded in Egypt in order to teach Islamic law, and though it is not found unmodified there today, its use has been revived from time to time in other Arab countries such as Sudan, Libya and Pakistan under General Zia.

With the French Revolution was introduced the idea that the law ought to be the common property of all citizens, and capable of being understood by them. Hence it should be codified, and the 'Code Napoléon', completed in 1806, stands as a monument to the success of this ideal, having been adopted as the basis of the legal system of many other countries in Europe (Belgium, Netherlands, Spain), in the former French Empire and in Latin America. The Spanish case is particulary interesting, since the Laws of the Indies, first codified in 1682, pre-dated the Code Napoléon by more than a century, and were probably no more difficult to understand (Haring, 1952: 100).

Code law restricts the role of the judges in interpretation, but leaves them a wide range of powers in the conduct of cases, where the institution of the examining magistrate, who scrutinises every aspect of a case and hears witnesses before the case is formally tried, is particularly noteworthy. Anglo-Saxon common law, on the other hand, leaves the judges free to interpret according only to the precedents set by higher courts, but restricts their power in court by the institution for serious offences of a jury, whose task it is to decide simply on the question of guilt or innocence. Though judges in both systems are in general appointed from within the legal profession by a specially constituted committee or committees of the executive, lower judges in the United States are elected at popular elections, though officially on a non-partisan basis, giving them quite a different sort of popular authority for their actions. The general respect accorded to the judiciary is seen at its strongest in the case of the United States Supreme Court, where the power of judicial review of administrative decisions common to Anglo-Saxon legal systems has been transformed by custom into the additional power (in specific cases where the issue cannot be avoided) to declare acts of Congress unconstitutional.

In all cases, however, the formal operation of the judiciary represents only part of the structures associated with rule-adjudication. Decisions of government, such as appeals, the hearing and decisions of tribunals, and the arbitration of industrial disputes (where such are permitted), all involve the adjudication of rules and are normally performed by political or bureaucratic structures, into which the specialised personnel of the law need not venture. The operation of the police force or some similar structure is essential to bring certain classes of case before the courts. Those cases are those in which the government has decided as a matter of public policy that the general good, as it sees it, can be secured only by centralised enforcement of the law. Other cases, involving only the dispute between two persons or legal entities as to their respective rights, will be brought before the courts anyway, though the extent to which this is freely done – itself an indicator of the extent to which the authority of the government is accepted – depends also on the financial cost of justice and the amount of time it takes.

In France appeals against administrative decisions are handled by special courts under a separate code of administrative law, thus clearly distinguishing the public from private responsibility in the matter. In the Anglo-Saxon system, such recourse is through the normal courts. In closed societies, such as the East European states, such recourse is extremely difficult to obtain by any means, attempts to pursue one's rights being met with more or less forcible reprisals, in the belief that any criticism of government constitutes a threat to national security. In fact historical experience demonstrates that long-term survival of a regime and its elite is more securely established by guaranteeing cheap and speedy recourse to the victims of minor injustices, such as seem inseparable from the functioning of bureaucracies as from all human institutions. It is not for nothing that, in monarchies, the prerogative of mercy was seen as the distinguishing mark of a just ruler.

In the former Communist countries the popular notion of a legal code was retained and, indeed, elaborated, but the interpretation of it was placed in the hands of 'people's courts' where lay assessors sat with the judges to determine the guilt of the accused. Since it was widely assumed that the state knew what it was doing in bringing a case before the courts, acquittals were rare. 'Ordinary' criminals, however, though subject often to terms of imprisonment savage by Western European standards, were nevertheless better treated in the former Soviet Union than those whose supposed offence was political.

STATE OF EMERGENCY

The ultimate defence of a political ruler is to return to the pre-constitutional order and to proclaim a state of emergency. This is quite a simple everyday concept. In any country, from time to time, war or natural disaster creates a situation which, in the interests of the citizens, requires that a government acts without normal legal restraints. The ability to proclaim a national emergency is so much part of the normal functioning of government that it was used in Britain, for example, five times between 1970 and 1974 (*The Times*, 14 November 1973).

Its role as a response to war, or threat of war, internal or external, is better reflected perhaps in the Spanish term *estado de sitio* ('state of siege'), suggesting a condition in which a government is imminently under mortal threat from a hostile force (Stokes, 1959: 393–4).

The ancient Romans had already faced this problem. In their past they had overthrown their kings and had established a republican government. Therefore, they established a rather curious system by modern standards, a system in which all power was concentrated in two separate people, who checked each other. So when they were under serious military threat and needed to concentrate their power they instituted the emergency office of dictator. The dictator was given supreme power in the state for a period of six months (Cowell, 1956: 175), then at the end of that time he went back to being a private citizen.

The bad thing in ancient Rome was to be a king, not a dictator; to be a dictator was perfectly respectable. It was the attempt of Julius Caesar (as people thought) to make himself a king that led to the conspiracy of Brutus and Cassius and so to his assassination, not the fact that he held the Roman emergency office of dictator. So that when the idea of dictatorship as an emergency form of government was revived at the time of the French Revolution it was quite widely used. Dr José Rodríguez de Francia was elected Dictator of Paraguay in 1814, and Perpetual Dictator in 1816. Juan Manuel de Rosas was formally recognised as Dictator of the Argentine Confederation in 1835 by twelve provinces outside Buenos Aires (Wilgus, 1963: 65, 261). When he started an organisation to kill off his political opponents, insisted on everyone wearing red cockades to show they were on his side, and had his picture exhibited in all the churches for public veneration, Argentines finally rose against him, but only after eighteen years, and with foreign help. Even Simón Bolivar, deservedly regarded as the hero of South American independence, was Dictator of Peru (1825–6) at the same time as he was President of Colombia, and received, incidentally, no salary for either post (Salcedo-Bastardo, 1978).

Dictatorship, then, is a republican office which values the forms of legitimacy and is often ratified by plebiscite or acclamation. It originally was and has continued to be justified by its proponents as a response to serious national emergency. It was originally considered to be respectable and only after many decades of abuse and incompetence was discredited. Already, by the beginning of the twentieth century, the term had become pejorative.

Nevertheless, Western Europe had its age of dictators in the twentieth century, and not in the nineteenth, and specifically between 1920 and 1945. The redrawing of the map of Europe after the First World War destroyed political legitimacy and left a legacy of conflict. Adopted in this period in Germany, Austria, Hungary, Yugoslavia, Bulgaria, Greece, Italy, Spain and Portugal, the positive view of dictatorship was still not wholly dead in the post-war period, despite Mussolini's war in Abyssinia and Hitler and the Holocaust. Not only did Salazar survive in Portugal and Franco in Spain, but the Colonels seized power in Greece in 1967 and came to grief only when in 1975 they were foolish enough to become entangled in a war with another NATO ally, Turkey, over Cyprus. And dictatorship has had a great revival in the new states, though General Idi Amin of Uganda was, perhaps, unique in openly declaring himself an admirer of Hitler.

So, to sum up, what is characteristic of a modern dictatorship?

It is, first, something that values the forms of legitimacy, internally involving recognition by an elite group, particularly by opinion-leaders – the elders of the state and the military. It may not actually dare to seek mass recognition by plebiscite, but it usually does.

Second, dictators always enjoyed the kind of legitimacy they won externally, and today they like to be recognised by other heads of state. Lacking initial internal support as they do, external recognition by peer states is very important to them, especially that of the older, constitutional states, and of the great powers.

Third, the dictator does not recognise the rights of individual people. For instance, Napoleon I regarded the people as being the vehicle of his political programme, as it were, for France. He created the French Empire in the style in which it ought to be created, and with it the Ecole Polytéchnique, deliberately to obtain an elite to maintain the system (Ridley and Blondel, 1964: 40–1). That is why *polytechniciens*

('Les X') have been valued ever since by French governments, whether the government was a dictatorship, a monarchy or a republic. The idea of moulding the people to need is very much inherent in the idea of dictatorship – it is such an emergency office that all rights are given up to it, and those exercised in the name of the country as a whole.

Fourth, it has always shown a tendency to create a new form of 'aristocracy', in the shape of the active military. Because it is a military emergency office, the military tends to become the elite, and generals and colonels hold regional political power, in the way that earls and barons did in the Middle Ages, operating within a military command structure, and becoming a new 'aristocracy', as in Brazil since the inauguration of the republic (1889).

Last, dictatorship creates no regular form of succession. The emergency character of the dictatorship is absolutely incompatible with the idea that dictators can have successors. Happily, therefore, dictatorships are finite, and since 1989 there has been a marked shift in world opinion away from them and towards liberal democracy.

KEY CONCEPTS

cabinet du ministre: in France a small group of advisers surrounding a minister; not to be confused with the Cabinet.

clientelism: using patronage on behalf of one's family or friends.

co-option (*co-optation* in the United States): the bringing of new members into the political elite by appointing them to formal governmental positions.

dictatorship: emergency office given all power to deal with urgent threat; by extension, any authoritarian ruler.

patronage: appointment to jobs of office-seekers, also appointments on their behalf which act to strengthen their political position or to reward their supporters.

system maintenance: the power of a government or regime to maintain itself.

SAMPLE QUESTIONS

This field involves practical consideration of issues of *authority* and *legitimacy*, and the possible challenges that may arise to them.

Discuss the problems arising from nationalism and the treatment of national minorities in traditional Communist states.

Is there a contradiction between the goals of political democratisation and market-orientated economic reform in post-Communist countries?

FURTHER READING

On clientelism see Clapham (1982) and Randall and Theobald (1985). For studies of the pressures on governmental officials in semi-competitive states see Grindle (1977). For similar effects in the former Communist states see Dawisha (1980) and M. Matthews (1978).

10 Force and political stability

INTRODUCTION

We have already seen how the state can be defined as the entity holding the monopoly of force within a society. This monopoly presupposes that it has been obtained by the exercise of control over rival centres of force within the social system. These centres may either be regulated or suppressed, through the process termed here *interest arbitration*.

If they are regulated, then they are subject to specific restraints in a code of laws or etiquette, such as those governing the duel or feud in Corsica or Sicily. Beyond this point comes the development of the state in which, as in feudal times in England, the use of force is dispersed throughout many levels, but in each is subject to regulation by that immediately above, and the general arbitration of a code of behaviour recognising obligations to the community as a whole.

If the centres are completely suppressed, then force has to be used to suppress them. In either case, there will remain at the government's disposal a regular corps of specialist users of force to defend the national territory. This performs a useful dual function. Though the socialisation of the regulated community involves members inhibiting their aggressive instincts with the aid of mechanisms of sublimation such as sporting contests, there are always some members who lack the ability to fall in line. Some can be usefully employed in the police or armed forces.

POLICE FORCES

There are a number of distinct ways in which states use forcible restraints on adults, the principal of these being directed in all cases towards those who break the formal laws of society. In assigning to these a number of levels at which force is applied, the first and most effective, though of relatively recent origin, is that of the *police*.

A police force exists to provide for the use of actual physical constraints by the state to enforce its norms on others, in the belief that society's survival as a community is at stake. The law recognises the differences between offences by assigning stated penalties, but the fact that a penalty is fixed at all means that all are in some degree acts hostile to the accepted order of society, whether the crime is stealing a pile of old banknotes, or hitting an old lady over the head in a country post office. In theory all are punished appropriately, since the alternative is to allow the will of the anomic individual to prevail over that of society. However, in practice there are two stages in this process: identifying and capturing the criminal, and successfully bringing him or her to punishment, and the efficacy of all police forces, therefore, depends to a large part on the *indirect* effect the threat of arrest is believed to have.

Hence a great deal depends on what the norms of the society are, and what the successive regimes that direct the state choose to make laws about. Laws for the maintenance of the society or the state are in a different category from laws for the maintenance of the regime. Though there is general agreement that there will always be some laws to ensure the maintenance of regimes, there is a vast difference in the perceived desirability of regimes, and how far regimes see themselves as being indispensable.

There are two broad types of police organisation in modern states, often termed the 'Anglo-Saxon' and the 'Continental' (Cramer, 1964).

The 'Anglo-Saxon' form derives from the experience of medieval England as formalised in the Statute of Winchester (1285) which made citizens collectively responsible for aiding the King's officers in enforcing the apprehension of criminals. At the time when other European countries were developing a regular police force, however, in the seventeenth century, England was reacting to the unpleasant experience of martial law as administered by Cromwell's major-generals. Consequently the introduction of a uniformed constabulary was delayed until the beginning of the nineteenth century, and, characteristically, was tried out first in Ireland (1787). Even after the formation of the Metropolitan Police for the capital in 1829, the rural areas of the country had to wait nearly thirty years for the formation of a police force to be made compulsory (1856).

Characteristic of the 'Anglo-Saxon' police is that it is loose and decentralised in organisation; its members are limited in their powers, are normally uniformed and identifiable, and in Great Britain and the Republic of Ireland they do not carry firearms except with special training and specific permission. In England the Home Secretary is the police authority for the capital only; in the rest of the country his powers are those of an inspector rather than a commander. In the United States police are a state and not a federal responsibility. There is no national police force and a federal investigation agency, the FBI, was not created until 1924. Many cities have their own police force.

The 'Continental' form is derived from the experience of France above all European countries. There had been a police force in the capital, Paris, from time immemorial, but its powers began to increase dramatically at the end of the Middle Ages, and in 1667 the King's Lieutenant of Police 'ruled the city despotically and had jurisdiction over beggars, vagabonds and criminals' (Cramer, 1964: 292). The equation of crime, disorder and dirt is highly suggestive. The police had the power of summary arrest and fining on the spot for infringements of the law, and the Crown retained the right to hold prisoners without trial indefinitely. The French revolutionary governments, though they began by breaking this system, soon re-created it, and put in charge of the new and extended police organisation a Minister of the Police 'responsible for the safety of persons and property, for the maintenance of public order and for the security of the state'.

Hence in France there emerged three principal forces: the prefecture of police responsible for the Seine, the national *gendarmerie*, responsible outside the capital and major towns for the internal and external security of the state and so capable of being used as an auxiliary military force, and the *sureté nationale*, organised in urban areas under a Commissaire de Police working under the mayor and prefect of the department. These were merged into the *police nationale* in 1968 (Gregory, 1976). The 'Continental' system is heavily centralised, with responsibility for the whole in a minister. It operates not only in uniform but as a matter of course in plain clothes, its members having exceptional powers denied the ordinary citizen, including the power of imposing summary fines. In addition they are armed, sometimes heavily.

There is in France, in addition, a riot force, the Republican Security Companies (Compagnies Republicaines de Securité – CRS) used in 1958 and 1968 to defend the republic against real or imaginary insurrection, and on many lesser occasions besides to protect the government against the wrath of French farmers.

It should be added that the influence of the French form today derives primarily not from earlier times but from the unifying effect of the Napoleonic Wars, and the admiration for things French in other parts of the world, for example Eastern Europe, the Balkans and Latin America. It was for this reason that the system was copied by the Russians who, under Nicholas I, added the dreaded 'Third Section' or secret police. The term 'police' was so distasteful to the makers of the Russian Revolution, that Lenin and his colleagues (like the Irish) dropped it altogether, and replaced the police with a people's militia. After many vicissitudes the militia was placed under the Ministry of Internal Affairs (MVD) in 1946. Though decentralised somewhat in 1956 following the general move towards de-Stalinisation, it retained until the collapse of the regime in 1991 the general characteristics of the 'Continental' type.

An important difference, however, in the societies' respective attitudes to the police lay in the Soviet assumption of the common responsibility of all citizens to admonish or bring to justice any individual committing even a trivial crime (Cramer, 1964: 403–5). In Cuba after 1959, the organisation of the militia on a block basis, coupled with the trial of offenders before people's courts staffed by lay assessors, reminds us of the revolutionary origins of both systems. From this responsibility, it is only a very short step to the political offence, since the essence of a political offence lies not in its visible damage to person or property, but to the invisible assumptions of the society in question.

STATE SECURITY

If the maintenance of the regime involves the continual use of regular police action to restrain a substantial sector of the population, the legislation maintaining it must be political, and the state can be described as in some degree a *police state* (Chapman, 1970: 15ff.). Restraints of this kind, however, are common in many countries against large groups who are defying the government of the day, such as strikers on railways or in docks, or students demonstrating against what they conceive to be the follies and iniquities of their elders. In South Africa under apartheid, however, the use of police restraint went far beyond this point to involve the persistent regulation of the movement and communication of an unparalleled majority of the population. Pass laws, residence restraint, segregation, were all enforced by the same mechanisms as control parking or apprehend thieves. This use involves the conscious moulding of society by the creation of attitudes and behaviour alien to it. It also had an inevitable effect on the attitudes of the majority of the population towards the police, who were seen as an alien force of occupation.

In response the South African Government justified its use of police power in the name of state security. Any opposition to it could be and frequently was attributed by government apologists to the actions of foreign agencies. This is significant, since almost all societies recognise a special responsibility of police behaviour for state security, and have created specialist branches to handle security matters.

Special police organisations for state security exist to restrain infiltration and espionage activities by foreign nationals who might, using these means, achieve the sort of result normally to be expected only from an overt hostile act of war, or which would enable such an attack to be launched with an effectiveness significantly greater than might otherwise be expected. As befits a complex nation with a traditional distrust of power, the United States divides this function between two main agencies, the FBI and CIA, and several minor ones. In Britain the responsibility rests with a Special Branch of each police force, and above all with that of the Metropolitan Police. In either case, however, the operation of these agencies is supposed to be subject to the overriding control of the state. It is also supposed to be concerned with an *external* threat and not with internal political affairs, though in practice the line between the two gets blurred. It is now known that under its first head, J. Edgar Hoover, the FBI maintained extensive files on the personal affairs of leading politicians (in Britain, too, the Labour Government of Harold Wilson appears to have been the target of hostile activity from self-appointed agents of the security services). It is also known that the CIA, initially concerned with gaining information from and denying information to the Soviet Union (Dulles, 1964), became increasingly involved in clandestine operations of sabotage, assassination and insurrection (Agee, 1975).

A *secret police* is something very different, an organisation that applies the same techniques to the civil population because it fears danger from them regardless of outside influences. The distinction between a secret police and a police force engaged in secret activities may, however, be purely conceptual. The term 'secret' too is misleading. It is not the existence of the secret police that is secret – otherwise it would hardly instil the degree of fear that it does.

In Europe, within living memory, almost all states have suffered from the attentions of a secret police. Its characteristic is that it is no longer merely a body ancillary to the rule-enforcement agencies – the public prosecutor, the courts, and so forth – but is a rule-enforcement agency, having its own volition as to the assignment of prosecution and punishment. It is directly responsible through its bureau chief to the head of government, regulates its own hierarchy, and is concerned with a wide range of activities in the day-to-day operation of the state which are not disclosed to other members of the community. Its ability to use forcible sanctions is thus limited only by the resources available, and the ingenuity of its members.

The secret police, therefore, is an output mechanism entirely divorced from the input functions generated in the society as a whole. Not only, however, does it act to screen out pressures on the decision-makers, but it performs an even more difficult task in attempting to create the impression of spontaneous political support from the masses for a policy prefabricated by the elite. This particular form of output activity can conveniently be termed *input control*. As such, it does not fit exactly within either the terminology of Easton or of that of Almond's developmental model of the extractive and regurgitative processes of government (Calvert, 1969b). Easton, it is true, does make provision for the concept of 'gatekeepers' limiting the degree to which pressures affect the decision-making process, but the context makes it clear he is primarily concerned with the orderly transaction of business as represented by forms, procedures, committees etc. (Easton, 1965: 122). Like him, Almond retained the basic assumption that the original fount of power is located in the mass, and not in the elite (Almond, in Almond and Coleman, 1960: 7). While this may be true in fact in most cases, and in theory in all, it is not true in fact in all. Input control ensures that only favourable inputs, e.g. supports, are felt in the system as a whole, that is, among all citizens in their political roles.

The other important attribute of secret police, apart from the free use of forcible restraints, is the acquisition and monopoly of a centralised bank of data on members of the community, available for manipulation by the elite for political purposes – that is to say, their own maintenance. The nature of this information is not known to the individual from whom it has been secured. Gossip, misunderstanding, error therefore maintain a status in it equivalent to fact, and may be preferred to it as more exactly conforming to the needs of the state.

The maintenance and extension of this sort of information are greatly enhanced by quasi-military status, such as that enjoyed by the SS in Hitler's Germany (1933–45) or the NKVD in Stalin's Russia (1928–53), both of which maintained paramilitary units as political 'shock troops' for use in actual warfare. The NKVD's successor, the KGB, still maintains frontier troops among its responsibilities. In turn, these are to be distinguished from military intelligence organisations such as the German Field Security Police or the Chief Intelligence Directorate of the Soviet Army; military units on the regular establishment engaged in military intelligence duties. They are also different from the category of paramilitary forces other than secret police (Wolin and Slusser, 1957).

PARAMILITARY FORCES

There is nothing particularly secret about the paramilitary police forces of Malaysia and Thailand. Nevertheless, they exercise very different political roles within the community, despite their common origin in the intention to maintain a force other than the military which could be engaged in counter-terrorist activities and the suppression of 'bandits'. That of Malaysia is a professional organisation, used openly in armed combat against insurgents during the Malayan Emergency (1948–59) (Short, 1973: 285–91; Wang, 1966). That of Thailand is a paramilitary police force similarly engaged and similarly equipped with sophisticated weapons, such as tanks and machine-guns, but which, because of the nature of the political process in that country, additionally became an alternative power base after 1946 and as such the major strength of Luang Pibul, who dominated Thai politics for a generation, and was fully engaged in both the abortive coup of 1949 (Coast, 1953) and the successful revolution of 1957.

Paramilitary force can be used against a wide range of possible 'enemies of the government', and in certain circumstances very effectively. Equally it can form the active force of a militia-based revolutionary organisation, perhaps the type example being the *fasci di combattimento* (fighting bands) from which the Italian Fascisti of Mussolini took their name. Hitler's stormtroopers (SA) similarly played a key role in destroying his enemies in the early stages of his rise to power. Once he had succeeded they became a danger to him and were in turn annihilated by the rival SS in the Röhm *putsch* of 1934. The consequences for the unnecessary weakening of the system were particularly well exemplified by the rivalries of the Cicero affair (Delarue, 1964), which rendered much of the high-quality intelligence gained from it totally useless.

MILITARY FORCES

The last resort of government, in internal as well as external matters, is the military, the 'ultimate argument of kings'. Their employment within the community, however, is restricted by a number of factors: their need to maintain combatant status in the event of foreign attack, the disproportionate effect of their powerful weapons, and their size, not easily accommodated in the absence of special barracks and cantonments in the appropriate regions of the state. These attributes are capable of generating a considerable amount of hostility, as when the billeting of troops on the local inhabitants of the American colonies became a major grievance of the American Revolution. At the same time they give rise to important theoretical considerations which must be considered in the broader context of the phenomenon known as *militarism*.

It should be noted in passing, however, that effective as the military may be at dispersing demonstrations and strike-breaking, by substituting for the strikers in the performance of distribution functions, in protecting the personnel of government against a *coup d'état* or assassination they are not only useless, but are themselves dangerous as a focus for disaffection.

Militarism

The phenomenon of militarism is hence of great importance in the understanding of politics over the greater part of the earth's surface. It is normally found in the army, rather than in the other armed forces. Navies, vital to, and therefore of vast weight in, the politics of Britain, the United States, Portugal, Greece, Argentina, Brazil and Chile, have in general acted symbolically through their admiralty establishments, rather than from actual physical strength, since ships once at sea were effectively out of touch with domestic affairs. Air forces had little independent weight before 1945. They remained (and remain) critically dependent on highly specialised land bases for refuelling and maintenance. The army formed the ultimate defence in most other countries, and being land-based and stationed usually close to the capital, could exercise all their power if they chose to do so, and in fact frequently did. They were, after all, equally open to the influence of politicians anxious to obtain their support (Stepan, 1971).

There are two types of militarism which must be carefully distinguished. There is 'military' militarism – militarism among the military personnel themselves, and 'civilian' militarism – militarism among the civilian population, a distinction first made by Alfred Vagts (1959).

Military militarism is a caste pride, a pride in the glory, honour, power and prestige of the military forces. This type of militarism, however, is not just the normal pride of belonging to a well organised force, but an exaggerated sense of remoteness and of superiority over the outside world in all aspects, so that those things which the military do not undertake are considered to be things not worthwhile for society as a whole. Military militarism, then, tends to arise in one of two sets of circumstances.

The first is when, for whatever reason, their ambitions become extended to the point of becoming conterminous with the limits of the ambitions of the state itself; that is to say, when the whole end, existence and pride of the state is seen by them to be the concern of the army and the army alone. Such was the case in Imperial Germany (Craig, 1955), or in Japan after the Meiji Restoration, both ambitious to become 'Great Powers' in the fashion that a rather oversimplified view of European history had taught them was the approved method. This was to wage wars of imperial expansion, and the view was oversimplified because it was not necessary in fact to wage war with any real vigour in order to succeed, but only to give the impression of doing so.

The alternative situation is when the military feel that they have been betrayed by the civilians – as in the United Kingdom under Lloyd George (Callwell, 1927), in France following the disaster of 1940 (Werth, 1956), or in Egypt after the humiliation of 1948, when their government accepted the Anglo-Egyptian Treaty, and their forces were so conspicuously and ridiculously ineffective against the apparently amateur army of the nascent state of Israel (Neguib, 1955). This belief can easily lead to the conclusion that the army should take over the state to regain its position, as did José Antonio Primo de Rivera in Spain following its military defeat at the Riff in North Africa (1923);

to a long-term process of military politicisation, as in Egypt before 1952; or to an effort by the military to provide alternative bases for 'grandeur' as in Egypt with Israel in 1970, or in France with Algeria in 1958.

Civilian militarism is something rather different. It may afflict either the elite or the mass of the society, or in extreme cases both. It is a nationalist pride in crude power – in Vagts' words 'self-immolation on the altar of violence' (1959: 22) – a feeling that the army is well deserving of the state, and should be rewarded with the unconditional support of the population on whose behalf it fights. This state of mind, a vital prerequisite of total war in modern states dependent for their deployment of force on conscript armies, has great drawbacks even then.

There have, of course, in every age been people who are exceptionally bellicose. There are thousands more who like vicarious excitement. There are also, in modern times, millions more who in times past have taken part in military service or training; of these some join the ranks of the armchair strategists and others (despite the evidence of their eyes) would be prepared to think the efficiency of a state could be improved by its militarisation. It may not be just nostalgia, of course, for it all depends on what aspect of civilian life they are using for comparison. But civilian militarism goes beyond approval of the military or even beyond applause. It implies extremism in its support, being more militaristic than the soldier in the front line.

There are four main examples of civilian militarism:

1. Extreme civilian support for the armed forces in time of war. In the First World War in Britain women pinned white feathers on men in civilian clothes, to shame them, as they thought, into fighting. In the United States sauerkraut was renamed 'liberty cabbage'. In the Second World War, allied insistence on unconditional surrender, though morally well-intentioned, helped prolong the war by offering no incentive for other German leaders to overthrow Hitler.
2. The belief of civilian politicians that they have special qualities as military leaders, strategic planners or even tacticians. In the Second World War each of the major Allied leaders, Churchill, Roosevelt and Stalin, assumed military expertise he had not got, though not surprisingly each was, on occasion, right to overrule more specialist advice in the light of political strategy (Vagts, 1959: 463–9). Fortunately, their chief opponent had even less knowledge, not solely because of his own inadequacies but also from the struggles of his lieutenants, though the nominal leader of Japan was a sailor and a military appointee. In 1956 Khrushchev complained that Stalin planned the defence of the

Soviet Union on a globe rather than on a proper map, while historians have attributed at least part of the responsibility for Allied disasters in Italy to Churchill's desire to relive the unsuccessful Gallipoli expedition of 1915.

3. The voluntary election by civilians of a military leader as civil head of state or of government, often after a successful war. Examples from the United States alone are George Washington, Andrew Jackson, William Henry Harrison, Zachary Taylor, Ulysses S. Grant, James Garfield, Theodore Roosevelt and Dwight D. Eisenhower. In major crises the military virtues are those sought for – the willingness to make quick decisions and the zest for action. But in day-to-day matters, it seems clear that military training is regarded as an essential part of citizenship for a political aspirant, as witness the effect of 'PT 109' on the fortunes of John F. Kennedy or the emphasis on his own military record by President Bush when seeking re-election.
4. Support by civilians for military dictatorship, whether or not coupled with aggressive war, concentration camps and so forth.

The incidence of militarism is variable, and though it depends greatly on time and historical circumstance, it clearly has an important relationship to the society in which it is found and hence to that society's political system. S.E. Finer argues that the tendency to intervene will vary, as between liberal democracies, developing states, or the Communist regimes (Finer, 1962: 86–9).

In a developing country the perceived emergency implies a strong tendency towards the adoption of democratic Caesarism. The prevalent form of militarism is military. The forces in such countries – whether in Asia, Latin America or Africa – have a pride in their prowess which does not necessarily derive from recent combat as, in many cases, for geographical or other extraneous reasons, the opportunity has not arisen. Until recently, however, the fact of independence implied an important historic role for the forces. They had the role of guardians of the state thrust upon them, in their opinion, because they saw themselves as the ones who had given birth to it. Second, the forces in those countries – primitive as they might appear in the light of modern technological innovations – have an important claim to the principal reservoir of technological expertise within them. Their capacity for force is quite high enough, for the rifle as a marksman's weapon has not improved substantially in the last fifty years and the aeroplanes and machine-guns of the Second World War were quite good enough to kill more people than form the entire population of any African country but Nigeria. But it is the developments ancillary to these that matter.

The chief aim of education in developing countries tends to be towards the well-qualified specialist. The shortage is so great that the scientist must be given precedence over the technician, while the technicians are so scarce that the military can easily monopolise them. The services need medicine, communications, engineers, surveyors, and they have to supply them for themselves. The example of the US Corps of Engineers, and the way in which the provisions of Congress on the delimitation of land were actually carried out by the bowie knife, the Colt 45, the telegraph, the heliograph and coils of barbed wire, or the role of the soldier in developing north west India and modern Pakistan, Iraq and Egypt, has its parallels in the Amazonas region of Brazil today. Here the army maintains communications, surveys geographical formations, watches for infiltrators, and teaches civics classes by turn. In Ecuador, Bolivia and Peru too, the army is often the sole agency of government apparent to the tribesmen, who see it as the agency of miracles in an inscrutable mixture of condign punishment for misdeeds and sudden cures of sick children and animals (see Bourricaud, 1970: 313–15). The military of developing countries have been viewed as the chief agency of national unity (Yugoslavia) or even of revolution (China).

In consequence, the defence ministers of such states are in a particularly strong political position, which they do not fail to take advantage of as often as they might. The opposite situation, of course, may be found in the liberal democracies. There the military have been subordinated to the civilian power because of the professionalisation made necessary by technical advances. This professionalism removes the military from the community in a way equivalent to that in which the conditions of service overseas on behalf of an expanding power have removed them in a physical sense. Such remoteness, of course, goes far to end military interference in government. No one would expect, however, that it would be totally removed.

The liberal democracy finds that the military operates at once as the largest consumer of finance and as the most powerful lobbyist. Since Elizabethan times the navy has exercised a powerful influence on politics in Britain, and its maintenance and development have been key issues. But in modern times the sophistication of weapons makes the forces dependent on a range of specialist services of little relevance to civilian needs, while its vast weapons procurement needs call into play the typically 'modern' preoccupation with economics and the organisation of state production for defence needs. The rivalries between needs, especially between land, sea and air, do however act against one another in the call on political resources.

The Communist states were in a middle situation. Most Communist states were underdeveloped in an economic sense, and so their armed services could be expected to follow the behaviour patterns appropriate to this situation. However the role of the military as the major power in retaining the Communist Party in power in nearly all of them was anomalous. Even as an elite the military could not hope to displace the Communist Party in power, because that would have destroyed the regime's claim to popular support. Moreover the rule of the Party was backed up by a capacity for paramilitary force and rendered more powerful by the ability to exercise the state's right to socialise even within the caste itself, and the schismatic effects of the political police. It could, however, hope to displace individual leaders if they failed to give it due credit and budgetary support. An interesting example is the intervention of Marshal Zhukov in the USSR who positively supported Khruschchev against the 'anti-Party group' in June 1957, and was duly rewarded with a place in the Politburo. He was demoted in October 1957 on charges of 'Bonapartism', and of using his position to weaken Party primacy within the military (Conquest, 1961: 338–9). General Jarusielski used his position as military commander in Poland to intervene to 'protect' his country from direct Soviet intervention.

Militarism in the liberal democracy, therefore, tends to be predominantly a civilian attribute, while in the Communist state it could be either military or civilian.

Military intervention

In his analysis of military intervention in politics, S.E. Finer rightly starts by pointing out that the armed forces have such a substantial advantage in politics that what is surprising is not that they take over governments, but that they ever relinquish them. Intervention, he argues, will depend on both the *opportunity* and the *disposition* of the armed forces to intervene. Almost all forces have the opportunity, but not all have the disposition, and the relationship between the two is a complex one.

Second, he argues, intervention can take place on any one or more of four *levels*.

1. All armed forces act as a *lobby*. Even in NATO the high spending profile of the armed forces make them formidably effective at maintaining their position, as witness the failure of civilian governments since 1989 to recover the so-called 'peace dividend'.
2. Many armed forces have secured virtual *independence from civilian control*, but retain the right to assert a military voice in executive decisions. In modern presidential states the minister of war is often a military appointee or a cypher approved by them, while the armed forces speak though their chiefs of staff directly to the president, whether military or civilian.

3. Intervention by direct military action is commonly used to *displace* civilian governments (or even military ones) through the real or implied use of force, as repeatedly seen in recent years in Haiti.
4. Only rarely, however, as in Brazil (1964), Argentina (1976), or Ghana (1982), do the armed forces choose to *supplant* civilian government completely (Finer, 1962: 70–1).

Finer relates these levels of intervention broadly to types of what he terms 'political culture'. This presents obvious difficulties. Military intervention differs considerably over time in any one country; in 1964, for example, Chile as a democratic presidential state choosing its leaders in competitive elections in a highly aware literate society, would have been regarded as a country of high political culture; by 1974 it was under military dictatorship and all political expression had been suppressed. It seems, therefore, that 'political culture' is the product of military intervention (and other factors) rather than the reverse and the decline in military rule since the early 1980s (see Table 10.1) will bring about long-term changes in political culture only if given time to do so. Moreover it is difficult to see how such a general and imprecise concept can be measured with accuracy.

Other of the now extensive literature on the military role in politics has focused on the nature and origins of the armed forces themselves, and their relationship to the society in which they serve. In Nigeria, for example, the military takeover of 1966 owed much to the persistence of tribal consciousness in the army, among the northerners who felt excluded by the commercially active and politically dominant Igbo (Ibo). The fall and death of William V. Tubman in Liberia in 1980 was born of resentment of the dominant tribe of the interior at the domination of Americanised settlers on the coast. More recently the Serbs and Montenegrins who dominate the officer corps of the former Yugoslav National Army (JNA) have had no hesitation in putting their expertise,

Table 10.1 *Countries with military heads of state at 1 January 1983*

Argentina	Equatorial Guinea	Madagascar	Suriname
Benin	Ethiopia	Mali	Syria
Bolivia	Ghana	Mauritania	Togo
Brazil	Guatemala	Niger	Turkey
Burma	Guinea-Bissau	Pakistan	Upper Volta
Burundi	Indonesia	Paraguay	Uruguay
Central African Republic	Iraq	Portugal	Yemen Arab Republic
	Korea (South)	Rwanda	Zaire
Chile	Liberia	Somalia	(37)
Congo	Libya	Sudan	

backed by heavy weapons, at the disposal of their fellow Serbs in Croatia and Bosnia.

To argue, as some writers have done, that the military act only as the armed wing of a tribe, or indeed of a class, is, on the other hand, to underestimate the profound importance of the army *as an institution* to soldiers, and in particular to the elite who command them (Howard, 1958). The majority of armies are dominated by a relatively small, professionally-trained officer corps. Its recruits are, in terms of their respective societies, largely middle-class, and hence in many cases are drawn from a wide area, and are bound together primarily by institutional ties. It is through the service as an institution, moreover, that they obtain their access to a system of substantial personal privileges, such as pensions, mortgages, credit, cheap goods, clubs, medical attention and, above all, government positions, for it is membership of the institution that guarantees at one and the same time the safety of a general standard, and the opportunity through promotion to gain access to much greater rewards. Military intervention in politics is guaranteed by the need to maintain this institutional structure in the face of competing civilian interests; its persistence is due to the complex interrelationship between the three levels of the *social, institutional* and *personal* interest of the intervenors, such that no one of them can be singled out as *the* cause, nor wholly disentangled from the others (Calvert, 1979, reviewing Luttwak, 1979).

Despite the serious difficulties the political scientist faces in amassing information about active military personnel in many of the most interesting cases, there is much information available. The need to gather information begins with the pre-recruitment stage in an officer's career. What sort of family background, what sort of education, how he came to be chosen for military service, and from what sectors of society, for what reasons he took up arms as a career – all these are questions of great importance, but most countries lack documentation on attitudes of individual soldiers to set beside Morris Janowitz's *The American Soldier* (1960), itself now three decades old. What can be known is what is partly or wholly in the public domain: how well integrated they are, what sort of regiments they form, and what sort of training process is standard, what their officers are like in relation to them, and whether they have special relationships with the officers of other armies. It is also relevant whether or not they are stationed near civilian communities, and if so what sort of arms they have and how they practise with them, and so forth. For the only states in which the military–civilian relationship can be entirely businesslike are those which have maintained a purely alien army, such as the Turkish Janissaries, or have an entirely alien subject population, such as ancient Sparta or modern South Africa. In all other cases the relationship is a two-way one. Nationalism in the citizenry gives the military a key to national sentiment in time of crisis. But the military pay for having an alert militarised populace by becoming subject to the tides and currents of uninformed opinion, so that they themselves become politicised and divided, and so lose their power to alter governments at will.

This power is most often exercised indirectly, by pressure from the military authorities on the constitutional authorities to alter either personnel or policies. If this pressure is unsuccessful, the last resort is to intervene. Intervention, therefore, does not come out of a clear sky; like a thunderstorm, it is preceded by obvious signs of discontent, and often by an ultimatum which leaves the government in no doubt as to the army's view. Only if this is unsuccessful does the last stage of the process of disaffection follow, when the high command of the armed forces agree among themselves how to intervene and what is to follow. When they do act it will then normally be done in such a way as to minimise any chance of civilian obstruction or involvement until the military phase of the action is over, the existing government deposed and a new interim government ready to take over. In fact the efficiency of a military coup lies in precisely this: that the government can be changed without civilians becoming involved. Where common, the process has become so ritualised that in Latin America in the twentieth century no less than three-quarters of all military coups have been carried out without casualties, though considerably higher levels of bloodshed are to be expected in Africa and the Middle East (see Table 10.2).

Though military intervention in this sense is commonplace over much of the earth's surface, only comparatively rarely does it lead to the formation of a *military government*. Having military officers in

Table 10.2 *Stages of military intervention*

Preparation
Alienation of armed forces
Bargaining between major interest groups
Ultimatum to government
Decision to intervene: pre-positioning of troops
Action
Capital sealed off and strong points seized
President siezed and deported
Manifesto issued
Curfew and imposition of martial law
Consolidation
Negotiation for formation of interim government
Decree-laws etc.

government, or even a military president, does not in itself make a government a military government, since civilians are needed to carry out many of the major functions of government whoever is officially in control. Nowhere is this more noticeable than in the economics ministry. Despite the fact that so many military coups are 'justified' on the grounds of the incapacity to manage the economy, almost invariably the person chosen to hold this position after a military coup is also a civilian.

However, in the 'developmentalist' era of the 1960s there was a noticeable shift in attitudes and a new phenomenon emerged, starting with Brazil in 1964. This phenomenon has often been termed 'bureaucratic authoritarianism', a term originally invented by the Argentine Guillermo O'Donnell (1988), whose views derive from Marxism and more particularly from dependency theory.

O'Donnell's theory envisages three stages of development of political systems. In the *oligarchic* stage the popular sector is not yet politicised, and so is neither mobilised nor incorporated in the state structure. In the *populist* stage, the popular sector is mobilised and incorporated. In the bureaucratic-authoritarian state it is then demobilised and excluded. For O'Donnell the bureaucratic-authoritarian state 'guarantees and organizes the domination exercised through a class structure subordinated to the upper fractions of a highly oligopolized and transnationalized bourgeoisie' (O'Donnell, 1988: 31). Within the state structure two groups have decisive weight: specialists in coercion (the armed forces), whose job it is to exclude the 'popular sector' from power, and finance capitalists, whose role is to obtain the 'normalisation' of the economy, which performs the dual purpose of excluding the popular sector from economic power and promoting the interests of large oligopolistic interests. As part of the exclusion policy, social issues are depoliticised by being treated as a matter of narrow economic rationality, and direct access to government is limited to the armed forces, the state bureaucracy and leading industrialists and financiers.

Though applied in the first instance to Brazil, O'Donnell's model was derived from the experience of Argentina between 1966 and 1973, and, not surprisingly, fits it closely. Having failed in 1955 and 1962 permanently to exclude the Peronists from power by simple military coup, the promoters of what was grandiloquently (but not altogether inaccurately) termed 'the Argentine Revolution' in 1966 sought to stay in power for long enough to achieve that objective. However, the term itself is misleading, in that it is military rule not bureaucracy that was its distinguishing characteristic, and the model does not fit the authoritarian regimes imposed in Brazil in 1964 (reinforced in 1968), in Uruguay and Chile in 1973 or in Argentina again in 1976 (Linz and Stepan, 1978). Not only were these states at very different levels of economic development, but in each, Collier (1979) noted, ideological polarisation was so marked that an adequate explanation had to take account of political factors such as the nature of the party system and the strength of organised labour.

Nor were these authoritarian regimes universal. Venezuela's mobilisation came at the end of its period of dictatorship and was accompanied by a deliberate and successful attempt to establish consensus as a basis for democratic government. The same was originally true also for Mexico which, though authoritarian, is closer to the liberal-democratic model than it is to the pattern envisaged by O'Donnell, and has been particularly successful in co-opting potential opposition. Both have relatively diversified and well-developed economies.

Last, the phrase gives insufficient emphasis to the military aspect of these governments, for what distinguished them was not their bureaucratic nature, nor (as O'Donnell argues) the 'transnationalization' of production (for that has also happened in Western Europe, for instance) but the fact that the process was directed by the army and gained its distinctive features from the army's ability to make use of force. For this reason the present writer has suggested the term 'military developmentalism', a term which stresses its analogies with, for example, the military regimes of Egypt, Pakistan or even Thailand.

FORCE AND POLITICAL STABILITY

Revolution, as will be seen in Chapter 11, is often associated with military action and inevitably with military alienation. But it is always a strategic process capable of modification in response to tactical needs. It can therefore be averted by governments by approaching it on an entirely military level, and preventing the combination of the elements which are essential to the use of force against an armed opponent.

No revolution can occur successfully unless it has an efficient leader, an adequate number of followers, a cause to fight for, and means to make its numbers effective. Of these four, the easiest to avoid is the last. The classic instance is the case of the troops that marched through Baghdad on the night of 13–14 July 1958 on their way to the Israeli frontier. For the first time in the history of the state of Iraq they were not disarmed before entering the capital, and the result was the dramatic revolution which dethroned the Hashemite dynasty and established the republic. If the means had not been available, there can be reasonable doubt that this revolution would not have taken place – at least, not in the way that it did (Finer, 1962: 79).

This poses two questions: when military intervention takes place in politics, how far is this a real expression of popular wishes? Is anomic interest articulation the necessary consequence of the blockage of other channels? As already suggested it has been the peculiar sophistication of the twentieth century that men have been able to devise methods of creating the appearance of support, and so isolating the individual who might wish to express views hostile to them and their political programme. In the real world, if a man finds the country is run by the army, and he dislikes the way it is run, he may join the army and try to become a general, or he may take a gun and make for the hills, but he is much more likely to stay at home and mind his own business.

CONCLUSION

Few people who read the press intensively can fail to be impressed, even in Western countries, with what a one-sided picture it presents. When, as in 1967, the news on China comes entirely from Japanese journalists trying to read wall posters in Peking without being seen to look at them, we can all see the difficulties. Only the vote, as the 1970 and 1992 general elections in the UK showed, can tell which, if any, of the public opinion polls has made a correct prediction. When there is no vote, or the vote is invalidated by the fact that military intervention is the normal or even the sole method of changing governments or government personnel, no safe deductions can be drawn. In any case, many years pass without any such intervention succeeding.

Turbulence as such represents part of a very wide nexus of interactions, which in point of fact may only incidentally be concerned with demands on the government. If people are not orientated to expect things from government they may direct their energies towards getting them from one another, and yet be in general agreement that the government is doing the small minimum they want of it as well as can be expected. Political stability is not the same thing as freedom from violence, and it is not as remarkable a thing as the perspectives of journalism sometimes suggest.

KEY CONCEPTS

bureaucratic authoritarianism: for O'Donnell a repressive political system characterised by the institutionalised role of the armed forces in control of the civilian population.

civilian militarism: a feeling among civilians that the army is well deserving of the state, and should be rewarded with the unconditional support of the population on whose behalf it fights.

force: the use of physical coercion.

gatekeepers: for Easton persons or agencies regulating demands on the political system.

military militarism: a caste pride in the glory, honour, power and prestige of the military forces.

secret police: in an authoritarian state a rule-enforcement agency, having its own volition as to the assignment of prosecution and punishment.

socialisation: formal and informal processes by which young people acquire political attitudes and opinions.

violence: the unregulated use of force.

SAMPLE QUESTIONS

What is political stability? How far is it threatened by economic development and change?
Why do Latin American governments have a reputation for instability?
Are newly independent states inherently politically unstable?
Why, despite its traumatic political past, has the stability of the Federal Republic of Germany never seriously been challenged?
Examine the problems in either *Nigeria* or *Ghana of securing the withdrawal of military regimes and the restoration of civilian politics.*
'Power grows out of the barrel of a gun' (Mao Zedong). Discuss.

FURTHER READING

On the police, Brewer (1988) is a good recent comparative study of the police in liberal democracies. Cramer (1964) is dated but spreads its net widely. On the general concept of the 'police state' see Chapman (1970). For intelligence and secret police organisation in the former Communist states, see Wolin and Slusser (1957) and Adelman (1984). Both annual and special reports of Amnesty International give ample evidence (if it were needed) of the use of force by governments to coerce political opponents.

On the role of the military in politics the literature is extensive. Finer (1962) gives a straightforward general framework. Clapham and Philip (1985), Johnson (1964) and Stepan (1971) deal specifically with Latin America and Decalo (1976) with Africa, though each has value for other areas also. The argument for the concept of 'bureaucratic authoritarianism' can be found in O'Donnell (1988).

11 Violence and political change

INTRODUCTION

No political system is ever likely to satisfy the needs of all its citizens. However, where substantial numbers are denied what they believe to be their rights over a long period of time, they are likely to seek a justification for using force to overthrow the existing order and to establish a new one. If they are unsuccessful their actions will be termed a 'rebellion' and they may well pay for their presumption with their lives. If they succeed, they may become the new government, proclaim their movement a 'revolution', order major social changes and rewrite history with themselves at the centre of it.

Comparative politics is concerned with three issues:

1. Why do people rebel?
2. Why do some rebellions succeed and others fail?
3. How likely is it that rebellion will lead to real social change?

THE RIGHT TO REBEL?

The problem of the citizen confronted with a repressive government is one that has been discussed by political philosophers since Plato. The 'right to rebel' has been considered by many to be the ultimate right available to citizens whose civic rights are consistently denied. But it is a different question deciding on what occasion the citizen may legitimately exercise this right, and how, if it is exercised, all the consequences of the action can be legitimate. There are essentially two different and nearly opposed viewpoints.

According to the view of St Thomas Aquinas, accepted today in most countries of Catholic heritage, rebellion is justified provided that the rebel can show – after his achievement – that his action was legitimate; that it had involved the use of the minimum possible force by which its ends could be achieved; and that no other resort was open to him (d'Entreves, 1959: 161, 181–5). A similar view was arrived at independently by Islamic writers (Rosenthal, 1962: 97).

According to the later view of John Locke, however, at the time of the so-called Glorious Revolution in England, legitimacy is an attribute fixed before the event. Rebellion is only justified because the government of the day has lost its legitimacy, and the will of the people at large is more exactly represented by its successor. Any action tending to reduce the influence of the people on their own destinies is not legitimate and is to be opposed (Locke, 1964: 202). This is the view held in Anglo-Saxon countries and their derivates.

Marxist–Leninists were in an anomalous position. They believed that the overthrow of bourgeois government was preordained by the forces of history, and justified by their previous exploitation of the proletariat. On the other hand, once a 'socialist' revolution had taken place, they believed (erroneously, as it turned out) that it could not be reversed and that fellow Communist states had a right and a duty to support the new order (the Brezhnev Doctrine). This shows one of the problems inherent in the study of revolution and rebellion, most of which come back to the basic point that rebellion creates its own legend or *myth*.

For example, it has long been dogma in conservative circles – following Burke and Carlyle – that the French Revolution of 1789 was an upsurge of primitivism among atavistic plebeians. To them, mobs of dirty illiterates delighted in destroying a social order too educated and complicated for them to understand. Recently, the detailed research of the historian George Rudé among the papers of the Paris sections has shown that crowd composition in the street demonstrations was principally drawn from the educated artisan class (Rudé, 1964: 195ff.). Similarly, Marx greeted the Paris Commune of 1871 as the first example of the rising of a self-conscious proletariat, though in fact the *communards* were drawn from all social classes.

The reason for the myth, in the case of a successful revolution, is to support the legitimacy claim of the new government, and in the case of an unsuccessful rebellion, to denounce the action taken as a deviation from the prevailing norms of society. All systems of political thought except the anarchist agree that if a government is legitimate it has the 'right' to suppress those who use force against it. Where violence is 'normal', then the use of force against violence is also 'normal'.

Not surprisingly, therefore, there is a clear relationship between the ability of a government to use coercion and the amount of political violence with which it is likely to be confronted. But the relationship is not a linear one (see Figure 11.1).

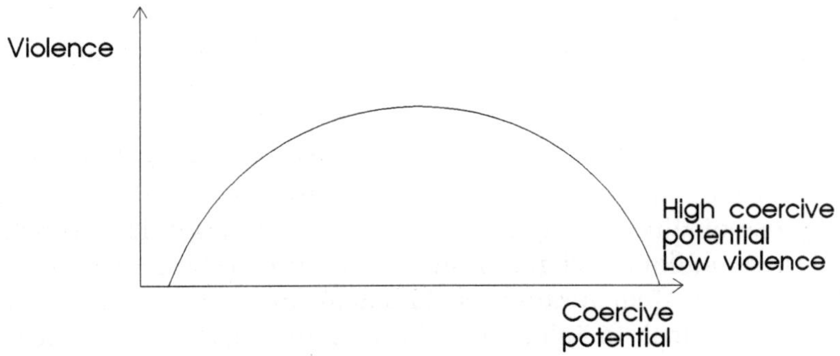

Source: based on Duff and McCamant *Violence and Repression in Latin America*, 1976, pp. 119–22

Figure 11.1 *State coercive potential and political violence*

VIOLENCE AND SOCIAL CHANGE

There is a great deal of anomic activity in any society which is not articulated, the goals of which are not clear in political terms, and which is not so clearly formulated as being within either of these two spheres of justification, if only because, if it does not succeed, it cannot obtain subsequent approval. Indeed any anomic movement which did not aim to strike down the government without delay would probably be suppressed by an efficient government determined to maintain its own power.

It is widely assumed that political and social change are bound up together. Unfortunately this is not the case, and it is therefore very important to distinguish between terms. For the political scientist, the first concern must be with political change: change in government or in regime by the use of force by its own citizens (cf. Tilly, 1978). This may or may not be an act which is a prerequisite of deep-reaching social change. Historically the overthrow of a government was itself termed a 'revolution'. However, for many years there has been a tendency to restrict the term 'revolution' only to those rare historical events in which the fall of governments is followed by profound social change. Hence writers as diverse as Edwards (1927, reprinted 1970), Pettee (1938), Brinton (1938, reprinted 1952), Johnson, C. (1964) and Skocpol (1979) concur on one thing: only movements involving such change qualify for the glorious title of revolution (Calvert, 1970a: 121ff.).

There is much less agreement on just how many instances there are of what have been termed 'the great social revolutions' (Edwards, 1970), but there is almost universal agreement that there have been very few of them. Those that would be generally accepted include England (1640–59), America (1774–89), France (1789–95), Mexico

(1910–20), Russia (1917–29), China (1949–78?) and Cuba (1959). Perhaps a dozen more would be fairly generally recognised – these range from China (1911) and Turkey (1923) through the Nicaraguan and Iranian Revolutions of 1979 (Brinton, 1952; Leiden and Schmitt, 1968; Calvert, 1990a: 4) to the events of 1989 in Eastern Europe and, perhaps, the collapse of the Soviet Union itself in 1991. Many might add the rise of Hitler in Germany (1933). But they would not include long-term evolutionary changes, such as the rise of the gentry in Tudor England or the Meiji Restoration in Japan, in which the element of violence is minimal. In Table 11.1, those more generally recognised are capitalised.

This leaves us the problem of what to call the many political revolutions which occur each year and have no important social consequences, most commonly since either they do not seek to obtain them or have been carried out in order to pre-empt social change and not to achieve it. These events, which are referred to by a variety of names – palace revolutions, coups etc. – can be regarded as being within the norms of society and certainly not as spectacular breaks in its continuity, but they are none the less very important to a student of politics.

Table 11.1 *The great social revolutions?*

Date	Country
1581	The Netherlands
1642	ENGLAND
1688	England
1775	UNITED STATES
1789	FRANCE
1910	MEXICO
1911	China
1917	RUSSIA
1919	TURKEY
1933	Germany?
1949	CHINA
1952	Bolivia
	Egypt
1958	Algeria
1959	CUBA
1968	Peru
1969	Libya
1974	Portugal
1979	IRAN
	NICARAGUA
1989	Czechoslovakia, East Germany, Romania etc.
1991	RUSSIA etc.

WHY DO PEOPLE REBEL?

Violence as such does not necessarily have much political significance. Broadly speaking, the main concern here is with what Russett *et al.* term 'domestic group violence' (Russett, 1964). That is to say, it will arise within the domestic context and not involve foreign intervention; it will involve groups rather than individuals; and either its objectives or its scale or both will be such that it affects the political system significantly. J.C. Davies argues that revolution is most likely to take place when an intolerable gap opens up between what people want and what they actually get (Davies, 1962), and illustrates a common form of this with his well-known 'J-curve' (Figure 11.2).

On the other hand *sub-revolutionary violence* will, by definition, not result in a change of government. There are three forms it is likely to take.

1. *Demonstrations*. Demonstrations are anomic groupings of people moved by a single common interest, controlled either by their own agreement or by leaders, with a limited target of applying pressure to part or whole of the political system and a fairly low level of accompanying violence, at least in the early stages. They may occur anywhere within the territorial limits of the state, but should they occur in the capital the pressures themselves can be sufficient to bring down a weak or discredited government or even topple a regime – as in France in 1830 and 1848, or more recently in Argentina in 1982 following the defeat of the military government in the South Atlantic. Otherwise they

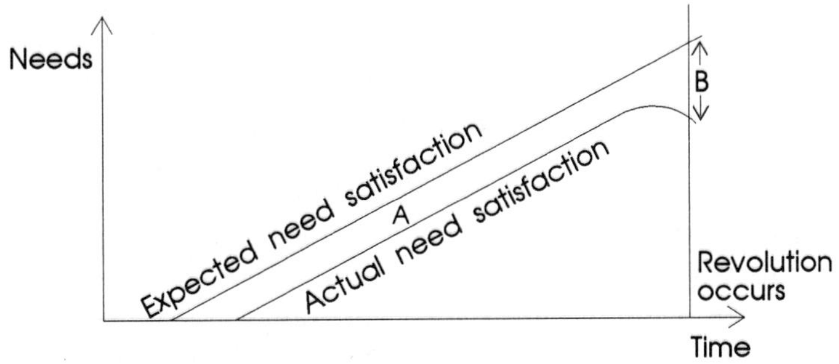

A Tolerable gap between what people want and what they get.
B Intolerable gap between what people want and what they get.

Source: J. C. Davies (1962)
Figure 11.2 Davies' J-curve

are best regarded as short-lived interest groups (see Chapter 5).

2. *Riots.* Demonstrations, however, must be distinguished from riots, which are uncontrolled movements of frustrated opinion, undiscriminating in target. In the countryside such movements are sometimes given the French name *jacquerie*, but in modern states they are unlikely to bring about political change, being removed from the centres of power around the capital. Their methods depend on the nature of weaponry in the country, and their articulation as a movement varies with this and the location of their strength. In the past, when weapons were more or less interchangeable with agricultural implements, it was possible for peasants to take their pitchforks and flails and march upon the local 'Big House' to enforce their demands. Nowadays the farm labourer driving a combine harvester is not in a position to do this. But over the greater part of the world peasants still retain the need to use some kind of cutting or slashing instrument as well as firearms in order to stay alive in tropical or semi-tropical conditions (Stokes, 1959: 300–12). The general opportunities for rural violence on a national scale are very much limited also by the intricate nature of the state and modern industrial society.

Riots in cities show great differences in their political effects, but seldom pose a serious challenge to a confident government sure of the support of its armed forces and police. In Colombia in 1948 the capital was out of control for three days of unrestrained violence and looting (the 'Bogotazo') without the President yielding to it. In Greece in 1965 extensive riots took place in Athens, but had no result in terms of change of government or regime. The riots of 1967 and 1992 in the United States helped discredit the incumbent power-holders, but the frustrations they expressed were speedily absorbed into the normal pattern of presidential campaigning. However, where, as in the United States, there is free sale and distribution of firearms, a new element enters the picture: the possibility of long-term urban violence. Without firearms, this cannot exceed the level of sporadic incidents at weak points in the presence of city government – in dark streets, waste lots, or deserted buildings not subject to regular police patrol, for example. The introduction of firearms clearly amplifies the possibilities considerably, but it has yet to be proved how far it is actually effective outside closed communities such as those of the Chinese in Hong Kong or the dwellers in the shanty towns of Caracas. However, it is sobering to recall that in 1964 Yugoslavia was at the bottom of Russett's list (Russett, 1964: 100) for domestic group violence, together with the United Kingdom.

3. *Terrorism.* Terrorism is the use of force to impart fear with a view to bringing about political or social change. In the quite recent past it has been endemic in at least parts of most of the countries of the world. The nature of terrorism, which may in fact be either spontaneous or organised, is that it is widespread and effective across the political spectrum in securing publicity and influencing public opinion. However, terrorism is a strategy born not of strength but of weakness in political terms, and it seldom if ever results in a change of government without the assistance either of external intervention or of a mass uprising.

REVOLUTION AND POLITICAL CHANGE

There are, therefore, many reasons why people rebel, but all these actions fall short of revolution. Revolution is violence *plus political change*: it brings about a fall of government or a change of regime. As long as violence falls short of this point it is a means of interest articulation and aggregation, though of a nature in the long run incompatible with the maintenance of ordered government. It corresponds, therefore, to levels of activity within the regular political system: demonstrations being similar in action to pressure groups, riots to the parliamentary aspect of the political party, and terrorism to the mass organisation attempting to build a groundswell of political support. It therefore can be politically significant in application to regular processes as well as those of violence. The key factors that differentiate revolution from rebellion, therefore, are *leadership* and *organisation*; that is to say, its political attributes.

This raises the question of how to assess resultant changes in the long term. Any theory of the development of the political system first has to deal with a number of snags. For one there is the problem of identifying the conceptual boundary of the political system in application to the real world. Then there is the problem of delimiting the period within which development is to be considered and its relationship to earlier political formations in the same area. Third, there is the question of how the units of development are to be measured. 'Development' is itself a complex of concepts only some of which can be reduced to expressions in terms of quantifiable indicators. If there is no general agreement as to what the system is, or how long it has lasted, there is not likely to be much that can usefully be said about its development.

This is the problem facing Almond in his essays on developmental theory. As has been shown, he goes some way towards considering the third, avoids the first, and leaves practical application to the reader.

Using the concept of revolution used by him elsewhere – in *The Politics of the Developing Areas,* 1960 – it seems likely that the major discontinuities, and hence the 'start' and 'finish' of his conceptual systems, are in the major revolutions, in periods of social rather than political change. This concept of discontinuity is clearly inapplicable. Two things stand in the way of its acceptance: the prevalence of political change through violence, and the prevalence of violence without political change. For if neither violence nor political change is separately the mark of discontinuity in a political system, no combination of the two can effect such a discontinuity. To put it in terms of an example, the French Revolution marks a discontinuity in the history of France, but not in its political system, which continued to exist throughout, since it was broken neither by the violence employed nor by the changes of government which occurred during it.

If sub-revolutionary violence forms a 'normal' part of the political process, the process of political change that results from it, or from the actual transition between government, may be distinguished from it. Under the umbrella term 'revolution' there are four concepts to be distinguished.

1. A *process* by which social changes occur, leading towards political change through violence or the convincing threat of violence.
2. The political *event,* in which a government or regime is actually changed.
3. The *programme* that a post-revolutionary government pursues, which has links with both process and event.
4. The *myth* of revolution, the symbolic value it holds in the integration or disintegration of the community. The special quality of the myth, which seems to be embodied in the sociologists' concept of social revolution, is that it suggests in aggregate that political order is at once permanent and discontinuous, since it owes its final form to a species of consensus between conservative and radical interpretations (Calvert, 1970b: 4).

An integrated model of this kind recognises most usefully the functional role of revolution in society. It rests on conflict: the conflict between demands and supports, the conflict between elite (decision-makers) and mass (the public), the conflict, above all, between the political system and the social system as a whole. In the flow pattern of such a model, revolution forms one kind of interaction among the many patterns of positive and negative interchange between these last: the maximisation of demands (or negative inputs) and the minimisation of supports (or positive inputs).

In the political sense, then, revolution is first and foremost an *event*, and may be suspected in any violent change of ruler by subjects. There are obviously vast variations in the surrounding events, but in the actual change a certain rigidity is apparent. Certain attributes can be recognised as being important, and can be used therefore for classification.

To begin with the event implies the use of a certain amount of violence by revolutionaries, opposed on occasion by a quantity of force on the part of the regime. The fact of success implies that the revolutionary violence has attained a point which can be termed the *minimum necessary force (MNF)*. This point is crucial to the differentiation of revolutionary from sub-revolutionary activity. Failure to reach MNF implies the failure of the movement in question: excess over it, it may reasonably be hypothesised, will result in ancillary phenomena in the political or social consequences of the event (Calvert, 1970a: 32). After all, those revolutions which have been associated most closely with developed social phenomena have been those in which the government overthrown exercised power at so low a level that any force used to overthrow it was proportionately almost infinite. The force employed is a measurable quantity, measurable either as the number of troops mobilised or as the number actually deployed at any given moment, multiplied by their capacity to use force and the degree of their spatial concentration.

A revolutionary event must occupy a certain time period. Within this, three time phases can be distinguished:

1. a period of *preparation* integral with and related to the social process of disaffection;
2. the *action* itself, which can be termed *the assault phase*; and
3. a period of *consolidation* with the promulgation of the post-revolutionary programme (Goodspeed, 1962).

The nature of the assault period is the determinant of the transition itself, and the duration of it – usually brief – is a second criterion for classification. The reason is that the superiority of power to be obtained by the revolutionary force has to be effective during this period or, more specifically, during a period, termed the critical time, which in a successful revolution falls wholly within this period. Beyond the conclusion of the assault phase, it should be noted, the use of force is no longer directed specifically at the defeated government, but as in the case of any other government of whatever age, against all possible and probable enemies of the new regime.

A third attribute is the *level* on which force is deployed, that is to say the extent of the geographical space over which the action takes place, which can be termed the *arena*. This action must be related to the force available if MNF is to be achieved, and the option may exist for initiating hostilities on either of two levels, or on any level, depending on resources. In order of power required, revolutionary action may be directed against the executive, the government, the capital or a province. Each brings its particular hazards.

The immobilisation of the *executive* requires speed and secrecy of planning, but the least actual force.

Capture and overthrow of the *government* involves a number of personnel, some of whom are of little importance, but others of whom have authority without formal rank. These have to be rapidly and accurately located and captured, and synchronisation of action becomes a major consideration if reinforcements are not to become a hazard. Failure to do so results in the sort of consequences that followed the breakdown of the plot to overthrow the government of Abraham Lincoln, which was successful only in so far as it resulted in the death of Lincoln himself (Havens, Leiden and Schmitt, 1970: 43). A major social revolution of such a type was the Bolshevik seizure of power in November 1917.

A movement directed at securing control of the *capital* involves a number of considerations, but that of force is obviously most important. Since it assumes that a complete superiority of force will be achieved in the key administrative area of a country, which will not be challenged in the critical time by forces brought in from the provinces, it is the form normally favoured by military movements. It is effective because it gains control of the area from which the people at large expect leadership, and that on which the communications net is centred. It was also the scene of the French Revolution of 1789 and hence of its many nineteenth-century imitators.

The seizure and exercise of governmental functions in a *province*, which requires the most force of any type of revolution, is intended to put pressure on this area indirectly. It can therefore start with small beginnings, but depends on remoteness from the centre of power to attract superior forces before government troops arrive to engage it. It can then hope, if the government does not yield, to strike at the capital and put it out of action directly. This is the principle behind the guerrilla warfare that led to the Chinese Revolution of 1949 and the Cuban Revolution of 1959.

For obvious theoretical reasons, the Marxist writers on revolution advocate movements in which large-scale mobilisation occurs of the masses. Since Marxists have traditionally been opposed, for fear of Bonapartism, to the coup, they have laboured under the necessity of maintaining unusually high force levels in their attempts to gain power. Lenin himself was prepared to adopt the coup as an opportunistic short cut, however, with outstanding success (Goodspeed, 1962: 70ff.). Significantly, none of the so-called Communist 'revolutions' in Eastern Europe after 1945 took place independently of the presence of a large occupying force of Soviet troops.

Reliance on peasant guerrilla movements, advocated by Mao Zedong (Schram, 1963: 202–88) and Che Guevara (1967: 15), appeared both in China and Cuba to succeed through direct pressure in bringing about the collapse of central resistance. However, in both cases other factors have to be taken into account. In China the collapse of the Kuomintang came only after eight years of war against the Japanese, and the power vacuum left by the Japanese surrender. A similar power vacuum was largely responsible for the success in 1945 of the Communists in Vietnam, and the followers of Sukarno in Indonesia, their government being established in each case before the return of the colonial power and thus able to provide a geographical base for guerrillas' resistance to reconquest (Kahin, 1964: 392–5). In Cuba, the guerrilla war formed the pretext for a massive urban uprising, and it was the combination of the two, and not just the guerrilla campaign on its own, that led to governmental collapse. It was the fact that the Cuban revolution occurred in an area that was already acquainted with revolutionary movements on all levels which pointed up its regularities, and made possible the assimilation of Marxist revolutions to a general theory.

It should be added, however, that difficulties lie in the way of precise application of force analysis (even retroactively) which have nothing to do with the type advocated, but are purely practical. Information about troop numbers and movements is classified information, and by the time security has been lifted, the recollections of witnesses may be unable to rectify the propaganda versions of numbers engaged. In any case, actual numbers of forces employed are rarely used, vague expressions such as 'regiments', 'companies', 'detachments' being capable of multiple interpretations, even assuming that they were regular formations up to their roster strength. It is for this reason that Lewis F. Richardson chose to set the precedent of measuring the impact of violent events in terms of 'magnitude'. The magnitude of an event is simply the total number of casualties caused by it, as measured on a simple logarithmic scale (Richardson, 1960: 6–7).

What sort of statements can this analysis enable us to make on the nature of actual revolutions? First of all, there is from observation alone no clear link between economic development and the absence of violence in politics, though it is clear that there is some link. Comparison on the one hand between Argentina and Uruguay indicates that a highly developed agricultural country, backed by a substantial industrial complex with money to spend on social and other services, does not necessarily enjoy peaceful politics, or even civilian government. Comparison on the other between Chile and Mexico suggests that it is not necessary to have a large-scale social revolution in order to achieve equality and social justice. Personalities in power are very important, as the destruction of civilian rule in Chile after 1973 demonstrates.

The presence of violence, however, imposes its own necessities. In particular, given the need to adapt to changing times, military intervention all too easily becomes essential where it is normal. Otherwise the operation of a system in which political change is achieved substantially by violent means cannot be continued in face of the non-participation of the monopolists of the means of coercive force. Contrary to the impression that violence is a sign of instability, governments seem to change sometimes more and sometimes less frequently in countries in which violent politics is the norm. It does not seem to make much difference in either case how the change is achieved provided that it is seen to have occurred. A dictator who changes his Cabinet frequently may fulfil the desire for new faces as effectively as the process of frequent elections in other countries, and the value of federalism where it operates, or elective local government where it does not, must at least partly be the facility it offers for frequent lesser changes and the channelling of the impulse into manageable form. But evidently not all states value leadership changes, preferring to demonstrate one leader of accepted skills or outstanding personal qualities, such as Mao, Nasser or Kenyatta.

Third, it should be noted that the impulse towards violence results in frequent and fairly simple coups, sometimes following one another in a *sequence*. The 'great social revolutions', as Lyford P. Edwards named them, such as the French, English and Russian, and even in some states the American, were composed in part of coups. As discussed above, the relationship between these coups and social reform is contradicted on both sides, but on sequential grounds Haiti, Panama and the Dominican Republic all offer equally dramatic examples without the social change (Calvert, 1970b: 181ff.).

The difference is often attributed to a particular combination of social circumstances, which impelled into power a set of moderate social reformers who succeeded in arousing expectations and making the burden of the past intolerable, without at the same time taking steps sufficient to satisfy resultant demand. This was the pattern of Brinton's (1938) comparative historical study of the English, American, French and Russian Revolutions. In it he drew parallels between the four periods studied, each of which had been characterised by a move towards political extremism. He concluded that the Russian Revolution, too, might in due course be expected to enter the period he termed 'Thermidor', the winding-down of revolutionary fervour and consolidation of a new and more efficient state system.

But moderate reform does not necessarily result in the rise and successful accession to power of extremists; it may, and often does, result in a counter-coup by irate conservatives. Besides, history abounds with examples in which moderate reform satisfied demands of a potentially revolutionary character: the passage of the Great Reform Act in Britain in 1832 was one. Even if extremists accede to power, they need not necessarily follow their first reprisals with that organised reign of terror, of which Iraq and Egypt are recent cases in point (Khadduri, 1970: 137), but may, like the Nicaraguan Sandinistas (FSLN), seek to maintain a dialogue with their political opponents. The presence of a threatening external enemy, however, does appear to have been a factor in cases in which terror has been adopted, despite the great weakness of the internal opposition, but external enemies have acted to exacerbate suspicion that this weakness was feigned (but see also Walt, 1992). The numbers however, are small, and the suspicion remains that the revolutionary by nature expects to find hostility, and if he does not tends to create it in order to justify his philosophy of violence. There is, after all, the temptation to extend an apparently easy (because successful) method of achieving power into a means of maintaining it.

There must also be taken into account the panic reaction of people who do not wish to be 'liberated' from the traditional ways that they know which, after all, are basically the means by which they have been taught to survive (Fromm, 1960). In such circumstances even leaders may be nervous about unpredictable changes of opinion.

REVOLUTION AND SOCIAL CHANGE

The very limited number of examples of the so-called 'great social revolutions' has strengthened the tendency to study them through the methodology of comparative history. Since the Second World War the emergence of new states has been accompanied by the occurrence of new social revolutions, but as the number of cases available for study has expanded, authors have still tended to study them in the same traditional context, using much the same criteria. Thus Leiden and Schmitt (1968) basically repeated the work of Brinton, taking as their case studies four examples that had either not previously been studied in a comparative context or which had occurred too recently: Mexico, Turkey, Egypt and Cuba. In a theoretical introduction they did, however, recognise the work of social scientists in seeking to derive from such case studies some more general propositions which would be useful in application to other cases.

Moore (1969) is not really concerned with modern societies or the theory of revolution at all, but the way in which pre-modern societies had evolved in the way they had. His book, which was widely popular, uses six case studies, contrasting the experiences of Britain, France and the United States, with those of Japan, China and India, and throughout lays special emphasis on the importance of land-ownership and the role of the peasantry. Moore, moreover does not hesitate to assert that violence and coercion have played as much of a role in the formation of Western democracies as in the making of Communist states or the rise of fascism: the differences between them, he asserts, can be found in the different nature of their revolutionary experiences.

Dunn (1972, 2nd edition 1989) uses eight case studies: Russia, Mexico, China, Yugoslavia, Vietnam, Algeria, Turkey and Cuba. Though treated on the basis of secondary sources and hence on a rather high level of generality this book is informative, and the introduction and conclusion do challenge many of the traditional generalisations about revolution in an interesting and provocative way. Dunn describes the variety of methods by which power has actually been achieved. But he does not link the achievement of power to the nature of the outcome, except in the sense that both are recognised to be authoritarian.

Unlike earlier 'comparative' studies, such as those of Brinton and Dunn, Skocpol (1979) does not examine each of her case studies in turn and them sum up her findings. Instead, following a theoretical introduction, the first part of her book is a very detailed comparative treatment of three revolutions: the French Revolution of 1787–1800, the Russian Revolution of 1917–21 and the Chinese Revolution of 1911–49. The Marxist concept of class relations and class conflict forms the basis of the analysis in each case. She emphasises, however, that this concept can become effective only through the modification of political structures. All existing theories of revolution she claims are voluntarist; this modification, she argues, must be seen in structural terms and hence non-voluntarist. Second, revolution cannot be understood simply on the national level. International as well as national conjunctures have to be favourable for a major social revolution to occur. But international conjunctures alone are not a sufficient explanation, so there is no support here for Immanuel Wallerstein and the world systems' theorists. Third, classes are not the sole actors, and states not simply the agents of the dominant class. States are both potentially autonomous and coercive. In fact, influenced by Ellen Kay Trimberger, Skocpol's concept of the great social revolutions is one of 'revolutions from above' led by elites in the name of the masses. Though social revolutions arise from mass action in the pre-revolutionary situation, the programme of reform that follows them is seen as imposed by elites operating not only within the limitations of the domestic context but the international conjunctures of the world economic system, in particular, the structures of the world economy and the changing range of models available for borrowing. These are important, not because they influence the people, but because they influence their rulers.

Among social scientists, there are three main interpretations of revolution to be found: psychological theories, sociological theories and political theories.

Psychological theories help explain the motivation of individuals in revolutionary situations, but are not really appropriate as modes of explanation of mass action. Early writers focused on the actions of crowds, but today at least these play a limited role. The role of 'relative deprivation', stressed by William Gamson (1975) and T.R. Gurr (1970), is, however, undoubtedly significant, as it relates directly to the applicability of the Davies J-curve mentioned earlier.

Sociological theories of revolution assume that the stability of society depends on the social order continuing to fulfil the requirements of its citizens. If it fails to do so, consensus on the values of society is lost, and with the failure of consensus the way is open for a mass rejection of the existing order. Thus for one of the first of the comparative writers, Lyford P. Edwards, revolution was of social rather than political significance, and this led him to play down the elements of physical violence and transfer of power. 'The overthrow of the monarchy and feudal system in France was not caused by the French Revolution,' he argued. 'The Revolution simply made evident the fact that the real power in France had passed into the hands of the middle class.'

George Sylvester Pettee introduced as an explanation of revolution the term 'social disequilibrium'. Employing the terminology of Parsonian sociology, society is here seen as fundamentally stable, and equilibrium is that normal state of society to which it will tend to return after crises or disturbances. However, societies are constantly changing. If the equilibrium point is moving, how is it possible to determine when a society has become so disequilibrated that fundamental change is inevitable?

A more systematic view is that of Chalmers Johnson (1964, 1966), to which Gurr relates his notion of progressive deprivation. Johnson adopts as his provisional definition of revolution that of Sigmund Neumann: 'a sweeping fundamental change in political organization, social structure, economic property control and the predominant myth of a social order, thus indicating a major break in the continuity of development'. He then develops a typology of revolution in six rather oddly assorted categories, which involve the use of four criteria: the targets of the activity, the nature of the revolutionaries, the goals of the revolution, and whether it is planned or develops spontaneously. The categories are:

Jacquerie – a mass rebellion of peasants with the limited aim of redressing grievances.
Millenarian rebellion – urban or rural, a rising in the hope of a radical change in the world in which all will be made anew.
Anarchistic rebellion – a reaction to modernisation opposing governmental authority and seeking to return to an older order regarded with nostalgia.
Jacobin Communist revolutions 'are the "great" revolutions', and the French Revolution is given as the classic example of this very small category.
Conspiratorial coup d'état – a sudden seizure of state power by a small group of plotters
Militarised mass insurrection – a mass-based, countrywide campaign to overthrow a government by guerrilla warfare.

The weakness of this classification is obvious. The first three involve mass action and much spontaneity. In the other three categories, elites lead masses and plan action accordingly. But there is no obvious reason why these six categories *and no others* have been selected. Indeed many of the examples of the first three (*jacquerie*, millenarian rebellion, anarchistic rebellion) can hardly be regarded as revolutions at all, since they failed either to bring down governments or to change the social system. Its value lies in its perception of the social background of revolution, and the essential unity of forms of violent political change.

Political theories of revolution focus on the conflict between government and opposition. Tilly (1978) defines the *sine qua non* of revolution thus: 'A revolutionary outcome is the displacement of one set of power holders by another.' The present writer would term it a *revolutionary event* and hence prefer the definition used in his *A Study of Revolution* of 'a change of government (transition) at a clearly defined point in time by the use of armed force, or the credible threat of its use' (Calvert, 1970b). Instead of using the terms *process* and *event* Tilly distinguishes between *revolutionary situations* and *revolutionary outcomes*. He sees the revolutionary outcome as the product of the emergence of multiple sovereignty in what he terms a *revolutionary situation*.

In doing so he correctly recognises the fundamental point about revolution, that it is the product of a contest. Whether the outcome is no change, a coup, a silent revolution or a great revolution depends on circumstances and the amount of power mobilised by the contenders. No view that seeks to explain revolution solely from the point of view of the government or solely from the point of view of the opposition will therefore be able to explain properly what is going on.

There are, he argues, three causes for the emergence of multiple sovereignty:

1. the appearance of coalitions of contenders advancing 'exclusive alternative claims' to power;
2. a commitment to those claims by a substantial sector of the public; or
3. the unwillingness or inability of the government forces to suppress the contenders or those who support their claims.

Tilly correctly recognises (with Gurr and others) that the greater the use of force the more probable far-reaching structural change becomes, and hypothesises (though he does not carry this argument very far) that the more change that occurs in the first short stage of consolidation the more likely it is that the changes will be extensive and permanent – these are, he suggests, the 'great revolutions'. Like many other writers, however, he tends to support the widespread and incorrect assumption that the converse is the case by the comment: 'Military coups almost never produce any significant structural change . . . *because* [emphasis added] they involve minor rearrangements among extremely limited sets of contenders,' despite the fact that, as he goes on to explain, where such a contender achieves power and makes an alliance with previously unrepresented social groups (Turkey, Japan) then far-reaching change is possible.

INSTITUTIONALISATION

Finally, therefore, revolutions can be said to be *institutionalised.* When this term is used, it refers not to the process or the event, but to the programme and the myth of revolution. Both are established as permanent essentially by the passage of time. There are no specifically 'revolutionary' institutions, only institutions designed to carry out the revolutionary programme, and the routinisation of these is the process of state formation itself. All modern states contain institutions owing their origin to a revolutionary event and a new programme.

The nature of the new system-balance, however, depends on the forces it brings into unity or counterpoise. This in turn is necessarily dependent on the social milieu on the initiation of the revolutionary process. The precise form depends on the number of major interest sectors within the ruling elite. If there are only one or two, turbulence remains almost inevitable for the future, while a multiplicity brings the problem of coalition against the possible independence of the instruments of power, for example, the army or the police. A tripartite division seems very nearly ideal (Calvert, 1969a). A strong tradition of personalism in the ruling elite can lead to the overwhelming desire for a Bonaparte, the most dramatic form of the democratic Caesar, but otherwise the routinisation of charisma seems to be less a feature of post-revolutionary times than the routinisation of concepts. Individual action can still play an important part, however, in the acceptance of forces and the way in which the rise of new ones is received.

On the other hand, the similarity between post-revolutionary times and primitive politics must not be overstressed. This recollection of the past is dominant in the minds of those establishing the new government. It is their concept of what a government should be. Those who rebel against it are as always few compared with those who seek guidance on forms and precedents. But the event of revolution is of only marginal importance in creating this problem; its myth obscures the lesson that in every age governments are continually evolving to meet new challenges with new responses.

KEY CONCEPTS

arena: geographical space over which political action (including the use of force) takes place.

demonstrations: anomic groupings of people moved by a single common interest with a limited target of applying pressure to part or whole of the political system.

disequilibrium: for functionalists the absence of a stable state.

rebellion: unsuccessful attempt to use force to overthrow the existing order and to establish a new one.

relative deprivation: the perception of lacking what others have.

revolution: change in government or in regime by the use of force by its own citizens.

terrorism: the use of force to impart fear with a view to bringing about political or social change.

'Thermidor': for Brinton the winding-down of revolutionary fervour and consolidation of a new and more efficient state system.

SAMPLE QUESTIONS

Questions in this area are most likely to call for a review of the available literature. Thus the question 'How far does the pattern of the French Revolution of 1789 still influence our understanding of politics?' invites discussion of the various models of social revolution propounded by

Brinton, Edwards, Moore, Skocpol etc., while a topic such as 'Was 1989 a year of revolution?' invites the candidate to apply these or similar models to events which are still current. Alternatively, in an individual case the question may arise of how far the social changes associated with the period can be seen to have been effective (e.g. in the case of Russia/the USSR).

General questions on political violence may invite the candidate to consider possible differences between the incidence of violence in different societies or states.

FURTHER READING

Calvert (1990a) deals with the principal debates on the origin and meaning of revolution; see also Calvert (1970a).

Comparative historical treatments of revolution include Brinton (1952), Dunn (1972, 2nd edition 1989), Moore (1969) and Skocpol (1979); all deal exclusively with a selection of the so-called 'great social revolutions'. The main sociological approaches were foreshadowed by Edwards (1970), Pettee (1928; reprinted 1963) and Johnson (1964, 1966). Gurr (1970) and Gamson (1975) seek to probe into the psychological causes as well. Goodspeed (1962) lays special emphasis on the military aspects of political change. For a political explanation of revolution see Calvert (1970b) and Tilly (1978). On the question of external influence and involvement in revolution see Calvert (1984) and Walt (1992).

12 Conclusion

THE END OF HISTORY?

Following the end of the Cold War, it has been widely argued that liberal democracy and the free market now reign supreme. In the United States, Francis Fukuyama has gone so far as to say that in the Hegelian sense we are witnessing 'the end of history' (Fukuyama, 1989). How much credence should we place on these claims?

Certainly a principal objective of Western European states, in the tradition established at the time of the French Revolution, has been the maintenance and spread of pluralist, representative democracy. The characteristic feature of modern political systems has been the emergence of the *assembly* as the prime instrument of mass mobilisation. As we have seen, the systems generated by this development have in many cases more recently undergone further modification. Such modifications usually result from the attempts of governments to substitute for the assembly forms of representation, such as by a party or the military, more easily directed in the perennial task of mobilising the population in support of its government, and in the performance of tasks which many of its members do not really want to perform. Occasionally this brings about a successful reaction among the population for a greater say in their own government. Sometimes, as at the fall of Ceausescu in Romania in 1989, this is gained by popular uprising, and very rarely, as in former East Germany and Czechoslovakia, is it grudgingly conceded.

But the irruption of the assembly into the political structure of France in 1789 has had such wide consequences that it still forms the basic point of departure for all later developments. This is because its claim to power is based on a very simple principle, its representation of the people.

The establishment of pluralist democracy has coincided with first a decline and then a revival in the belief in the market economy. However, it is quite incorrect to believe, as some have argued, that these two objectives are necessarily connected, or that one is dependent on the other. As Hannah Arendt points out, political liberty is an absolute good and hence its own justification (Arendt, 1963: 219–20). To believe either that liberty will necessarily result in prosperity, or that an unregulated market economy is a prior objective and a requirement for liberty, would be in each case to make a most serious mistake.

There are two reasons for this. First of all, as is now all too clear, the sacrifice of freedom in the Soviet Union did not result in prosperity and the attainment of freedom will not necessarily do so either. A market economy may or may not be a desirable goal in itself, but it is an objective quite separate from that of political liberty.

Second, in recent years the proponents of the market economy have presented a wildly romantic picture of the 'free market' as an independent force, superior to the power of the state and not in any way to be trammelled by state regulation. In fact this picture is not only misleading, it is the exact opposite of the truth. No market can exist without political power to regulate and protect it. An unregulated market is no market at all, since the essence of a market is a bargain which both parties know is going to be kept. It is because political authority is able to give this stability and assurance to private individuals that in turn it is able to demand of them their obedience.

Historically markets originated in a variety of ways and had a variety of patrons, but in the modern world the whole world is parcelled out among nation states. It is they and they alone which issue money, create credit and provide the legal framework within which the market can operate. But for most of the world the fact that their states are weak and unpredictable places citizens at a considerable disadvantage, both politically and economically, compared with their more fortunate neighbours.

All governments seek to the best of their capacities to be efficient, rich and successful. This in turn involves external obligations such as maintaining a surplus on their balance of payments on overseas trade, and keeping their currency strong against the US dollar (unless, of course, they already have dollars). And for internal reasons they want, as visible signs of their success, such things as new motorways, airlines, shipping fleets, oil wells and public buildings.

But there are two problems. All of these things cost money and inconvenience people, so there is a latent conflict between what people need and what they would vote for if they were actually asked – who, for example, might be yachtsmen, railway users, householders or gardeners. Since it is impossible to build a motorway with a kink in it to avoid someone's cabbage patch, or to allow people to eat Swiss chocolate if it unsettles the balance of trade, governments tell their citizens that their sacrifice is necessary for the good of the nation at large. However, they are not always convinced, and sometimes they become sufficiently aroused to try to do something about it.

Second, therefore, there is an innate conflict between the desire for economic success for the society as a whole and the narrower needs of the political elite themselves. What this means, in plainer terms, is the maintenance of the government itself in its existing framework of political obligation, by promises to benefit those who support them at some unstated time in the future. The problem is, unfortunately, that most governments are not very good at keeping their promises. This does not matter too much in a very rich country, but in a very poor one it is a recipe for disaster.

THE NORTH–SOUTH DIVIDE

For the disappearance of the Soviet Union has not helped diminish the North–South divide, and of the majority of the world's states, which are in what used to be called the Third World, many are still autocracies, and a substantial number can be confidently said to have a long way to go before they settle down as stable liberal democracies.

Even in Latin America, most of whose states have enjoyed political independence for more than a century and a half – longer than Italy, or Ireland, or Israel – political democracy has yet to come to Haiti and is currently under serious threat in Peru. One-fourth of the world's population live under the authoritarian system of the People's Republic of China, and it is not at the time of writing showing any signs of emulating its neighbours in the former Soviet Union.

However, even this powerful state cannot suspend the laws of nature, and the remorseless pressure of population growth is driving its citizens into an extreme form of the Third World 'short-termism' which has seriously degraded the environment of Mexico, Thailand or the Philippines and now threatens Malaysia. In such countries political control is purchased by allowing unrestrained exploitation of land and forests. The immediate returns are promising, but soon the inevitable happens and irreplaceable soil washes away in the tropical rains. Disconsolate settlers abandon their holdings and swell the crowds in the shanty towns on the edges of the great cities, where despite all their efforts the pressure of space creates an unhealthy and dangerous environment, fertile of resentment and ready to be mobilised in support of any populist leader who promises a quick and easy solution to their problems.

Ethiopia was once one of the most fertile countries in the world, and the seat of civilisation for thousands of years. Today it is a dust-bowl, and in neighouring Somalia public order has totally broken down. While tens of thousands starve, the functions of the state have totally ceased to exist and there is no one to bring the hordes of independent leaders, armed with Soviet and American weapons in the days of the Cold War, under control. The United States Government, indeed, has been persuaded to breach the state-centred tradition of non-intervention and to send in troops to protect the United Nations relief operation, but it is a dangerous precedent and the new administration is understandably not very happy about the number of obligations it has inherited.

In these circumstances it is, unfortunately, all too easy for elites to divert attention from their own shortcomings by blaming 'foreigners' for all their country's problems. It is much more satisfying to believe that one is the victim of vast external forces. Furthermore, the rulers of the rich countries have everything to gain in the short term from looking after their own domestic political support, keeping taxes down and allowing their companies to make money abroad. The future of the former East European states is still very much an open question. The same sort of forces that have led to the semi-unification of Western Europe may yet lead to the reconsolidation, not of the old Soviet Union – that has certainly gone for ever – but of a new regional grouping in North Central Asia. Other regional groupings are emerging in other parts of the world. But future relations between these regions, and the states of which they are composed, are still very unclear. One thing is certain: political conflict existed for centuries before Marx was born or the Soviet Union was invented. It can confidently be expected to be with us for a long time yet.

THE UTILITY OF COMPARATIVE POLITICS

For this reason, in a world of nation states, anyone who may at any time, for any reason, seek to venture outside their own country, whether to do business, to travel or to go on holiday, will benefit from a better understanding of the very considerable variety of state systems of which the modern international world is still composed. But it is no less important in broadening the general standard of civic understanding, and so enabling the citizen to play a more informed, and hence more effective part in public debate.

Comparative politics is concerned with identifying both similarities and differences. Above all, it teaches to do so *in a systematic way*. And it is this that demonstrates just how much the political scientist can help the practitioner of politics, the politician.

Like many other professionals, politicians over the years develop abilities to size up and guide a situation. These abilities, which, as noted above, are generally self-taught, are often of a high order, but they are not without their faults. Apart from those errors which creep in unconsciously over the years, as they grow tired or careless, politicans have a specific limitation to their knowledge in that they are trained to think in adversarial terms, and a general limitation that the deeper their knowledge is in their chosen field, the less adequate their knowledge will be in others. These other fields political scientists have the freedom to explore, and in other countries or in other times they can seek out and examine patterns of behaviour generally rare or unknown in the politician's society, but ones with which – in changed circumstances – the politician may some day have to deal.

And political scientists, while they cannot answer all the questions a politician might wish to put to them, can answer, or help to answer, some very useful questions.

- How can we choose a leader who will have the support of most of the people?
- How can we devise an electoral system for a given desired result?
- How can we decide a difficult political issue and avoid responsibility for the outcome?
- Why do other people seem to get all the money?
- How can formerly hostile states live alongside one another in close proximity?

These are only a few of the questions the comparative study of politics helps to answer. It is obvious how practical they are.

Bibliography

Adelman, J. (ed.) (1984), *Terror and Communist Politics: The role of the secret police in the communist states*, Boulder, CO: Westview Press.

Afrifa, A.A. (1966), *The Ghana Coup*, London: Cass.

Agee, Philip (1975), *Inside the Company: CIA diary*, Harmondsworth: Penguin.

Akzin, Benjamin (1967), 'Israel Knesset', *Israel Yearbook 1967*, Tel Aviv, cited in Milnor, A.J. (1969), *Elections and Political Stability*, Boston, MA: Little, Brown, p. 85.

Albrow, Martin (1970), *Bureaucracy*, London, Pall Mall and Macmillan.

Alexander, Robert J. (ed.) (1973), *Aprismo: The ideas and doctrines of Víctor Raúl Haya de la Torre*, Kent, OH: Kent State University Press.

Allan, Graham, and Skinner, Chris (eds) (1991), *Handbook for Research Students in the Social Sciences*, London: The Falmer Press.

Allardt, Erik, and Rokkan, Stein (eds) (1970), *Mass Politics: Studies in political sociology*, New York: The Free Press.

Allen, C.K. (1947), *Law and Orders*, London: Stevens.

Allison, Graham T. (1971), *Essence of Decision: Explaining the Cuban missile crisis*, Boston, MA: Little, Brown.

Almond, Gabriel A. (1968), 'Comparative politics', *The International Encyclopedia of the Social Sciences*, New York: Macmillan.

Almond, Gabriel A., and Coleman, James S. (1960), *The Politics of the Developing Areas*, Princeton, NJ: Princeton University Press.

Almond, Gabriel A., and Powell, G. Bingham (1966), *Comparative Politics, a Developmental Approach*, Boston, MA: Little, Brown.

Almond, Gabriel A., and Verba, Sidney (1963), *The Civic Culture*, Princeton, NJ: Princeton University Press.

Anderson, Patrick (1968), *The President's Men*, New York: Doubleday.

Annual Abstract of Statistics, annual, London: HMSO.

Annual Register of World Events, annual, Harlow: Longman.

Apter, D.E. (1965), *The Politics of Modernization*, Chicago, IL: University of Chicago Press.

Apter, D.E. (1987), *Rethinking Development: Modernization, dependency, and postmodern politics*, Newbury Park, CA: Sage.

Arendt, Hannah (1963), *On Revolution*, London: Faber & Faber.

Aristotle (1968), *The Politics*, trans. and ed. Ernest Barker, Oxford: Clarendon Press.

Aron, Raymond (1967), 'Social class, political class, ruling class' in R. Bendix and Seymour Martin Lipset (1967).

Auty, Phyllis (1970), *Tito: A biography*, London: Longman.

Bahro, Rudolf (1978), *The Alternative in Eastern Europe*, London: New Left Books.

Bailey, F.G. (1969), *Strategems and Spoils*, Oxford: Basil Blackwell.
Baker, Gordon E. (1966), *The Reapportionment Revolution*, New York: Random House.
Ball, Alan, and Millard, Frances (1986), *Pressure Politics in Industrial Societies*, Basingstoke: Macmillan Education.
Baran, Paul A. (1957), *The Political Economy of Growth*, New York: Monthly Review Press.
Barghoorn, Frederick C. (1972), *Politics in the USSR*, Boston, MA: Little, Brown.
Barker, Ernest (ed.), *see* Aristotle.
Barnard, Chester (1938), *The Function of the Executive*, Cambridge, MA: Harvard University Press.
Beetham, David (1987), *Bureaucracy*, Milton Keynes: Open University Press.
Bell, Daniel (1961), *The End of Ideology: On the exhaustion of political ideas in the Fifties*, new rev. edn, New York: Collier Books (1988).
Bendix, R., and Lipset, Seymour Martin (1967), *Class, Status and Power*, 2nd edn, London: Routledge & Kegan Paul.
Berger, Peter L., and Luckmann, Thomas (1972), *The Social Construction of Reality: A treatise in the sociology of knowledge*, Harmondsworth: Penguin.
Bernstein, Basil (1973), *Classes, Codes and Control* (4 vols), London: Routledge (1973–6).
Binder, L. *et al.* (1971), *Crises and Sequences in Political Development*, Princeton, NJ: Princeton University Press.
Black, Duncan (1958), *The Theory of Committees and Elections*, Cambridge: Cambridge University Press.
Blau, Peter, and Duncan, Otis Dudley (1967), *The American Occupational Structure*, New York: John Wiley.
Blondel, Jean (1973), *Comparing Political Systems*, London: Weidenfeld & Nicolson.
Blondel, Jean (1985), *Comparative Legislatures*, London: Sage.
Bloodworth, Dennis (1969), *Chinese Looking-glass*, Harmondsworth: Penguin.
Bosanquet, Nick, and Townsend, Peter (eds) (1979), *Labour and Equality: A Fabian study of Labour in power, 1974–79*, London: Heinemann.
Bourricaud, François (1970), *Power and Society in Contemporary Peru*, London: Faber.
Brewer, John D. (1988), *The Police: Public order and the state policing in Great Britain, Northern Ireland, the Irish Republic, the USA, Israel, South Africa and China*, Basingstoke: Macmillan.
Bridges, Edward (1956), 'The reforms of 1854 in retrospect', in William A. Robson (ed.), *The Civil Service in Britain and France*, London: Hogarth Press.
Brinton, Crane (1952), *The Anatomy of Revolution*, New York: 1938, reprinted New York: Vintage.
Brittan, Samuel (1976), *The Economic Consequences of Democracy*, London: M.T. Smith.
Brodbeck, May (1968), *Readings in the Philosophy of the Social Sciences*, New York: Macmillan.
Brogan, D.W., and Verney, D.V. (1963), *Politics in the Modern World*, London: Hamish Hamilton.
Brzezinski, Zbigniew, and Huntington, Samuel (1964), *Political Power, USA/USSR*, London: Chatto & Windus.
Bury, J.B. (1956), *A History of Greece to the Death of Alexander the Great*, 3rd rev. edn, London: Macmillan.

Butler, David (ed.) (1959), *Elections Abroad*, London: Macmillan.
Byrd, Peter (1987), 'Great Britain: Parties in a changing party system', in Alan Ware (ed.), *Citizens, Parties and the State*, Cambridge: Polity Press, pp. 205–24.
Callwell, Charles E. (1927), *Field Marshal Sir Henry Wilson, His Life and Diaries*, London: Caseel.
Calvert, Peter (1967), 'Revolution: The politics of violence', *Political Studies*, **15**, No. 1, February, p. 1.
Calvert, Peter (1969a), 'The institutionalisation of the Mexican Revolution', *Journal of Inter-American Studies*, **11**, No. 4, October.
Calvert, Peter (1969b), 'The dynamics of political change', *Political Studies*, **17**, No. 4, December.
Calvert, Peter (1970a), *Revolution* (Key Concepts in Political Science), London: Pall Mall and Macmillan.
Calvert, Peter (1970b), *A Study of Revolution*, Oxford: Clarendon Press.
Calvert, Peter (1979), 'The coup: A critical restatement', *Third World Quarterly*, **1**, No. 4, October, p. 89.
Calvert, Peter (1982), *The Concept of Class: An historical introduction*, London: Hutchinson.
Calvert, Peter (1983), *Politics, Power and Revolution: An introduction to comparative politics*, Brighton: Harvester.
Calvert, Peter (1984), *Revolution and International Politics*, London: Frances Pinter.
Calvert, Peter (ed.) (1987), *The Process of Political Succession*, Basingstoke: Macmillan.
Calvert, Peter (1990a), *Revolution and Counter-revolution*, Milton Keynes: Open University Press.
Calvert, Peter (1990b), 'Argentina: Goodbye to Peronism', *The World Today*, **46**, Nos 8–9, August–September, pp. 170–5.
Calvert, Peter (1990c), 'The US intervention in Panama', *Small Wars and Insurgencies*, **1**, No. 3, December, pp. 307–14.
Calvert, Peter, and Calvert, Susan (1990), *Latin America in the Twentieth Century*, Basingstoke: Macmillan.
Calvert, Susan, and Calvert, Peter (1989), *Argentina, Political Culture and Instability*, London: Macmillan.
Campbell, Peter (1951), 'Remarques sur les effets de la loi electorale française du 9 mai 1951', *Revue française de science politique*, **1**, October–December, p. 498.
Canovan, Margaret (1981), *Populism*, London: Junction Books.
Cardoso, Fernando Henrique, and Faletto, Enzo (1979), *Dependency and Development in Latin America*, trans. M.M. Urquidi, Berkeley, CA: University of California Press.
Carstairs, Andrew McLaren (1980), *A Short History of Electoral Systems*, London: Allen & Unwin.
Carsten, F.L. (1967), *The Rise of Fascism*, London: Methuen.
Carter, Gwendolyn M. (1958), *The Politics of Inequality: South Africa since 1948*, London: Thames & Hudson.
Cattell, R.B., and Stice, G.F. (1954), 'Four formulae for selecting leaders on basis of personality', *Human Relations*, **7**, p. 493.
Cerny, Philip (1980), 'The new rules of the game in France' in Philip G. Cerny and Martin A. Schain (eds), *French Politics and Public Policy*, London: Methuen.
Cerny, Philip G., and Schain, Martin A. (eds) (1980), *French Politics and Public Policy*, London: Methuen.

Chapman, Brian (1970), *Police State*, London: Pall Mall and Macmillan.
Churchward, L.G. (1975), *Contemporary Soviet Government*, London: Routledge.
Clapham, Christopher (ed.) (1982), *Private Patronage and Public Power: Political clientelism in the modern state*, London: Pinter.
Clapham, Christopher (1985), *Third World Politics: An introduction*, Beckenham: Croom Helm.
Clapham, Christopher, and Philip, George (eds) (1985), *The Political Dilemmas of Military Regimes*, London: Croom Helm.
Coast, John (1953), *Some Aspects of Siamese Politics*, New York: International Secretariat of the Institute of Pacific Relations (mimeo.).
Cohen, Emmeline (1941), *The Growth of the British Civil Service, 1780–1934*, London: Allen & Unwin.
Cole, Alistair, and Campbell, Peter (1989), *French Electoral Systems and Elections Since 1789*, Aldershot: Gower.
Collins, David (ed.) (1979), *The New Authoritarianism in Latin America*, Princeton, NJ: Princeton University Press.
Condon, John C., Jr (1966), *Semantics and Communication*, New York: Macmillan.
Congressional Quarterly Weekly Report, Washington, DC: Congressional Quarterly.
Conquest, Robert (1961), *Power and Policy in the USSR*, London: Macmillan.
Cornford, F.M. (1970), *Microcosmographia Academica, Being a Guide for the Young Academic Politician*, Cambridge: Bowes & Bowes.
Cowell, F.R. (1956), *Cicero and the Roman Republic*, Harmondsworth: Penguin.
Craig, Gordon A. (1955), *The Politics of the Prussian Army, 1640–1945*, Oxford: Oxford University Press.
Cramer, James (1964), *The World's Police*, London: Cassell.
Crick, Bernard (1964), *In Defence of Politics*, London: Routledge & Kegan Paul.
Crick, Bernard (1973), *Basic Forms of Government: A sketch and a model*, London: Macmillan.
Dahl, Robert A. (1964a), *Modern Political Analysis*, Englewood Cliffs, NJ: Prentice-Hall.
Dahl, Robert A. (1964b), *A Preface to Democratic Theory*, Chicago, IL: University of Chicago Press.
Davies, James Chowning (1962), 'Toward a theory of revolution', *American Sociological Review*, **43**, No. 1, February, p. 5.
Davies, Morton R., and Lewis, Vaughan A. (1971), *Models of Political Systems*, London: Pall Mall.
Dawisha, Karen (1980), 'The limits of the Bureaucratic Politics Model: observations on the Soviet case', *Studies in Comparative Communism*, **13**, pp. 300–26.
Decalo, Samuel (1976), *Coups and Army Rule in Africa*, New Haven, CT: Yale University Press.
Delarue, Jacques (1964), *The Gestapo*, New York: Morrow.
del Castillo, Pilar (1989), 'Financing of Spanish political parties' in Herbert E. Alexander (ed.), *Comparative Political Finance*, Cambridge: Cambridge University Press, pp. 172–99.
D'Entreves, A.P. (ed.) (1959), *Aquinas' Selected Political Writings*, Oxford: Blackwell.
Deutsch, Karl (1966), *The Nerves of Government, Models of Political Communication and Control*, New York: The Free Press.

Díaz Guerrero, R. (1975), *Psychology of the Mexican, Culture and Personality*, Austin, TX: University of Texas Press.
Diedrich, Bernard (1978), *Trujillo, the Death of the Goat*, London: Bodley Head.
Diedrich, Bernard (1982), *Somoza and the Legacy of US Involvement in Central America*, London: Junction Books.
Di Tella, Guido (1983), *Argentina Under Perón, 1973–1976: The nation's experience with a labour-based government*, London: Macmillan.
Djilas, Milovan (1957), *The New Class: An analysis of the communist system*, London: Thames & Hudson.
Dobzhansky, Theodosias (1971), 'Race equality' in Richard H. Osborne (ed.), *The Biological and Social Meaning of Race*, San Francisco, CA: W.H. Freeman & Co.
Dogan, Matthei, and Pelassy, Dominique (1984), *How to Compare Nations*, Chatham, NJ: Chatham House Publications.
Dollard, John, Doob, Leonard W., Miller, Neal E., Mowrer, O.H., and Sears, Robert R. (1939), *Frustration and Aggression*, New Haven, CT: Yale University Press.
Duchacek, I.D. (1970), *Comparative Federalism: The territorial dimensions of politics*, New York: Holt, Rinehart & Winston.
Dulles, Allen (1964), *The Craft of Intelligence*, London: Weidenfeld.
Dunleavy, Patrick, and O'Leary, Brendan (1987), *Theories of the State*, Basingstoke: Macmillan.
Dunn, John (1989), *Modern Revolutions: An introduction to the analysis of a political phenomenon*, 2nd edn, first publ. 1972, Cambridge: Cambridge University Press.
Durkheim, Emile (1964), *The Division of Labor in Society*, trans. George Simpson, New York: The Free Press.
Duverger, Maurice (1959), *Political Parties*, 2nd edn, London: Methuen.
Easton, David (1957), 'An approach to the analysis of political systems', *World Politics*, **10**, pp. 383–400.
Easton, David (1965a), *A Systems Analysis of Political Life*, New York: John Wiley.
Easton, David (1965b), *A Framework for Political Analysis*, Englewood Cliffs, NJ: Prentice-Hall.
Eckstein, H.H. (1960), *Pressure Group Politics*, London: Allen & Unwin.
Edwards, Lyford P. (1970), *The Natural History of Revolution*, Chicago, IL: University of Chicago Press (first publ. 1927).
Eisenstadt, S. (1963), *The Political Systems of Empires*, New York: The Free Press.
Evans-Pritchard, E.E. (1940), *The Nuer: A description of the modes of livelihood and political institutions of Nilotic people*, Oxford: Clarendon Press.
Eysenck, Hans (1963), *Psychology and Politics*, London: Routledge.
Eysenck, Hans (1964), *Crime and Personality*, London: Routledge & Kegan Paul.
Falk, R. (1970), *This Endangered Planet*, New York: Random House.
Farb, Peter (1968), *Man's Rise to Civilization, as Shown by the Indians of North America from Primeval Times to the Coming of the Industrial State*, New York: Avon.
Feinberg, Richard E. (1972), *The Triumph of Allende: Chile's legal revolution*, New York: Mentor Books.
Fejtö, Francois (1974), *A History of the People's Democracies*, Harmondsworth: Penguin.
Figueiredo, Antonio de (1975), *Portugal: Fifty years of dictatorship*, Harmondsworth: Penguin.
Finer, S.E. (1962), *The Man on Horseback: The role of the military in politics*, London: Pall Mall; 2nd edn, Harmondsworth: Penguin, 1975.

Finer, S.E. (1970), *Comparative Government*, London: Allen Lane.
Finer, S.E. (1979), *Five Constitutions: Contrasts and Comparisons*, Brighton: Harvester, and Harmondsworth: Penguin.
Fitzgerald, C.P. (1976), *Mao Tse-tung and China*, London: Hodder & Stoughton.
Fluharty, Vernon Lee (1957), *Dance of the Millions: Military rule and the social revolution in Colombia, 1930–1956*, Pittsburgh, PA: University of Pittsburgh Press.
Foley, Michael (ed.) (1993), *Political Ideas*, Manchester: Manchester University Press, forthcoming.
Frank, André Gunder (1978), *World Accumulation 1492–1789*, London: Macmillan.
Frankel, Joseph (1963), *The Making of Foreign Policy, an Analysis of Decision-making*, London: Oxford University Press.
Frankel, Joseph (1964), *International Relations*, Oxford: Oxford University Press.
Friedrich, Carl (1972), *Tradition and Authority*, London: Pall Mall.
Friedrich, Carl J. and Brzezinski, Zbigniew N. (1975), *Totalitarian Dictatorship and Autocracy*, Cambridge, MA: Harvard University Press.
Fromm, Erich (1960), *The Fear of Freedom*, London: Routledge & Kegan Paul.
Fukuyama, Francis (1989), 'The end of history', *National Interest*, **16**.
Gallagher, Michael, Laver, Michael, and Mair, Peter (1992), *Representative Government in Western Europe*, New York: McGraw Hill.
Galtung, Johan (1971), 'The structural theory of imperialism', *Journal of Peace Research*, **8**, No. 2, p. 81.
Gamson, William A. (1975), *The Strategy of Social Protest*, Homewood, IL: The Dorsey Press.
Gauhar, Altaf (1983), *Talking About Development*, London: Third World Foundation for Social and Economic Studies.
Gehlen, Michael P. (1969), *The Communist Party of the Soviet Union: A functional analysis*, Bloomington, IN: Indiana University Press.
Gerlich, Peter (1987), 'Consociationalism to competition: The Austrian party system since 1945' in Hans Daalder (ed.), *Party Systems in Denmark, Austria, Switzerland, the Netherlands and Belgium*, London: Frances Pinter.
Gerth, H.H., and Mills, C. Wright (1946), *From Max Weber: Essays in sociology*, London: Routledge & Kegan Paul.
Gibb, C.A. (ed.) (1969), *Leadership*, Harmondsworth: Penguin.
Gil, Federico G. (1965), *The Political System of Chile*, Boston, MA: Houghton Mifflin.
Goldenberg, Boris (1965), *The Cuban Revolution and Latin America*, London: Allen & Unwin.
González, Edward (1976), 'Castro and Cuba's new orthodoxy', *Problems of Communism*, **25**, January–February, p. 1.
Goodspeed, D.J. (1962), *The Conspirators: A study of the coup d'etat*, London: Allen & Unwin; New York: Viking Press.
Gott, Richard (1970), *Guerrilla Movements in Latin America*, London: Nelson.
Gregory, Frank (1976), *Protest and Violence: The police response*, London: Institute for the Study of Conflict.
Grindle, Merrilee S. (1977), *Bureaucrats, Politicians and Peasants in Mexico*, Berkeley: University of California Press.
Grofman, Bernard, and Lijphart, Arend (eds) (1986), *Electoral Laws and Their Political Consequences*, New York: Agathon Press.
Guevara, Ernesto Che (1967), *Guerrilla Warfare*, New York: Monthly Review Press.

Gurr, Ted Robert (1970), *Why Men Rebel*, Princeton, NJ: Princeton University Press.

Gustafson, Thane (1980), *Reform and Power in Soviet Politics: Lessons of Brezhnev's agricultural and environmental policies*, Cambridge: Cambridge University Press.

Ham, C., and Hill, M. (1993), *The Policy Process in the Modern Capitalist State*, 2nd edn, Hemel Hempstead: Harvester-Wheatsheaf.

Hansard Society (1976), *The Report of the Hansard Society Commission on Electoral Reform*.

Haring, C.H. (1952), *The Spanish Empire in America*, New York: Oxford University Press.

Havens, Murray Clark, Leiden, Carl, and Schmitt, Karl M. (1970), *The Politics of Assassination*, Englewood Cliffs, NJ: Prentice-Hall.

Hawgood, John A. (1939), *Modern Constitutions Since 1787*, London: Macmillan.

Hazard, John N. (1964), *The Soviet System of Government*, 3rd edn, Chicago, IL: University of Chicago Press.

Heidenheimer, Arnold J. (1971), *The Governments of Germany*, 3rd edn, New York: Crowell.

Held, David (1988), *Models of Democracy*, Cambridge: Polity.

Henige, David P. (1974), *The Chronology of Oral Tradition: Quest for a chimera*, Oxford: Clarendon Press.

Herz, John H. (1959), *International Politics in the Atomic Age*, New York: Columbia University Press.

Hewitt, Patricia (1982), *The Abuse of Power: Civil liberties in the United Kingdom*, Oxford: Martin Robertson.

Heywood, A. (1992), *Political Ideologies: An introduction*, Basingstoke: Macmillan.

Hill, Ronald, and Frank, Peter (1983), *The Soviet Communist Party*, 3rd edn, London: Allen & Unwin.

Hillyard, Paddy, and Percy-Smith, Janie (1988), *The Coercive State*, London: Pinter.

Hirsch, Fred (1977), *The Social Limits to Growth*, London: Routledge & Kegan Paul.

Holden, Barry (1988), *Understanding Liberal Democracy*, 2nd edn, Hemel Hempstead: Harvester-Wheatsheaf, 1993.

Hollander, Paul (1973), *American and Soviet Society: A reader in comparative sociology and perception*, Englewood Cliffs, NJ: Prentice-Hall.

Hong Yung Lee (1978), *The Politics of the Chinese Cultural Revolution: A case study*, Berkeley, CA: University of California Press.

Hoover, Kenneth, and Plant, Raymond (1989), *Conservative Capitalism in Britain and the United States: A critical appraisal*, London: Routledge.

Hough, Jerry F. (1974), 'Political participation in the Soviet Union', *Soviet Studies*, **27**, No. 1, January.

Hough, Jerry F. (1977), *The Soviet Union and Social Science Theory*, Cambridge, MA: Harvard University Press.

Howard, Michael (ed.) (1955), *Soldiers and Governments*, London: Eyre & Spottiswode.

Howells, William W. (1971), 'The meaning of race' in Richard H. Osborne, (ed.), *The Biological and Social Meaning of Race*, San Francisco, CA: W.H. Freeman & Co.

Huberman, Leo, and Sweezy, Paul M. (1968), *Cuba, Anatomy of a Revolution*, New York: Monthly Review Press.

Huntington, Samuel P. (1965), 'Political development and political decay', *World Politics*, **17**, No. 3, pp. 386–430.
Huntington, Samuel P. (1968), *Political Order in Changing Societies*, New Haven, CT: Yale University Press.
Inkeles, Alex (1968), *Social Change in Soviet Russia*, Cambridge, MA: Harvard University Press.
Ionescu, Ghita (1967), *The Politics of the East European Communist States*, London: Weidenfeld & Nicolson.
Janowitz, Morris (1960), *The American Soldier*, Glencoe, IL: The Free Press.
Jennings, Sir Ivor (1951), *Cabinet Government*, Cambridge: Cambridge University Press.
Johnson, Chalmers (1964), *Revolution and the Social System*, Stanford, CA: The Hoover Institution on War, Revolution, and Peace, Stanford University, Hoover Institution Studies 3.
Johnson, Chalmers (1966), *Revolutionary Change*, Boston, MA: Little, Brown.
Johnson, John J. (1964), *The Military and Society in Latin America*, Stanford, CA: Stanford University Press.
Kahin, George McTurnan (ed.) (1964), *Governments and Politics of South-East Asia*, 2nd edn, Ithaca, NY: Cornell University Press.
Kautsky, John H. (1972), *The Political Consequences of Modernization*, New York: John Wiley.
Keesing's Contemporary Archives, monthly, Harlow: Longman.
Keeton, George W. (1960), *Trial by Tribunal*, London: Museum Press.
Kelley, Donald (1976), 'Environmental policy-making in the USSR: the role of industrial and environmental interest groups', *Soviet Studies*, **28**, No. 4, October.
Khadduri, Majid (1970), *Political Trends in the Arab World: The role of ideas and ideals in politics*, Baltimore, MD: Johns Hopkins Press.
Kirkpatrick, Jeane (1982), *Dictatorships and Double Standards*, New York: Simon and Schuster.
Kolinsky, Martin, and Paterson, William E. (eds) (1976), *Social and Political Movements in Western Europe*, London: Croom Helm.
Kornhauser, William (1959), *The Politics of Mass Society*, Glencoe, IL: The Free Press.
Kuhn, Thomas S. (1970), *The Structure of Scientific Revolutions*, 2nd edn, Chicago, IL: University of Chicago Press.
Lakeman, Enid (1970), *How Democracies Vote, A Study of Majority and Proportional Electoral Systems*, London: Faber.
Lane, David (1971), *The End of Inequality? Stratification under state socialism*, Harmondsworth: Penguin.
Lane, David (1976), *The Socialist Industrial State: Towards a political sociology of state socialism*, London: Allen & Unwin.
Lane, David (1978), *Politics and Society in the USSR*, 2nd edn, London: Weidenfeld & Nicholson.
Lane, Jan-Erik and Ersson, Svante O. (1991), *Politics and Society in Western Europe*, London: Sage.
LaPalombara, J. (ed.) (1963), *Bureaucracy and Political Development*, Princeton, NJ: Princeton University Press.
Lees, John D., and Kimber, Richard (eds) (1972), *Political Parties in Modern Britain, an Organizational and Functional Guide*, London: Routledge.

Leiden, Carl, and Schmitt, Karl M. (1968), *The Politics of Violence: Revolution in the modern world*, Englewood Cliffs, NJ: Prentice-Hall.

Lembruch, Gerhard (1967), *Proporzdemokratie: Politisches System und politische Kultur in der Schweiz und in Österreich*, Tübingen: Mohr.

Lenin, Vladimir Il'ych (1967), 'What is to be done?', in *Selected Works*, vol. 1, Moscow: Foreign Language Publishing House.

Lenz, Guenther H., and Shell, Kurt (eds) (1986), *The Crisis of Modernity: Recent theories of culture and society in the United States and West Germany*, Frankfurt: Campus.

Lessnoff, Michael (1974), *The Structure of Social Science: A philosophical introduction*, London: Allen & Unwin.

Lijphart, Arend (1969), 'Typologies of democratic systems', in Arend Lijphart (ed.), *Politics in Europe*, Englewood Cliffs, NJ: Prentice-Hall.

Lijphart, Arend (1974), *The Politics of Accommodation: Pluralism and democracy in The Netherlands*, 2nd edn, Berkeley, CA: University of California Press.

Lijphart, Arend (1977), *Democracy in Plural Societies: A comparative exploration*, New Haven, CT: Yale University Press.

Linz, Juan J., and Stepan, Alfred (1978), *The Breakdown of Democratic Regimes: Latin America*, Baltimore, MD: Johns Hopkins University Press.

Lipset, Seymour Martin (1979), *The First New Nation: The United States in historical and comparative perspective*, New York: W.W. Norton.

Lipset, Seymour Martin (1960, repr. 1983), *Political Man*, New York: Basic Books.

Locke, John (1956), *The Second Treatise of Government*, ed. J.W. Gough, Oxford: Basil Blackwell.

Locke, John (1964), *Two Treatises on Government*, ed. Peter Laslett, Cambridge: Cambridge University Press.

Lorenz, Konrad (1966), *On Aggression*, London: Methuen.

Lumley, F.A. (1976), *The Republic of China Under Chiang Kai-shek: Taiwan today*, London: Barrie & Jenkins.

Luttwak, Edward (1979), *Coup d'Etat, a Practical Handbook*, London: Wildwood House.

Machiavelli, Niccolo (1950), *The Prince and The Discourses*, intro. Max Lerner, New York: Random House.

MacIntyre, Alisdair (1983), 'Is a science of comparative politics possible?' in A.G. MacIntyre (ed.), *Against the Self-images of the Age: Essays on ideology and philosophy*, 2nd edn, London: Duckworth.

Mackie, Thomas T., and Rose, Richard (1991), *The International Almanac of Electoral History*, 3rd edn, London: Macmillan.

Macpherson, Crawford B. (1977), *The Life and Times of Liberal Democracy*, Oxford: Oxford University Press.

McQuail, Denis (1969), *Towards a Sociology of Mass Communications*, New York: Collier-Macmillan.

Mair, Peter (1987), *The Changing Irish Party System*, London: Frances Pinter.

Mannheim, Karl (1946), *Ideology and Utopia: An introduction to the sociology of knowledge*, London: Routledge & Kegan Paul.

Marceau, Jane (1980), 'Power and its possessors', in Cerny, Philip G., and Schain, Martin A. (eds), *French Politics and Public Policy*, London: Methuen.

March, James, and Simon, Herbert (1958), *Organizations*, New York: John Wiley.

Marcuse, Herbert (1972), *One Dimensional Man*, London: Sphere Books.

Marx, F. Morestein (1967), *The Administrative State*, Chicago, IL: Chicago University Press.

Marx, Karl (1852), letter to J. Weydemayer, in Karl Marx and Frederick Engels, *Selected Works*, Moscow: Foreign Languages Publishing House (1962), p. 452.

Marx, Karl, and Engels, Frederick (1848), 'The communist manifesto' in Karl Marx and Frederick Engels, *Selected Works*, Moscow: Foreign Languages Publishing House (1962).

Matthews, Herbert L. (1957), *The Yoke and the Arrows*, London: Heinemann.

Matthews, Mervyn (1978), *Privilege in the Soviet Union: A study of elite life-styles under Communism*, London: Allen & Unwin.

Mayer, Laurence C. (1989), *Redefining Comparative Politics: Promise versus performance*, London: Sage.

Meadows, Donella H., Meadows, Dennis L., Randers, Jorgen, and Behrens, William W. III (1974, first publ. 1972), *The Limits to Growth*, London: Pan.

Melville, Thomas, and Melville, Marjorie (1971), *Guatemala – Another Vietnam?* Harmondsworth: Penguin.

Merritt, Richard L. (1970), *Systemic Approaches to Comparative Politics*, New York: Rand McNally.

Mezey, M. (1979), *Comparative Legislatures*, Durham, NC: Duke University Press.

Michels, Robert (1959, first publ. 1915), *Political Parties: A sociological study of the oligarchical tendencies of modern democracy*, New York: Dover Publications.

Migdal, Joel S. (1988), *Strong Societies and Weak States*, Princeton, NJ: Princeton University Press.

Mill, John Stuart (1958), *Considerations on Representative Government*, ed. Carrin V. Shields, Indianapolis, IN: Bobbs Merrill.

Miller, George A. (1963), *Language and Communication*, New York: McGraw Hill.

Mills, C. Wright (1956), *The Power Elite*, New York: Oxford University Press.

Milne, R.S. (1967), *Government and Politics in Malaysia*, Boston, MA: Houghton Mifflin.

Milnor, A.J. (1969), *Elections and Political Stability*, Boston, MA: Little, Brown.

Mitford, Nancy (1966), *The Sun King*, London: Hamish Hamilton.

Montagu, Ashley (ed.) (1973), *Man and Aggression*, New York: Oxford University Press.

Montesquieu, Charles-Louis de Secondat, Baron de (1966), *The Spirit of the Laws*, trans. Thomas Nugent, intro. Franz Neumann, New York: Hafner.

Moore, Barrington, Jr (1969), *Social Origins of Dictatorship and Democracy: Lord and peasant in the making of the modern world*, Harmondsworth: Penguin.

Myrdal, Gunnar (1972), *Asian Drama: An enquiry into the poverty of nations*, New York: Vintage Books.

Needler, Martin C. (1963), *Latin American Power in Perspective*, Princeton, NJ: Van Nostrand.

Needler, Martin C. (1990), *Mexican Politics: The containment of conflict*, 2nd edn, New York: Praeger.

Neguib, Muhammad (1955), *Egypt's Destiny*, Garden City, NY: Doubleday.

Neumann, Sigmund (1965), *Permanent Revolution: Totalitarianism in the age of international civil war*, London: Pall Mall.

Neustadt, Richard E. (1964), *Presidential Power*, New York: Signet.

North, Robert C. *et al.* (1963), *Content Analysis*, Evamston, IL: Northwestern University Press.

Nurmi, Hannu (1987), 'Political succession as policy succession: Why so much stability?, in Peter Calvert (ed.), *The Process of Political Succession*, Basingstoke: Macmillan.

Nutting, Anthony (1967), *No End of a Lesson: The story of Suez*, London: Constable.

O'Brien, Phil, and Cammack, Paul (1985), *Generals in Retreat*, Manchester: Manchester University Press.

O'Donnell, Guillermo (1988), *Bureaucratic Authoritarianism: Argentina, 1966–73, in comparative perspective*, Berkeley, CA: University of California Press.

Osborne, Richard H. (ed.) (1971), *The Biological and Social Meaning of Race*, San Francisco, CA: W.H. Freeman & Co.

Osgood, Charles E., Suci, George J., and Tannenbaum, Percy H. (1957), *The Measurement of Meaning*, Urbana, IL: University of Illinois Press.

Page, E.C. (1992), *Political Authority and Bureaucratic Power: A comparative analysis*, 2nd edn, Hemel Hempstead: Harvester-Wheatsheaf.

Pareto, Vilfredo (1965), *Works*, ed. S.E. Finer, London: Pall Mall.

Parkin, F. (1971), *Class, Inequality and Political Order: Social stratification in capitalist and communist societies*, London: McGibbon & Kee.

Parkinson, C. Northcote (1958), *Parkinson's Law, or the Pursuit of Progress*, London: John Murray.

Parry, Geraint (1969), *Political Elites*, London: Allen & Unwin.

Parsons, Talcott A., and Shils, Ed B. (eds) (1962), *Towards a General Theory of Action*, New York: Harper.

Partridge, P.H. (1971), *Consent and Consensus*, London: Pall Mall and Macmillan.

Paterson, William E., 'West Germany: Between party apparatus and basic democracy' in Alan Ware (ed.) (1987), *Political Parties: Electoral change and structural response*, Oxford: Basil Blackwell, pp. 158–82.

Pettee, George S. (1928), *The Process of Revolution*, New York: Harper and Brothers.

Pierce, J.R. (1962), *Symbols, Signals and Noise, the Nature and Process of Communication*, London: Hutchinson.

Pierson, W.W. and Gil, Federico G. (1967), *Governments of Latin America*, New York: McGraw Hill.

Plamenatz, John (1970), *Ideology*, London: Pall Mall & Macmillan.

Plant, Raymond (1991a), *Modern Political Thought*, Oxford: Blackwell.

Plant, Raymond (1991b), *The Plant Report: A working party on electoral reform*, London: The Guardian.

Pool, Ithiel da Sola (ed.) (1957), *Trends in Content Analysis*, Urbana, IL: University of Illinois Press.

Przeworski, Adam, and Teune, Henry (1970), *The Logic of Comparative Social Inquiry*, New York: John Wiley.

Pulzer, Peter G.J. (1975), *Political Representation and Elections in Britain*, 3rd edn, London: Allen & Unwin.

Rae, Douglas W. (1967), *The Political Consequences of Electoral Laws*, New Haven, CT: Yale University Press.

Rae, Douglas W., and Taylor, Michael (1970), *The Analysis of Political Cleavages*, New Haven, CT: Yale University Press.

Randall, Vicky (ed.) (1988), *Political Parties in the Third World*, London: Sage.

Randall, Vicky, and Theobald, Robin (1985), *Political Change and Underdevelopment: A critical introduction to Third World politics*, Basingstoke: Macmillan.

Rappaport, Roy A. (1968), *Pigs for the Ancestors: Ritual in the ecology of a New Guines people*, New Haven, CT: Yale University Press.
Richardson, Lewis F. (1960), *Statistics of Deadly Quarrels*, London: Stevens.
Ridley, F.F., and Blondel, J. (1964), *Public Administration in France*, London: Routledge & Kegan Paul.
Riggs, Fred W. (1964), *Administration in Developing Countries*, Boston, MA: Houghton Mifflin.
Riker, William H. (1982), *Liberalism Against Populism: A confrontation between the theory of democracy and the theory of social choice*, San Francisco, CA: W.H. Freeman and Co.
Robinson, Joan (1969), *The Cultural Revolution in China*, Harmondsworth: Penguin.
Robson, William A. (ed.) (1956), *The Civil Service in Britain and France*, London: Hogarth Press.
Rose, Richard (1971), *Governing without Consensus, an Irish Perspective*, London: Faber.
Rose, Richard (ed.) (1974), *Electoral Behavior, a Comparative Handbook*, New York: The Free Press.
Rose, Richard, and Suleiman, Ezra N. (1980), *Presidents and Prime Ministers*, Washington, DC: American Enterprise Institute for Public Research.
Rosenthal, Erwin I.J. (1962), *Political Thought in Medieval Islam: An introductory outline*, Cambridge: Cambridge University Press.
Rostow, Walt Whitman (1960), *The Stages of Economic Growth: A non-communist manifesto*, Cambridge: Cambridge University Press.
Rostow, Walt Whitman (1971), *Politics and the Stages of Growth*, Cambridge: Cambridge University Press.
Rotberg, Robert I. (1971), *Haiti, the Politics of Squalor*, Boston, MA: Houghton Mifflin.
Rousseau, Jean-Jacques (1958), *The Social Contract and Discourses*, trans. and intro. G.D.H. Cole, London: Dent.
Rubenstein, Alvin Z. (1965), 'Yugoslavia's opening society', *Current History*, **48**, March, p. 149.
Rubenstein, Alvin Z. (1966), *Communist Political Systems*, Englewood Cliffs, NJ: Prentice-Hall.
Rudé, George (1964), *The Crowd in History*, New York: John Wiley.
Runciman, W.G. (1963), *Social Science and Political Theory*, Cambridge: Cambridge University Press.
Russett, Bruce M. (ed.) (1964), *World Handbook of Political and Social Indicators*, New Haven, CT: Yale University Press.
Rydon, Joan (1956), 'Electoral methods and the Australian party system, 1900–1951', *Australian Journal of Politics and History*, **2**, November, p. 82.
Sahlin, Michael (1977), *Neo-authoritarianism and the Problem of Legitimacy: A general study and a Nigerian example*, Stockholm: Reben & Sjögren.
Salcedo-Bastardo, J.L. (1978), *Bolívar, a Continent and Its Destiny*, Richmond: The Richmond Publishing Co. Ltd.
Sartori, Giovanni (1970), 'Concept misformation in comparative politics', *American Political Science Review*, **54**.
Sartori, Giovanni (1976), *Parties and Party Systems, a Framework for Analysis*, Cambridge: Cambridge University Press.

Scalapino, Robert A., and Masjumi, Junnosake (1962), *Parties and Politics in Contemporary Japan*, Berkeley, CA: University of California Press.
Schapiro, Leonard (1970), *The Communist Party of the Soviet Union*, London: Eyre & Spottiswoode.
Schapiro, Leonard (1972), *Totalitarianism*, London: Pall Mall and Macmillan.
Schattschneider, E.E. (1961), *The Semi-sovereign People: A realist's view of democracy in America*, New York: Holt, Rinehart & Winston.
Schram, Stuart (ed.) (1963), *The Political Thought of Mao Tse Tung*, New York: Praeger.
Seton-Watson, Hugh (1956), *The East European Revolution*, New York: Praeger.
Seton-Watson, Hugh (1977), *Nations and States: An inquiry into the origins of actions and the politics of nationalism*, London: Methuen.
Short, Anthony (1973), *The Communist Insurrection in Malaya, 1948–60*, London: Frederick Muller.
Skilling, Gordon, and Griffiths, F. (eds) (1971), *Interest Groups in Soviet Politics*, Princeton, NJ: Princeton University Press.
Skocpol, Theda (1979), *States and Social Revolutions: A comparative analysis of France, Russia and China*, Cambridge: Cambridge University Press.
Solomon, S. Gross (ed.) (1983), *Pluralism in the Soviet Union*, London: Macmillan.
Sorenson, Theodore (1965), *Kennedy*, London: Hodder & Stoughton.
Stacey, Frank (1978), *Ombudsmen Compared*, Oxford: Clarendon Press.
Stanyer, Jeffrey (1976), 'Irresistible forces: the pressure for a science of politics', *Political Studies*, **24**, No. 3, September.
Statesman's Year Book, annual, Basingstoke: Macmillan.
Steiner, Jürg (1972), *Politics in Austria*, Boston, MA: Little, Brown.
Steiner, Jürg (1974), *Amicable Agreement versus Majority Rule: Conflict resolution in Switzerland*, Chapel Hill, NC: University of North Carolina Press.
Stepan, Alfred (1971), *The Military in Politics: Changing patterns in Brazil*, Princeton, NJ: Princeton University Press.
Stodgill, R.M. (1948), 'Personal factors associated with leadership: A survey of the literature', *Journal of Psychology*, **35**, p. 35.
Stokes, William S. (1959), *Latin American Politics*, New York: Thomas Y. Crowell Co.
Talmon, J.L. (1961), *The Origins of Totalitarian Democracy*, London: Mercury Books.
Thomas, Caroline (1987), *In Search of Security: The Third World in international relations*, Brighton: Harvester Press.
Thomas, Caroline (1992), *The Environment in International Relations*, London: The Royal Institute of International Affairs.
Thomas, Hugh (ed.) (1959), *The Establishment*, London: Anthony Blond.
Thomas, Hugh (1966), *The Suez Affair*, London: Weidenfeld.
Tilly, Charles (1978), *From Mobilization to Revolution*, Reading, MA: Addison-Wesley.
Times, The (1974), *The Times Guide to the House of Commons, February 1974*, London: Times Newspapers Limited.
Tönnies, Ferdinand (1955), *Commmunity and Association*, London: Routledge & Kegan Paul.
Ullmann, Walter (1965), *A History of Political Thought, the Middle Ages*, Harmondsworth: Penguin.

Vagts, Alfred (1959), *A History of Militarism, Civilian and Military*, London: Hollis & Carter.

Vallenilla Lanz, Laureano (1919), *Cesarismo democrático: estudio sobre las bases sociológicas de la constitución efectiva de Venezuela*, Caracas: Empresa El Cojo; 4th edn, Caracas: Tipografia Garrido, 1961.

Verney, Douglas V. (1961), *The Analysis of Political Systems*, London: Routledge.

Vincent, A. (1991), *Modern Political Ideologies*, Oxford: Blackwell.

Vogt, Evon Z. (1969), *Zinacantan, a Maya Community in the Highlands of Chiapas*, Cambridge, MA: Belknap.

von Beyme, Karl (1985), *Political Parties in Western Democracies*, Aldershot: Gower.

Wang Gung-wu (ed.) (1966), *Malaysia*, London: Pall Mall.

Walt, S.M. (1992), 'Revolution and war', *World Politics*, **44**, pp. 321–68.

Ware, Alan (ed.) (1987), *Political Parties: Electoral change and structural response*, Oxford: Basil Blackwell.

Weber, Max (1964), *The Theory of Social and Economic Organization*, New York: The Free Press.

Weiner, Norbert (1967), *Cybernetics*, Cambridge, MA: The MIT Press.

Weinstein, Martin (1975), *Uruguay, the Politics of Failure*, Westport, CT: Greenwood Press.

Weller, Patrick (1985), *First Among Equals: Prime Ministers in Westminster Systems*, London: Unwin Hyman.

Werth, Alexander (1956), *France 1940–1955*, London: Robert Hale.

Werth, Alexander (1965), *De Gaulle*, Harmondsworth: Penguin.

Wheare, K.C. (1963), *Federal Government*, 4th edn, London: Oxford University Press.

White, Stephen *et al.* (1990), *Communist and Post-Communist Political Systems*, 3rd edn, London: Macmillan.

White, Theodore (1965), *The Making of the President, 1964*, London: Jonathan Cape.

Whiteford, Andrew H. (1964), *Two Cities of Latin America, a Comparative Description of Social Classes*, Garden City, NY: Doubleday.

Wilgus, A. Curtis (1963), *South American Dictators in the First Century of Independence*, New York: Russell & Russell.

Winch, Peter (1958), *The Idea of a Social Science and Its Relation to Philosophy*, London: Routledge.

Windsor, HRH the Duke of, KG (1951), *A King's Story*, London: Cassell.

Wolf-Philips, Leslie (ed.) (1968), *Constitutions of Modern States*, London: Pall Mall.

Wolin, Simon, and Slusser, Robert M. (1957), *The Soviet Secret Police*, New York: Praeger.

World Bank (1990), *World Development Report 1990*, New York: United Nations.

Wraith, R.E., and Simpkins, E. (1965), *Corruption in Developing Countries*, New York: Norton.

Yanov, Alexander (1978), *The Russian New Right: Right-wing ideologies in the contemporary USSR*, Berkeley, CA: Institute of International Studies, University of California.

Zaslavsky, Victor (1980), 'Socio-economic inequality and changes in Soviet ideology', *Theory and Society*, **9**, No. 2.

Index